DEDIC
To my big b

He was my buddy, my mentor, and an exemplary role model with knowledge that I could never equal. From an early age he was driven to be a doctor and his life was filled with schooling and intense studying but he always found the time to include me in his infrequent breaks. He taught me to swim when I was a toddler and I cannot remember a time when I was uncomfortable in the water. In fact, with him at my side, we swam to an island in the Potomac River when I was eight. Then, there were many enjoyable rides with him in his beloved Model A roadster, one of which he lovingly restored in later life.

He never stopped teaching me things that would eventually improve my quality of life and I believe that it started in 1929 with a crystal set radio and continued until 2013 when my ninety-four year big brother peacefully turned the last page of his life's story. All of his family was with him to see him off on his final journey. We maintained lively conversations with him and he did his best to respond. I joked with him about taking all of his good wine and I asked him if he remembered our listening to the crystal set when we were kids.

With his eyes still closed, a big smile brightened his face and with a fading voice he said,

" Yeah…I remember…we got Cincinnati."

To Pat Adams, an
old & dear friend!
Bob Parks

X

FROM A CRYSTAL SET TO HIGH SPEED JETS

Robert L. Parks

ISBN-13: 978-1503105676
ISBN-10: 1503105679

THE TRAIL

INTRODUCTION

The picture is familiar, a white-haired old goat in his rocking chair telling stories about " back when I was a boy." There is no rocking chair yet in our picture but the white hair, old goat, and stories are still a part of it. The old goat has been around for 88 years and he managed to remember most of the things that he did and he relishes the chance to tell his stories to anyone who has ears. And there are many things about which to tell because there was always something to dig into or to explore.

Picture household life 80 years ago. A one-eyed tabletop radio with a dimly lit orange dial staring at you was entertainment. Real entertainment was going to the movies but that was expensive, maybe $1.50 per person. Many of us read books and some of us little guys found our entertainment outside riding our bikes all over, playing hide and seek or kick the can. As life moved closer to the 40's our activities branched out to more widespread activities but the radio and movies were still the essential forms of entertainment. To me, they became boring and I had to find new things to experience or to learn so I never turned down an invitation to try something.

Some of the adventures weren't always safe or good but this is how grandfather stories are made to tell to your grand children and so far, they love them even as they grow up. Many times they have asked, "Grandpa, you really didn't do that, did you?" The answer is always, "Yes, I really did" and even now as adults they listen to the stories with a grin.

My wife has grown used to my stories and when an unusual subject is discussed in the news or on TV she sometimes flippantly offers," I suppose that you have done that, too." My answer isn't always, " Yes", but sometimes it's, "Well, I tried it once," and gatherings with family and friends provide a perfect setting to tell about past experiences that relate to the conversation and more than once I heard someone say, " You should write a book."

So I did.

It begins in 1929 when I was three years old and traces my journey for the next 86 years with many word paintings and some personal artwork. Looking at the date, one can see that the Depression started soon after I came along and our family was not spared. As a three year old I can remember our moving to an old farm where our new adventure was tempered by dire conditions and living close to poverty. The farm was located in Potomac, Maryland and it was under the routes of the fledgling airlines. I was fascinated when I watched the early airplanes that flew over then, never realizing that I was witnessing the birth of commercial air travel in our country.

Then the trace continues through post Depression, pre-war, WW2, a short stint in the service, and a long history with the Boeing Company where I participated in the birth of the jet transport age.

There is a lot of aviation in the story but there is also a wide variety of people, places, incidents, humor, and adventure because there was always something to see or to experience and we never ignored the opportunity to inject some fun into life. On the flip side of the games the inexorable aura of work forever lurks so it must be served. My jobs went from the depths of the Gulf of Mexico to the bowels of the Florida Everglades and eventually high in the sky. This allowed me to taste some of the many flavors of life and to meet many interesting people, some of whom will always remain in my heart.

Those with whom I was associated came from every walk of life and a variety of races with wide ranges of education. Attitudes and life styles in the 30's and 40's were very different then and every effort has been made to accurately describe the way it was. The following years from the 50's to the next century were exciting, fast moving, and hopefully described with clarity. The places, the people, and the language have been presented truthfully and without adulteration except for changing or eliminating some names in order to protect the guilty. There is some profanity sprinkled here and there and the "N-word" is mentioned because, as my dear black friend Levy always said, "Das jes de way it is." It was part of the scene then in the era of segregation and it was offensive then as it is now.

A lot of territory has been covered and a lot of subjects have been touched and I have no doubt that some of the readers will bored with some of the subjects. Fear not. There is something for everyone in the words that follow.

XXX

PART ONE
Chapter 1.

The good life in 1930.
The crash and farm life.
A ride in an airplane.

Sister Janet & Chickeebee, 1932

I'll bet that most of us have had a Granny who lived in an old house with an attic and up in that attic there was an old trunk full of pictures and letters. I have seen a lot of them in my time and most of them encapsulated the life of a family that has passed from the living to a collection of memorable keepsakes. Since our house doesn't have an attic or a trunk I have been able to keep a few boxed items but most of my collection is in my head and that means that I'm the only one who can visit the stacks of old stuff in there. But I like to share things, and I will so without having to rely on a plug or wire.

We are now living in a world where there is a cyber-electronic-digital-ethereal–spatial revolution taking place and at the age of 88 years, I find that it is very difficult comprehend all of it. The explosion of data collection and processing is simply overwhelming.

Alas, it is mostly beyond me and try as I may, it continues to race away adding more and more icons and synonyms that are, for the most part, meaningless. But I love it. It is exciting and fascinating but when I become lost in it, I take a look in my rear view mirror at the familiar times of my past. A vast expanse stretching back over 80 years, back into a life far different than today, slightly dimmer now but not obscure. If you're interested we can travel back there if you like.

You're interested? Good, then come with me, let's go back to 1929 when it all started and let me take you on a journey through some of the events and aviation happenings of which I was a part.

You'll see that these recollections are not those of one who has accomplished great things. No daring-do here, just someone who tried to lick every side of the lollypop of life and managed to complete some of it. I was always interested in the things that were happening around me -- be it airplanes, steam trains or boats with a few other adventures thrown in. My memorable journey began when I was three years old and more than 80 years later it continues. Come on, let's take a look at it, the trail is still fresh because I travel it every day.

I was born in 1926, the fifth child in a family of six, two boys and four girls. Our father was an architect and artist and was rapidly building a reputation in Washington, D.C. We lived in the northwest section of the city in a middle class row house on Ogden Street that I can still remember. It was a small two-story affair and my brother and I had to sleep year round on the back porch off the second story bedrooms in the back of the house because our sisters got the bedrooms inside. It was no problem for us because mom had made wonderful blankets and Afghans under which we snuggled in the cold winters. They worked well because I remember waking up on a winter morning with snow on them.

I'll never forget the thrill of listening to our crystal set radio while we were burrowed under the blankets when there was snow falling outside. Then, when one of our sisters left to live in the city I was allowed to sleep in the front bedroom and, oh, what a treat that was! Sometimes in the early morning I was awakened by the clip-clop sound of the milkman and his horse making his rounds to deliver the bottles that I could hear clanking in the wire basket that he carried. It amazed me that he never got into the wagon while he was making his deliveries. He simply loaded his basket from the back of the wagon and walked to the next houses to deliver the milk while his faithful horse moved ahead, unguided, and just far enough to be at the correct spot for the next delivery.

The glass bottles were left on the front stoop to be gathered by the customer several hours later but in the freezing months of winter, the frozen milk usually had popped the cardboard cap and produced an ice sickle of rich cream that was quickly placed in the icebox for mom to use in her cooking. Sometimes she mixed it into the milk when it wasn't needed for her delicious custards but it always separated from the milk when it sat near the block of ice.

Ah, yes, the block of ice. It resided in the upper tin-lined chamber of the oaken piece of furniture in the kitchen. Every other day as the ice melted the tray of water under the icebox had to be pulled out and emptied, often spilling some of its contents on the linoleum floor. Food didn't last very long when it was stored in there, so mom had to shop several days a week to replace food that was consumed. A hot summer required that the tray be emptied every day and when the warm days arrived there were other people plying their trades.

"Watermelon, watermelon mighty sweet and fine. Watermelon, watermelon fresh off the vine." A man pushing a cart ahead of him loaded with his produce out of which he would cut a plug for you to taste. A large watermelon might cost one dollar. Then there was the Ragman, "Any ol' rags, any ol' rags". He would take your rags and what he did with them was a mystery to me.

Mom would often have her knives and scissors sharpened by an old man who pushed a cart with a foot operated wiggly grinding wheel made of stone. Everything could be sharpened for fifty cents. One summer day my little partner, Snooky McGuire, and I sat on the curb and used mom's freshly sharpened scissors to cut our hair. We were equally talented as barbers and made a complete mess out of our locks without cutting anything else, just one of our episodes that kept our mothers entertained.

As a youngster I liked to try new things and to explore whatever came along and Mom told me that a few times I caused a bit of heartburn, one of her favorites was a summer day in 1930 when I was missing for an entire afternoon. After frantically searching for me in every place they could think of they saw a big Irish cop walking along Ogden Street toward the house. Holding his hand was a little blond kid, covered in melted chocolate ice cream and eating one that was rapidly adding to the stream of brown goo that had already reached his sandals. He had found me wandering around on 14th Street some six blocks away and I guess that I "remembered" a little bit more about how to get home after each ice cream cone.

FLORENCE, MY MOTHER

My mother is to blame for my adventurism and much to my benefit. She was an adventurist, a frustrated adventurist, but never denied or diverted. Even though she mothered six children and ran a taut ship at home, she never lost the desire to see and to discover what was 'out there'.

When I was four years old, she would put my baby sister and me in our black Hupmobile Straight Eight and drive to the airport to mail an airmail letter. To her, one did not put an airmail letter in a drop box. It must be mailed at the airport and put on an airplane. To get to the airport from our home on Ogden Street, NW, Washington, D.C., she had to drive down 14th Street through the city and cross the 14th street Bridge and turn right to reach the field. Then we could sit in the car for an hour and watch the airplanes. Oh yes, and to mail an airmail letter.

The airport was the old Hoover Field that served Washington, D.C. According to a statement by Charles Lindbergh, it was the worst in the country. It was situated on a small patch of swampy ground below the hill on which sat the Lee-Custis Mansion. The road to the mansion crossed the middle of the cinder-patch runway and when an airplane was taking off or landing, a red light and siren hopefully stopped vehicular traffic from crossing the runway. I have vivid memories of sitting in the "Hup" at the red light to see a Ford Tri-motor roar across the road in front of us and climb away.

I have a faint memory of many trips to the airport. We not only watched the airplanes, we visited the only hangar on the field where we went in to see a mechanic repairing a Curtiss Condor's fuselage fabric near the tail. How mother managed that, is lost to the ages. We stood there and watched him stitching the tear in the fabric while he explained that the airplane slid on the ice and hit something.

We never went straight home from there. Mom went either to the waterfront on the Potomac River to buy fish, or we went to the yards in back of the Union Station to watch the steam locomotives. There was always a lineup of those giants where they were washed and spiffed up. We saw the George Washington, a lovely Hudson-type locomotive dressed in olive green with white and gold trim. The Royal Blue was there sometimes as were the other beautiful locomotives that pulled the "Limited's."

So that's how it happened. That's how I became what we now call a "motor head", but I became an airplane nut and I my attention from then on was to the sky. I guess that is why I have been called an Airhead most of my life.

AFTER THE COLLAPSE OF '29

In 1932 we were living in the fashionable district of Bethesda, Maryland and we had a live-in maid, a wonderful black lady who cared for us kids and took care of the house. Dad was doing very well as a prominent architect and he had provided us with a beautiful three-story classic Colonial style home that he designed. Our stay there was short-lived because the bottom fell out of everything and soon we found ourselves on a defunct farm in Potomac, Maryland. Our life and survival there is a story of creative initiative and the resolve to do what had to be done. I don't recall any complaints, just grim determination on mom's face and terse orders to do her bidding.

The farm was out in the middle of nowhere on a hill northwest of Washington, D.C., under the route of the airplanes on their way to points like Cleveland and Pittsburgh. We moved there in the summer of 1932 and we had to muck out the house and the grounds around it since it was used for a drinking hideout during Prohibition. There was nothing around it but rolling open farmland as far as you could see. The front yard and the house were literally knee deep in empty bottles and it took weeks for us to get rid of them. We kids never realized the traumatic change in the life of the family going from a posh existence to the bare minimums. It was a big adventure for us except for the smelly and scary outhouse down by the chicken pen. We couldn't understand why we had to go out to the springhouse to get water because our old house had faucets that water came out of and here we had to work that big pump. The buckets were awful heavy and I had to use both hands to carry one and I spilled a lot on the way back to the kitchen. They scratched my legs, too.

When I had brought in three buckets of water, mom poured it in the kitchen sink and a washtub so that she could use it for cooking and washing clothes. That was my job until my big brother came home from school and, boy, was I glad! He could carry two buckets at once because he was 14 years old and a lot stronger.

Soon after we moved to the farm, dad came home with several boxes full of baby chickens. I couldn't count very fast but there must have been 100 of them, well, there were a lot of them peeping and huddling together. Mom and dad decided that we had to have some source of food since there were no grocery stores out here but my little sister and I were disappointed that they weren't purchased for us to play with. We helped to board the babies up in the old equipment shed so the foxes and other animals wouldn't get to them. We little children didn't realize it then but these chicks would keep us fed for several years.

Keeping us fed was uppermost in our parent's minds. Dad found work as a draftsman at the Washington Navy Yard and that brought in some much needed cash but it kept him away all week and we only saw him on the weekends. My big brother assumed the responsibilities needed to keep things running on the farm during the week because, after all, he was 14 and knew how to do anything that had to be done.

Soon after we had gotten the chicks mom went to the south side of the house, the sunny side, and started chopping and digging with the hoe and pick. This was an activity for which she was not accustomed. Mom was obese but she was out there doing the best that she could because she was determined to plant a garden for our vegetables. She was soon bathed in perspiration and breathing hard but she continued. The patch in which she was working appeared to have been a garden at one time and she was going to make it a garden again. My little sister and I pitched in and pulled weeds and tried to make it easier for mom and three days later she planted seeds for string beans, corn, and other things that she thought that we needed.

Looking back at this image, it is painful to think of this lady digging in the dirt when she was a classical musician who had played the piano and sang at the White House when she was younger. And dad, a gifted architect and artist, was reduced to work as a draftsman at the Navy Yard! We didn't have the maturity to consider these things then but looking back now, I can realize what a demeaning position into which my parents were forced. They did it and there were no complaints.

By the end of the summer we had some vegetables that would soon mature and the baby chickens had become real chickens that were put into the chicken pen. We weren't allowed to eat many of the vegetables because mom canned most of them. Picture a lady working over a wood fired range in the kitchen during the 100-degree summer heat boiling the jars and putting the vegetables into them. She kept at it for days until the shelves in the pantry were full of our winter supply of food. I still see her in her worn cotton dress, stained in the front and bathed in sweat, while she toiled over the range. That wood range was the only source of cooking heat, hot water for cleaning dishes, bathing, and heating the house in the winter. That scenario will be addressed later.

One of the sweeter memories of that summer was my little sister, Janet, and I sitting by mom on the cool concrete porch in front of the house while she snapped the string beans and peeled potatoes. Our wonderful big dog, Pal, enjoyed the coolness also and he peacefully lay there with some of the baby chicks climbing all over him.

A few days later Janet came in from the front and told mom that there was a colored man standing by the fence near the front gate which was a good 100 feet from the house. In those days, a colored man would NEVER approach a white man's farmhouse. Even though we were living in Maryland and the Civil War had ended 70 years before, segregation was alive and well. Stepping onto the porch, mom asked the man what he wanted. With his hat in his hand he said that he was looking for work for him and his two workhorses.

"I do plowin' an clearin' stumps and all kind of stuff like dat."

Mom's demeanor quickly changed when she asked his name he said," Russell, may-um "

"Is that your first name, Russell?"

"No may-um, it's Sam."

"Well, Mr. Russell, I think we can use your services because I would like to plant some corn and potatoes. How soon can you start?"

"I can be here fuss thing in the mornin' if'n that's alright. I hope that dog an' me can make friends"

"He'll be fine, he knows that you mean no harm. We will be ready for you early tomorrow morning."

"Yes may-um. I be here bright'n early"

Mr.Russell arrived at 7:00 a.m. sharp in a wagon pulled by his two horses, a black horse named "Snowball" and a brown and white named "Zoots". A plow was lashed to the back of the wagon and in minutes Mr. Russell had it on the ground and the horses aligned and hooked up, ready for work. Mom asked him to plow the field in front of the house, a perfect sunny place for potatoes to grow.

The next project was the plowing of the large plot on the south side of the house that sloped away to fence line. That is where she planned to plant corn, peas, and beans.

Mr. Russell's appearance couldn't have been planned any better than if he had dropped from heaven. Mom and dad had the answer to a crucial food problem and not only were the fields beautifully tilled, but Mr.Russell planted the seeds for us. Tilling the fields took the youth and beauty from dad's beautiful Huppmobile when it had to be used to help the horses pull some tenacious stumps out of their liars and after that it became part tractor and part automobile, hauling split wood on the weekends for mom's range and taking dad to work during the week. Like the rest of us, the Hupp had to earn its keep.

I don't recall when or how we got a duck but we soon had another playmate to join "Chickeebee", our Rhode Island Red rooster. Both those birds imprinted with Janet and they were her "dolls", since she only had one tattered ragdoll. She would put them in her rusty little baby carriage and go squeaking around in the barnyard with her "babies". Of course, the cracked corn that she put in the carriage was more than adequate enticement to keep them in the basket. I don't recall who named the duck but I believe that my sister, Jeanne, had something to do with christening her "Marlene Ducktrich".

So, we had a chicken, a duck, and a dog to play with when we weren't pulling weeds or attending to the chickens. They were constant companions and on rainy days when we were inside the kitchen with mom they took their station under the window, quacking and chirping for corn that mom threw out to them but on sunny days we were all over the property and by the end of the day we were pretty much done in. After dinner we sometimes had a bath in a washtub in front of the range, giving mom and big brother, Joe, the ideal time to check us for ticks. There was always one or two to be pulled off with tweezers and dropped into a jar of kerosene. Between checking us kids and the dog, we had quite a collection of the pests.

Ticks weren't the only problem. There were no screens on the windows and if they were opened in the summer, the mosquitoes made it unbearable if you weren't completely buried under the covers. Closing the windows and spraying the room with Flit helped but something else was biting me and I complained to mom and Joe. After several nights of whining and showing my bites to them, they figured that they should inspect the room and bed. Joe discovered that the mattress was infested with bed bugs and promptly threw it out of the window and burned it.

As the summer drifted into fall, dad, Joe, and I worked in the "bottoms" near the creek cutting and splitting wood for the range for we knew that it would be the only warm place in the house during the winter. My job was to haul the split wood up to the barn where it could cure a little bit before winter. One of my prized possessions was a pretty little red wagon and I had to use it to haul the wood. Since it would hold only four or five pieces, I had to make many trips up the rutted road to the barn and by the end of the summer the wagon suffered the same fate as dad's Hupmobile: beaten, dirty, and bent.

Late summer signaled the time to attend school and I was enrolled in the first grade at Bethesda Elementary. I looked forward to it and found school was to my liking but getting there was a perpetual problem when dad was at work in the city. When he was home he would sometimes drop me off at the school bus stop and sometimes at school. I had to ride the school bus when he was gone and that eventually became the only means of transport.

We have always heard the "grandpa story" of walking a mile in the snow to get to school. Well, our farmhouse was exactly one mile of dirt road from the hard surfaced road and that is what I walked every morning and evening on school days. In the middle of winter it was pretty dark and scary in the morning and the road seemed to get longer but it was mostly downhill. Coming home from school was even harder because it was a long uphill grind. I always feared the dark thick bushes and scrub trees that blocked the light along the edge of the road and I can't imagine allowing a 6 year old to do that nowadays but we didn't give it much of a thought then. Besides, there was no one available to meet me.

Winter finally forced fall out of our lives and settled in with the bland colors of land and darkening skies. The fall season triggered brilliant colors in the trees in the bottoms along the creek and even our apples trees and oaks up here on the hill were beautiful. But now we faced wind, rain, snow, and that made the hike to the school bus stop much more difficult. Any problems that we kids had were unimportant compared our parents who were city people and had never lived on a farm in good times much less in the grip of a depression.

At age six I had no idea why we had to move to the farm. I liked some things about the farm but the house in Bethesda was a lot warmer and I didn't like the outhouse very much. Later, I was told that dad's first employer, Mr. Milburn, graciously offered to rent the farm to dad for $25.00 a month. Milburn was not a farmer, he used it for a drinking hideout during Prohibition and that was his only interest in it. The house was a plain old wooden two-story structure built in 1917 so it wasn't fancy but it was huge. The living room stretched across the entire length of the house and measured 20 feet by 40 feet. On the right side behind a door there was a short flight of steps that reached a small landing from which the stairs went up to the second floor and to four bedrooms. The landing also had a short flight that went down into the kitchen.

The out buildings and springhouse showed that it was a functioning 425 acre farm at one time but one of the most interesting buildings was an old log cabin near the back of the barnyard. Dad said that it was built in 1860 to house slaves. This, then, established a deeper history of this place and gave evidence that the state line between Maryland and Virginia was blurred when it came to the use of slaves. Janet and I peeked through the window where we could see that it had a dirt floor and a loft in the back. An old ornate pot-bellied wood stove sat to the right to complete the sparse furnishings. I always wondered who was here in 1860 and what the slaves did then.

WINTER 1932-33

By December, the cold weather had us firmly in its grasp and the cold wind made it too uncomfortable to play outside so we pretty much lived in the house, mostly in the kitchen. I have dim memories of Christmas then, a small tree that we chopped down and set up in the living room. It had popcorn garlands that we strung, a few glass ornaments, and the ever- present tinsel. It was kind of scraggly but we loved it. There were two presents wrapped for each of the kids and the stockings full of goodies were hung on the mantel.

Tangerines, nuts, hard candies, and wool mittens that mom had made for us filled the stockings to bulging. Our presents from under the tree were filled with wool sweaters made by mom, flannel pajamas, and heavy socks. I remember a little tin train locomotive that I was thrilled to get.

We quickly gathered up everything and scampered into the kitchen to warm up by the range and much to our delight, mom gave us hot co-coa and some sweet buns.

It was a good Christmas.

The winter seemed to go on forever but finally it gave way to spring and thankfully, warm weather. However, that also brought mud, sticky mud that we had to stagger through on our way to the school bus but I somehow had been given some wonderful lace up high top leather boots. They were very special, with a little pocket on the side into which I could put my pocketknife and I was so proud of them! They were too large but they kept my feet almost dry and they looked just like the "Mounties" wore in Canada.

We worked our way through spring and by the time summer arrived we had the sprouts of corn, beans, peas, and potatoes pushing their way up through the rich earth. The chicken pen was full of chickens and hens were producing a good supply of eggs. We had settled into a different way of life and we were surviving. Dad was bringing home things from the city like fresh milk, oranges and seafood sometimes.

Big brother Joe had landed a job in Bethesda at McDowell Bros. gas station and made enough money to purchase a nice 1929 Model A Ford roadster. WOW! How did he do that? It cost $45.00 dollars! How did he do that and how did he learn to drive it? The only car that he ever drove was the Hupmobile when he was pulling stumps. Well, after all, he was 15 now and he could do anything...and he did. His aspirations to become a doctor became evident when he took it upon himself to treat a bad cut on the fore leg of our dog, Pal. Joe cleaned and stitched the laceration while we did our best to hold on to Pal who seemed to know that he was being helped but still struggled and whimpered. Then Chickeebee got some kind of blue colored cyst on one of his legs and Joe lanced it and cleaned it out without complications. Both patients survived without any infection.

INFECTION! Even as a six year old, I was acutely aware of the danger of getting an infection and we were under strict orders to go to mom immediately because she had a battery of medicines and tools that she coupled with a aggressive attack to clean a wound quickly and, to our discomfort, DEEPLY. Soap and hot water first then iodine or merthyolate, and hydrogen peroxide were freely swabbed down into a wound and she forced bleeding to keep the flow going out of the site instead of into it. Blood poisoning and lockjaw were always a worry and mom became our first line of defense.

So, a second car was sorely needed on the farm for numerous reasons. We were dangerously isolated since we didn't have electricity, a radio, a telephone, or transportation and there was no way to reach medical help in an emergency. There were no doctors nearby, at least that we knew about, so the Model A didn't totally solve our plight but it closed the gap somewhat. Joe also gave us a ride to school occasionally and that was special!

The summer of 1933 was good to us. Warm sunny days and enough rain to keep the corn and other vegetables growing. The chickens and ducks were laying eggs and everything else seemed to have established a rhythm and we had hit a stride where we seemed to know what we were doing as new farmers. Public enemy Number 1, John Dillinger was still on the loose along with Baby Face Nelson, and Al Capone. That was mildly interesting to me but much more interesting was watching the airplanes fly over every day. Ford Tri-Motors, Stinson Tri-Motors, Curtiss Condors, occasional military planes like Curtiss Falcons and even a DH4 once or twice. Civilian stuff like Waco's, Stinson SM8's, and Travel Airs often came by to show us their bright colors.

At night we could see the lights of Washington and those of the airplanes as they came clattering over. I wondered how in the world they could fly at night. We spent a lot of our summer evenings out on the big front porch watching the "Lightning Bugs"; Fireflies in classic terms. The lack of electric lights meant that inside activities were performed by the light of a kerosene lamp but that didn't stop me from sketching pictures of the airplanes that I knew. Apparently, I had inherited my father's artistic talents and I was drawing airplanes every chance I got. That often got me into trouble at school when I was drawing instead of conducting some other onerous activity.

The winter of 1932-33 was brutally cold and snowy and there were not many airplanes to see, but we could hear them in the clouds. Getting to school and surviving was more important. We got better established during the summer of 1933 and our mother resumed her trips to Hoover Field where we saw a new and exciting airplane. I couldn't take my eyes off the sleek grey metal design. Low wing, twin engines AND the wheels "folded up" into the wings! We had to wait forever for it to take off.

Finally the passengers boarded through the door on the right side and it cranked up with clouds of blue smoke and taxied to the south end of the oiled dirt field. After revving up the engines once or twice, it roared down the field and lifted smoothly into the air and "folded up" the wheels. That term was the way we described the retractable landing gear at the time and the Boeing Model 247 initiated us to the new concept.

The red light traffic signal and the man waving a flag where the road crossed the runway was still in effect. Then the coal tipple of the Griffon Fuel Company at the south end of the field still interfered with the landing approach. I remember that an airplane on approach clipped that coal tipple in bad weather and crashed on the field.

The other demeaning feature of the airport was the flooding in winter due to its proximity to the Potomac River. Wiley Post and Charles Lindbergh stated that it was the worst airport in the country and I think that they were correct. BUT, there was a public swimming pool across the road from the terminal and in the unlikely event that a flight was late you could go for a swim for twenty- five cents. We never did that, but we enjoyed our walking out to the low fence near the gate to watch the passengers board those big modern airplanes. There were no covered walkways then, you went through the gate and walked to the airplane through the rain or snow and for me that was okay.

We had a very bad winter in 1933-1934 with a lot of below zero cold and snow. We could hear the airplanes droning over us as they plied their work. One of my chores was to go out to the chicken coop every morning to get the eggs for breakfast. I was walking up the path to the house when I heard an engine in the cold fog that sounded way too low. It was coming fast and as I turned to look to northwest I could see the faint vision of an airplane between the log cabin and the barn.

The next instant, it was up on the right wing and zooming up just in time to miss the chicken house and the large apple tree behind the farmhouse. The image of the Curtiss O-1 Falcon is still fresh in my mind and I can still see the "U.S. Army" painted on the lower wing as it banked away from the house and disappeared in the cold fog. I then realized that I had dropped the bowl of eggs in the snow. Only one was cracked.

The army pilot was right on course, but 500 feet too low. I learned later that he was one of those poor souls who were assigned to fly the mail when Roosevelt took the contracts away from the more competent civilian operators. This ill-advised decision lasted only six months after killing ten poorly trained and ill-equipped Army aviators.

SECOND GRADE

"I am Miss McIntyre, I will be your second grade teacher!" I have no memory of what she said after her warm introduction to her new class but 80 years later I still have vivid memories of my incarceration in her classroom. She was a gaunt young woman with an active stride and a hatchet face that was barely wide enough to accommodate her thin-lipped grimace. She must have even frightened her hair because it looked like it was trying to escape her scalp in every direction. Soon after school began I felt uneasy in her presence and that I had to be careful. I did what I was supposed to do but as the weeks went by she made comments about my appearance and many times charged down the aisle to grab my arm in a steel grip when I made a mistake. I was at a loss to figure out what I had done to incur her wrath and it became a daily experience.

Finally one day she told me that I had to remove my boots and place them outside the door until the end of the day. It was early winter and the rains had come. I was still walking the muddy road to the bus stop so my boots were muddy and I had managed to get some on my pants. The door to which she referred was an outside door, every classroom had one door that opened to the schoolyard and there my boots sat all day while I was in my stocking feet. When it was time to go home I had to put on cold and sometimes wet boots.

The cold school bus ride ended with a long, muddy, cold, and dark walk to the house. There, my boots were removed and placed next to the warm range to dry and I sat cross-legged as close as I could get to the warmth that I didn't have all day at school. By morning the heat from the range had dried the mud on my boots and I was able to knock it off outside before I put them on for school. Then it all started over again.

One day, mom asked me why my socks were getting so dirty and I told her what I had to do at school. She looked at me for a moment and went on with folding clothes after they had dried in the kitchen. Several days later I was shocked to see her in her black coat and black hat march into our classroom and head straight for Miss McIntyre, dispensing with any protocol to see the principal beforehand. If I had had the power to shrink myself to the size of a pea I would have done it, but I had to sit there and watch mother chastise my dear teacher. I knew how mom was when she was angry and Miss M. never uttered a word.

Did it help? Not one bit. It got worse. I was the only "farm kid" in a classroom filled with city kids, some of whom were from well to do families. I was the only one who was dirty and perhaps smelled of smoke and animals, so maybe that had something to do with my displeasing my teacher. At least my friends didn't care and I had a heavy love affair, at least in my mind, with a pretty little blond girl named Barbara Johnson. She was the daughter of Walter Johnson, "Big Train", the famous pitcher for the Washington Senators. My big brother went to high school with his son, Eddie. So, I was the frog in the Punchbowl.

I unwittingly aided Miss McIntyre in her witchery by failing my first arithmetic test, and I mean FAIL. Unbelievably, I got all of the addition problems wrong! All of them! She ceremoniously held my test high for all the kids to see and then ridiculed me for being the only one in the class to get ALL of the problems wrong. If a hole had been handy, I would have dropped into it.

I had to take my paper home to show my parents and have them sign it to prove that they had seen it. Dad was an architect, my brother and sister were honor students and I figured that I had a serious head problem. I didn't like math in the first place but I never imagined that I was THAT dumb. I could have wet my pants when I gave my test to him. He studied it with concentration and concern without commenting while I sat waiting for my admonishment.

After what seemed like a week he said, "Well, I see the mistake. You added the number of the problem to the column of numbers beneath it. I don't see any mistakes in what you did except to ignore the decimal next to the number over the problem."

He signed the paper with a note explaining what I had done but my teacher still held it up for the class to see and announced that it was "completely wrong". After that, if I made the slightest infraction she would march back to me and squeeze my arm until it turned red.

One of my important chores year round was splitting kindling wood for the range and dad brought home several apple boxes made of thin pine. They were much easier to split than the small logs so happily went to work on them. I was careless and let the thumb of my right hand stick out too far from the hatchet handle when I split a thin board and jammed a long splinter under my thumb nail clear up to the first knuckle. I did the best that I could to remove the splinter while it was still a bit numb but mom had to complete the job.

There was no way to sterilize the deep wound so she made it bleed as much as possible and hoped for the best. The best came the next day when my thumb swelled and turned a reddish hue. The next several days there was pus and blood coming out of point of entry and my finger was stiff. Mom did everything to keep forcing the wound to drain but there was little else that could be done so she had me soak it in an Epsom salt bath. It seemed to stabilize after three or four days with no increase in swelling and the drainage continued.

Naturally, this affected my penmanship and left a little mess on my papers. Miss McIntyre loved it; she now had more ammunition with which she could continue her attacks. Several days later while I was mentally drifting away from my class work I started to pick at what appeared to be a white scab or a crust at the end of my thumb and I found that I couldn't pick it off. I pulled my little knife out the pocket of my boot and placed the point under the "scab" to lift it off and to my surprise, it was something solid. More prying revealed that it was wood. I worked it out enough to grasp it with my fingernails and pulled out another long splinter followed by a soup that dripped all afternoon.

I was panicked that I would REALLY mess up all my papers and asked to go to the boy's bathroom where I tried to wash and wrap my thumb in toilet paper. I kept my hand in my pocket the rest of the day, and the day after I pulled several more slivers out of the opening. Gradually it somehow healed without a lasting infection.

The winter of 1933-1934 was memorable in its brutal grip on our lives and cold or not our lives had to continue in as normal a manner as we could manage. Bathing in a washtub in the kitchen, eating in the kitchen, doing our schoolwork in the kitchen and then running upstairs to jump into an ice cold bed was routine. How ice cold? When mom became sick and was bedridden for weeks, my brother took a glass of water up stairs to her and spilled some on the steps. He came down and got a towel from the kitchen to wipe it up but it had already frozen. It stayed there until spring.

Things kept running when mom was ill because Joe, 15, and Jeanne, 12, did the cooking and all else that had to be done. Little Janet, 3 ½, and I, 7, had our duties also. One was to pick out the unburned coal from the ashes and return them to scuttle in the kitchen. Dad occasionally would bring home sacks of coal to supplement the wood that we burned, so we stretched it as much as we could. That wood range saved our lives with its bounty of heat. Most important for me was its keeping warmth in the board that I took with me to the outhouse when it was 20 degrees or lower.

Early spring of 1934 brought a lot of surprises for us kids. Mr. Russell told mom and dad that they were being evicted from their cabin and that he might not be able to work for us anymore. Mom and dad offered to let them occupy the old Civil War cabin rent free in exchange for helping on the farm. Of course, they accepted.

One dark and stormy night (I just had to do that) dad used Joe's Model A to go down to the Russells and I rode with him. Halfway there the car took a hard bump in the muddy rutted road and the steering wheel came off in his hands. Dad was never mechanically adept and he frantically tried to get the wheel back on the column but never took his foot off the throttle and the car careened down the road while dad struggled with his dilemma. The little car was like a train on a track, the wheels were locked into the deep ruts and simply went down the road as if it knew where we were going.

One would have thought so because we did arrive at the Russell's place that was just off the road to Potomac but dad had to leave the car in the middle of the muddy road. Mr. Russell reinstalled the steering wheel for us and helped to turn the car around for our trip home. The rain continued to pour down and dad drove home while grimly pressing the steering wheel down on the column.

Soon the Russell family of four moved into the log cabin. Sam, his wife Mary, and his two children had very little when they arrived so they weren't pressed for space. I recall a table and three chairs and several trunks in which they kept their clothing. The children slept on hay in the loft and Mary and Sam slept on hay that he fashioned into a bed by framing it with some small logs. The daughter must have worked elsewhere because we seldom saw her and I can no longer think of her name but I'll never forget Tommy, their little boy of 7. The best part of this arrangement was having a new playmate because Tommy was my age and we immediately became friends but we didn't forget little Janet. She still had Marlene Ducktrich and Chickeebee to play with.

As the months went by we all blended together and many times I ate lunch and sometimes dinner with the Russells after dad and Mr. Russell somehow found a small wood stove on which they could cook. I relished the grits, eggs, and country bacon that Mary cooked for breakfast. Biscuits, greens from the garden, fatback, and cornbread and molasses for desert after lunch. We all shared the garden, eggs, chickens, potatoes, and corn from the fields that Sam tilled with Zoots and Snowball.

I was too innocent then to think about their situation. They were barely surviving, toiling for someone else, and living in a shelter that was built for slaves long before them. Here they were, a short step from slavery seventy years after the Civil War. Not much had changed for their kind.

The early spring of 1934 brought some pivotal events to us with the sudden death of Sam's wife that saddened all of us. She was a helpful and cheerful assistant to mom as she helped with the house, garden, and cooking. Sam and Tommy were numb and looked hopelessly lost. Shortly after Mary's passing one of the workhorses sustained a terrible laceration over its left eye when he got tangled in a barbed wire fence and Sam was worried that he would lose half of his means to earn a living, meager as it was. Enter the doc! Joe to the rescue again! He examined Sam's horse and figured that he could suture the injury and close it. "Sew" the injury would be a more accurate description because he was planning to use needles and thread from mom's sewing kit.

He and Sam lashed the horse to a stanchion so that it couldn't move anything down to its hooves; the neck, head, legs, and body were immobilized. The 16- year old budding physician sterilized the wound and with pliers, with which to grasp the flaps of skin, and mom's needle and thread, successfully closed the cut. The poor horse suffered through it without anesthetic and he raised hell during the procedure. The cut quickly healed without infection, Snowball soon made friends with us again, and Sam put him back to work.

FINI

As with all things in life, they have an end and our saga at the farm came to a close in the fall of '34 when dad announced that we were moving back to Bethesda. I have no memory of this event. Perhaps it was so sad that I have shoved it in a dark corner of my mind. I have no image of Sam and Tommy leaving but they had to and where they went is a mystery. Janet and I missed our little friend and his gentle father. We missed Chickeebee and Marlene and our life on the farm. It was tough and hardscrabble but it was a good life to be able to swim in the creek in the summer, to eat the food from the garden, to have fresh eggs and chicken, and to play in the woods.

I wouldn't miss the cold winters when we had to walk so far in the mud and stand by the road in tears because our feet hurt from the cold. AND I certainly wouldn't miss the Witch, Miss McIntyre. My parting performance in her class involved some difficulty with spelling as well as arithmetic. For some reason I couldn't spell December or Thursday. Dad drilled me one evening and I had it thoroughly straightened out before I went to bed. When I came down for breakfast, dad asked me to spell December. My response. D-E-C-E-M-D-A-Y. Without a word, mom stopped cooking and looked at me. Dad said, "Spell Thursday". My response. T-H-U-R-S-B-E-R. Nothing more was said and I ate a silent breakfast, BUT I somehow spelled the words correctly at school.

So, that was the end of our days on the farm. We never went back there again but none of us forgot our time there and many times it was mentioned in our family conversations. It was mentioned somewhat with pride and relief, and amazement that we were able to survive it at all. Sometimes I think of our dog, Pal, sleeping outside near the house during the worst of the winter, nothing more than a lump in the deep snow. He was tough and would not enter the house. And why should he? It was as cold in there as it was outside. So, we all did what had to be done and, at the time, we didn't think much about it then.

But there are a few things that 80 years later are still a part of my persona. I cannot throw edible food away and I MUST eat all the food on my plate. I still keep too many "things" because I might be able to use them later.

That three-year test was a bright spot in my family history. I say "my" because I'm the only one left now but I speak for all who were there. We certainly weren't the only family challenged at that time but we had to face what was thrown before us and thank God we had strong and resourceful parents

BACK TO "CIVILIZATION"

We moved to the north end of Bethesda, Maryland just north of Washington. Our new home was sheer luxury with a furnace in the basement that heated every room in the house. Water came out of all the faucets in the bathroom and kitchen and we didn't have to out to an outhouse anymore. THAT was a wonderful improvement! We could simply move a switch and get electric lights again and we could see everything in a room at night. I could draw my pictures a lot better. I loved it! There were no more bed bugs, cockroaches, or mosquitoes at night and the floors were warm when we went to bed. The beds were warm when we got into them.

We did miss our little playmates, Marlene and Chickeebee, but not for long. Our new life offered so many things to do and so many things that were interesting and new. There were kids our age that lived in the neighborhood and we never had a moment when we were idle.

North of us was a wheat field that must have stretched to Rockville and I soon found out that there was an airport up there.

It was too far for an eight year old to hike to so I had to rely on the largess of those who drove the Model A's in the family. No one shared my interest in aviation so I resorted to my drawings and magazines. "G-8 and His Battle Aces" and "Bill Barnes Flying Aces" transported me into my own world of aerial adventures. THEN came my hero: "Jimmy Allen of The Airways" on the radio.

We now had a radio and what a wonderful thing that was! But to be able to listen to the adventures of Jimmy Allen put me in another world!

The Richfield Gasoline Co. sponsored my program and they offered the chance to belong to the JIMMY ALLEN OF THE AIRWAYS CLUB. Well. What could be better than that? A membership included a secret code ring, wings that you could wear, and a picture of Jimmy Allen's airplane that was a gleaming silver Stearman C3. You cannot imagine the thrill when a big manila envelope came in the mail for me with all the accouterment of the club: the wings, the secret code ring, and a picture of Jimmy and some other stuff. I was a real member of the aviation clan now and I wasn't just watching airplanes flying over the farm.

Then I learned that I could go to the Saturday matinee if I polished the silverware every Saturday morning. The movies cost 15 cents and I had to do ALL the silverware! But I did it. It was great fun to watch Tim Mc Coy and Buck Jones, but when the new serial came with TAILSPIN TOMMY I was in heaven! I simply could not wait for the Saturday matinee. After all, they were the greatest movies ever made! I wore my wings pinned to my sweater until some of the bullies made fun of me so I wore them under my sweater.

I wore my secret code ring until it started to turn my finger black so I put it in my pocket, but I never missed a Tailspin Tommy feature. He always won when he raced the steam locomotive and saved the girl. I really don't know how that image works, but it rests in my old head. I clearly remember his silver airplane, however. Even though I listened to Jimmie Allen on the radio during the week and watched Tailspin Tommy every Saturday, I never reached the saturation point.

AIRBORNE AT LAST!

Mid June is my birthday and in 1935 I turned nine. Life during the depression trained us to expect little and to work hard for whatever we got so I wasn't thinking about much of a celebration, maybe some cake and ice cream. One day my dad told me that we were going to take a drive and I got into our "Hup" without much thought; I always liked a ride. We drove north to Rockville and turned off at the grass strip there. Wonderful, I thought, we were going to watch airplanes. My dad got out of the car and spoke to someone in the little office and returned to tell me that he had arranged for me to take a ride in an airplane.

It is impossible to describe the incredible emotion that I felt when he said that. First, to fly was something that only the very special people did. Second, it was too expensive and I never dreamed that I could do it when I was so young. I realized it when I was greeted by a taciturn young man and asked to follow him. We walked to a little yellow airplane that I recognized as an Aeronca C-3. He adjusted something in the cabin and went forward and cranked the propeller until the airplane was running. He got in and motioned for me to get in. I climbed in and he fastened the seat belt and started to taxi down the grass strip without a word. It was then that I noticed a big hole in the floorboard and I spread my feet to make sure that I didn't let anything fall out.

The takeoff was exhilarating. I couldn't see anything forward, so I looked to the right and through the hole in the floorboard as the grass rushed by. We broke the surly bonds and I felt the wonderful sensation that comes with the freedom from the earth. The engine popped away with all the authority of its 36 horsepower. As we passed the hangar below, I waved to my parents who were standing by the car but they didn't wave back. We flew a rectangular circuit of the field and started the descent. Not a word from the pilot. I looked through the hole in the floor to see the trees as they began to rush by with increasing speed. Then the grass of the strip appeared and increased rushing by and then a bumpy landing. There was nothing from the pilot to encourage me or to invite me to aviation. But never mind, he got me into the air and I loved it.

I couldn't believe that my mom and dad would spend so much money on me. It cost 25 dollars for that 10-minute flight and it must have been tough for them to pull that out of the skimpy family budget. It was one of the most unforgettable incidents in my life.

The other startling incident occurred in the summer of 1936 when we were living in Bethesda. I don't recall exactly what I was doing at the time but I heard a foreign rumbling; a steady and increasing rumble of an engine sound that I had never heard. I ran outside in time to hear it grow louder and nearer. When I turned in the direction of the sound I saw an apparition that startled hell out of me. A huge shape emerged from behind the trees and continued to display itself for an astonishing long time. When it was three quarters exposed I could see that it was a huge dirigible, like a monstrous silver shark hovering over me looking for something to eat. The only thing that I could think that it could be was the Hindenburg and as it came into full view I could see the tail markings of the new German nation. The low steady beat of the engines never changed as it cruised by and headed south to the city. It cruised over Washington most of the day and we could hear it for hours. Now I have no doubt that many photos were made of the city and surrounding countryside that were slated for more nefarious uses in the future.

The summer of 1936 was warm and wonderfully lazy. There were no more onerous farm chores, just a few around the house so we had time to play with our new neighborhood pals. I also got a used bike for my birthday that I dearly loved but it wasn't complete without a wooden propeller on the handle bars, all the kids had one so I got some wood and gathered around with my friends and we started to carve some props for our bikes.

I got mine finished but it needed a hole in the hub for the nail so I started to carve one by spinning my knife around like a drill and what do you know? The wood split and I stabbed myself in my upper thigh. A quick trip home to get the well-known medical treatment, a firm admonishment, and orders to stay away from the knives!

I returned to my group and did what I was told and didn't touch a knife, so I was idling my time on the rope swing while another kid was trying to throw his knife to stick in the tree. Timing is everything in this world and mine was impeccable. As I swung on my way out, the knife bounced off the tree and intercepted my right foot where it DID stick up.

Here we go again not 20 minutes after one repair but this one looked a bit worse because blood was squirting out enough to make a squishing sound in my shoe as I walked home where I knew that I would receive the full force of mom's wrath. Even after I told her what happened she didn't believe me and commented that I had cut an artery and quickly applied a tourniquet. All her frantic work to prevent an infection was not enough this time and I spent a week looking at my swollen foot as the infection oozed from the wound. Mom worked on it every day, squeezing stuff out of it, soaking it in Epsom salt, and all the other desperate measures that she could think of.

Again, I somehow escaped from a serious conclusion of the infection and I slowly healed. I can still see the scar on my foot and think of that day.

Dad had a friend who owned a cottage on Chesapeake Bay and surprised us with a two-week vacation on the beach. After our dire life on the farm, this was something from heaven. Swimming, canoeing and exploring the creeks and marshes was wonderful, but when a huge flying boat came roaring over the cottage one day THAT was icing on the cake. Luckily I was on the beach and saw it coming along the shoreline straight for us and very low. A forest of struts and wires supported the wing on which were two engines that made a wonderful sound as it flew by. I didn't know it then but those two engines, Wright R-1820's, would become legend because they would power thousands of B-17's during WW2. This old bird was a Consolidated P2Y based near Annapolis. They came by almost every day---just for me.

I was ten years old now and 1936 saw many world changing events with Mussolini and Hitler showing the first signs of their depravity, but I wasn't really interested in them. I was building models, or trying to. I had to learn on my own because being the next to last in a family of six can be a lonely experience at times and no one shared my interest in airplanes. When I wasn't building models or drawing airplanes I was trying to somehow make my way to airports. My aunt Mimi lived on a farm northeast of Washington in Brooklands and our mother would load my sister and me into the "Hup" and visit her on weekends. I found out that the Queen's Chapel airport was within hiking distance and after receiving permission to walk there, my sweet aunt would always prepare a wonderful sack lunch to take with me and off I went.

Queen's Chapel Airport, unlike its royal moniker, was a dire patch of white dusty dirt and one rickety hangar. Its reason for existing escaped me even as a ten year old. It was in the middle of non-descript hardscrabble farmland crisscrossed with narrow dirt roads.

The few airplanes there looked the same as the scrubby surroundings, dirty old Waco's is all that I can recall. No one spoke to me as I examined the airplanes. One was being worked on and it fascinated me to watch the OX-5 engine with its rocker arms jumping up and down in their frantic dance. Oil and water dripped from hidden openings and blew back on the black and silver airplane adding to its grime. I watched for an hour or so and finally asked the owner if I could wash his airplane for him -- hoping for a ride in exchange.

"Why?" he answered. Why, indeed. There wasn't a patch of concrete to be seen or was there a hose faucet in sight. If there had been any water and a hose the washing process would have left the airplane in a sea of mud. Since my presence had been ignored, I walked back to my aunt's farm. The lunch was good.

I returned to that strip one more time the following year and saw a strange little plane with a roundish aluminum fuselage and a single high-mounted wing. It didn't look like much of an airplane to me with its tiny four-cylinder engine and toothpick propeller. Not much better than the Aeronca C-3 in which I flew two years before. No, that little Luscombe will never sell.

In 1937, we were living in the northwest section of Washington and I discovered that a neighbor two doors down from us was a pilot. Naturally we connected and talked about his flying a Travel Air and a Waco. He wasn't the most articulate young man or the best dressed, he was rather "common," as mom would say. BUT he was a pilot! So, his slovenly looks and manners were overlooked and I accepted an invitation to go flying with him so with mom's reluctant blessing I hopped into his Model A Ford one Saturday morning for our drive to Hybla Valley Airport south of Alexandria, Virginia. On the way he smoked one cigarette after another from a green pack of Lucky Strikes.

After driving forever, we finally pulled into the airport and stopped next to the large hangar in front of which were several Travel Air's, Waco's and some Stinson monoplanes. My cohort was warmly (and loudly) greeted by his friends and after some rather rakish bantering he motioned me out to an older Waco sitting on the grass in front of the hangar. While he was checking some things in the front of the plane he told me to get into the front cockpit and after a difficult climb I had a seat in a voluminous space bound by tubing framework and fabric. I don't recall any controls or instruments, just a hard cold wooden seat.

"Buckle up." I finally found the ends of the old leather belt and fastened them together, but I was too small for it to strap me tightly in the seat. My "friend" finally donned a filthy cloth helmet and greasy leather jacket and climbed into the rear cockpit. After he and the man cranking the propeller went through a rather lengthy yelling match the engine finally started.

We waddled out to a corner of the field and the pilot swung the airplane around into the wind and stared the takeoff. I couldn't see very much because I sat so low in the cockpit, but I quickly realized that my light sweater wasn't going to protect me from the cold wind swirling into my space. Stretching my torso to its limits allowed me to catch glimpses of the trees rushing by but again, the wind was too much for me and my eyes soon let me know that I should have had some goggles. The rumbling of the wheels ceased after a final bump and we were airborne.

For the second time in my life, I felt that wonderfully unique sensation that comes when you are free of the earth and the singular pull of gravity. The motion of flight comes from all directions at once, awakening the senses. My senses were certainly awakened from the cold air flowing around me. When I stretched up to see over the cockpit combing I was rewarded by the sight of a beautiful patchwork of bright green fields and the dark green of thick woods that stretched to the horizon. The pilot banked to the left and I could see the Potomac River's dark waters dotted with white boats.

The serenity was broken by some unannounced maneuvers that startled and frightened me. One unnerving gyration (that I think now was an attempt to perform a wingover) put the airplane on one wing tip at the peak of a steep climb and we went almost inverted. I'll never forget the shock of cold air on my buttocks as I left the seat and strained against the seat belt. A desperate reactive grab for the edge of the seat and some tubing in the fuselage didn't help much but as soon as I did it, the nose went down with the wires screaming. Then my first time to experience a high G pullout came and I was jammed down onto the seat, my body crumpling a bit. The only thing that I liked about it was the return of warmth to my bottom. "Ace" did a few more turns and headed for the airport.

I could sense that we were descending now and I could see the trees out to the side of the cockpit then, KER BLAMM! We collided with the earth and then a short bit of silence and another KA BLUMP, KA BLUMP and the characteristic rumble of the wheels. The airplane was swerving from side to side and finally we slowed and turned at the edge of the field. I couldn't see where we were taxiing as we returned to the hangar, but I felt relief as the engine was shut down.

No sooner than I put my shaky feet on terra firma I was handed a dirty towel and told to wipe the oil off the airplane. The pilot disappeared into the hangar and I wiped as much as I could and went to the car to wait for the driver. He finally appeared, lit up a Lucky Strike, and got into the Model A and we started our trip home. I could smell liquor on his breath and my eleven-year old brain told me that maybe this wasn't the best guy to fly with.

When we arrived at our homes he mentioned that he would be flying again the next weekend and asked if I wanted to go with him. I quickly said that we were going to my aunt's farm. Several weeks later he disappeared, leaving a pregnant wife who was fortunately living with her parents.

Chapter 2.

The move to Florida and another war.
The RAF in our home.

Whittacker Bayou | Robert Parks

TO A WONDERFUL NEW WORLD

That winter I was attacked by some sort of malady that was suspected of being tuberculosis. I was pulled out of school and spent my days at home building WW1 airplane models and sleeping. I had constructed an entire WW1 aerodrome complete with canvas hangars and tail wheel dollies for the six fighter planes that I had built from scratch. Spads, Nieuports and Fokkers all carved from balsa wood and correctly painted. After all, I was an avid reader of Flying Aces and Air Trails and I knew exactly what to do. I wish that I had that display now.

In February of 1938, my mother and I boarded a Greyhound bus and headed for Sarasota, Florida. I had no idea where we were going. My only concern at the time was a model kit that my father bought for me to build a beautiful free flight of a Miss America. It had a wingspan of 36 inches!

I believe that our trip was 3 days in duration. I can't remember where we stayed, but I recall our arrival in Sarasota on a cold February day. So for the next nine months we lived in a little cottage on the sunlit beach of Siesta Key while I ate and swam myself to good health. Much to my dismay, the only airplanes that I saw during that period was a flight of five Curtiss P-36's that made a loud demonstration over town as part of an Army Air force exercise to make certain that we knew they existed. Five Hamilton Standard props in flat pitch make wonderful noise at 900 feet.

Our father managed to find the wherewithal to build a small cottage on Siesta Key near where my mom and I stayed. So mom, my little sister and I moved back to Florida for the summer of 1940 to enjoy our new little house on the beach. That summer was one that will live with me forever. Before we left Washington, the war in Europe had started and I had started my first year of high school.

The city was on alert and the signs of our involvement were immanent. Military vehicles hurried about at times and there were blackout practices. I didn't understand it fully, but it was exciting to read about the aerial fights over Britain and to see photos of the Spitfires, Hurricanes and ME-109's.

THE SUNDAY PLANE

I spent a lot of time on the beach swimming, watching, walking, swimming and fiddling around. Believe it, living in paradise is boring when one has no one else to share the broad expanse of sugary–white sand, clear turquoise water, and gentle sea breezes.

One Sunday morning after breakfast, I was walking on the beach in front of the house when I heard some engines.

Our cottage was near a point where the deep water channel went into Sarasota Bay. There was a stand of Australian pines on the point and as I turned, an airplane came roaring around the trees on the point. Up on one wing and very low, it leveled off and flew by at probably 100 feet altitude. WOW! That was a marvelous surprise. BUT WAIT! Here comes another one! Another Stinson rounded the point the same way and unbelievably another one right behind it, a Waco CSO! WOW! I couldn't believe it! It was like they were hiding behind the trees waiting for me come out on the beach.

As I watched them fly away down the beach, the sound of another engine came roaring behind me and I turned just in time to see a silver Travel Air coming around the point very low and banking steeply. It leveled out as it went past and I could see that the pilot was a very tall man who literally sat head and shoulders above the edge of the cockpit, his thick black hair blowing back in the wind. I waved frantically in the hope that he would see me.

Just after he passed me, he executed a climbing turn to the right over the water. It was a beautiful chandelle that put him as high as he could get and facing in the opposite direction. His airspeed was just above stalling when the nose began to fall through and down he came in a steep diving turn. A brief flash of sunlight on his wings as he leveled off a few feet above the beach and with full power and wires screaming he flashed past me close enough to touch. Well, almost. Then climbing slightly, he gave a goodbye wave by rocking his wings.

Could that pilot ever realize what he had done? On that wide expanse of beach, he caught sight of a lone figure; a thirteen-year-old boy, jumping with glee and waving his arms at airplanes roaring by and he responded. In my excitement I must have yelled to myself, "HE SAW ME! HE SAW ME!" If I didn't, I sure felt it.

How does one describe the body-numbing experience that a young boy feels when he has connected with a stranger who is yet unknown to him but is an instant friend? It was a magical instant. An unforgettable thrill, I had connected with a real pilot whom I had never met and might not ever meet, but he saw me and saluted me, a small boy on the beach who had found his hero.

Things were never the same after that.

I watched them fly down the coastline until I could barely see them, but I caught sight of them circling out over the water. THEY WERE LANDING! I started to trot down the beach. I had to see them. This was Tailspin Tommy in real life! They were down on Crescent Beach about a mile and a half to two miles from me, so I trotted and walked as fast as I could. After running past Greer's Cottages and the old Siesta Casino, I trotted the last mile to my destination. And there they were! Seven of them were arranged in a semi-circle on the hard sand just above the water line and facing the Gulf. Their bright colors further illuminated by the bright white sand for which Siesta Key was well known.

A real airplane guy would never refer to the colors from the spectrum simply as green or blue. That would deny them of their colorful appellations. For example, cream was not just cream. It was "Diana Cream". Then there was "Stearman Vermillion", "International Orange", "Cub Yellow" and "Stinson" Blue. These bright colors were usually combined with a black or dark blue fuselage.

So, there they sat like a bunch of flowers on a white tablecloth. Sitting at the end of the lineup was the silver Travel Air, sans bright colors, but never mind, it sparkled in the sun like a diamond.

A picnic lunch was being spread on a blanket in the center and the fliers and their ladies were busy chatting so I stayed by the airplanes as they unloaded the baskets of food. Laughter and chatting filled the air as they began a day at the beach. Unlike the airplanes, their dress was conservative and unpretentious.

The ladies were dressed in light blouses and slacks, the men, of course, wore clean work shirts and dark dress pants. Several of the men outdid themselves and wore white long sleeved shirts. No one was wearing a bathing suit or shorts, for they simply were not worn then. Wisely, the women chose the best clothing for climbing in and out of an airplane.

At the time, we were barely out of the depression. Clothes were still a basic necessity and expressed nothing more than frugal personal choices and the need to be covered. We wore light cotton in the summer and dark wool in the winter and there was nothing left with which to be flamboyant unless you were a Hollywood star. The only wool that was worn in the summer was men's itchy bathing trunks and the day when they were replaced by Lastex and gabardine was a blessing.

Then I spotted the man in front of his silver biplane wiping the belly behind the engine. I was correct. He was tall and slim with a powerful athletic build. His tan face was lean and capped by a head of thick black hair. He was a handsome man dressed in a grey shirt and matching pants, all pressed. He was the only pilot in the group without a cigarette.

He moved with a deliberate grace that sometimes comes with tall people, but his muscular build showed strength and athleticism. He would not be someone to face in a confrontation, I thought. After thoroughly checking his airplane, he strolled over to his group, kicked off his shoes, stretched out on a blanket and reclined on one elbow to gaze out at the emerald colored water. The group showed no inclination to go for a swim and I thought that was odd, but then I realized that they had no place to change or to wash off before they dressed. They were simply having a picnic at the beach on their day off and they flew there with their airplanes.

We were taught that a child's mere presence wasn't automatically tolerated by others, so I stayed away from the group and looked at each of the planes, two Stinson monoplanes, SM2's or SM8's, a Waco CSO and the silver Travel Air. One important detail that I noticed was that all of them were equipped with Goodyear balloon tires so landing on softer sand was possible.

"You the kid on the beach?" the Travel Air pilot asked.

"Yes sir. You saw me and that was great flying what you did."

One of the group spoke. "Hey Tommy did you get some kind of promotion? Since when do people call you Sir?"

He thanked me and invited me to look at his airplane. He offered his hand, "I'm Tom, Tommy Livermore." I could feel the strength in his big hands and arms as he helped me get into the cockpit to show me the controls and instruments. I surprised him by reciting what the other airplanes were. We spent a lot of time talking about airplanes and flying and I recited the makes and engines of the airplanes that were present.

"Well, you certainly know your airplanes. How did you do that?"

"I have been crazy about them ever since I was a little boy."

"Ever since you were a little boy, huh?"

"Yes sir. I read Popular Aviation and Aero Digest whenever I can find an old one. I had my first ride in an Aeronca C3 and a flight in a Waco 10 when we lived up north. I really like your Travel Air 2000, too. It's very clean and neat."

"Thank you. I rebuilt that airplane from an original that had an OX-5 on it, but I decided to hang the new engine on it."

"Yes. I think that it's a Lycoming, isn't it?"

"Yep, right again!"

I found it easy to talk to this man in spite of his intimidating stature. He seemed genuinely interested in befriending me and after my tour of all the airplanes I thanked him and withdrew from their party. I walked up the beach but I didn't go far because I wanted to watch them leave. That should come pretty soon because the tide was coming in. Thirty minutes later as I was walking back, I heard the first engine come to life then followed by the others. By the time I reached them, all of the engines were idling to get warmed up. Tommy's airplane was at the end of the line nearest to me so I stopped to watch them leave.

My newfound friend saw me and signaled for me to come over to his plane. When I reached the cockpit, he said, "Try to get out to Johnny Lowe's airport some Sunday and we'll go for a flight."

I couldn't speak at first but I shook my head in the affirmative and smiled an okay. He pulled his goggles down and turned his attention to the airplane. I was no longer in his sphere of existence.

One by one they pulled out, lined up on the narrow hard part of the sand near the water and applied power evenly until they were wide open. The rudder flicking from side to side as they accelerated down the beach, blowing a cloud of sand and water behind them as they smoothly climbed away. Tommy was the last to leave. My eyes followed him until he was nothing but a glistening speck in the golden afternoon light.

I learned that he was a crop dusting pilot and that I had met a legend, Tommy Livermore. Before I left, he promised that he would fly by the house whenever he could in his "Sunday plane." While I was walking (floating) on the way home, all I could think about was the genuine invitation to go flying and how I was going to make it come true. I felt certain that I had made a good friend. After all, he gave me a hot dog before I left. Now all I had to do was to get some extra chores lined up in trade for having mom drive me out to the airport, wherever that was. If that didn't work, I would ride my bike.

It turned out that I had figured correctly. I ran the tires off that bike and with some extra labor around the house, I occasionally got a ride. The airport was six miles away and most of the time the journey there was in 80 to 90 degree weather, but I didn't mind, I was used to the heat and bright sun. My route took me from the north end of Siesta key, across the Siesta Key Bridge, through the town of Sarasota, and then two and half miles east to Johnny Lowe's Airport. On my first visit, there I was surprised to see the Ringling Brothers Circus winter training grounds across the road from the field. That sure opened up some new adventures for me, but I was anxious to meet my friend and to hopefully make some new friends.

That part of it took some time because Tommy wasn't there when I made my first visit and I had to introduce myself by hanging around and asking questions of the people who were busy working on their planes. Not an easy task when a squirt kid interrupts their work. I persisted in establishing my presence in a quiet way. The owner, Johnny Lowe, was a friendly gentleman of portly stature and accepted my intrusion with the comment that, "We don't get any kids out here so you be careful when the airplanes are running."

The airplanes of which he spoke were scattered about the grounds near the hangar and consisted mainly of the popular biplanes, Waco's, Travel Air's, Birds, Stinson Jr.'s and a few odd models and there were new "light planes" in the mix. Taylorcraft, Luscombe, Aeronca "K ", and a couple of Piper Cubs brightened the array with their yellow, orange and blue colors. There at the end of the line of airplanes south of the hangar, a silver colored Travel Air was tied down with a clean tarp neatly wrapped around the engine and a similar covering fastened over the cockpits.

Tommy Livermore wasn't there but his airplane spoke for him. Progress! I had made friends with the airport owner and some of the pilots. I wished that I could have met with Tommy and I wished that I could have stayed there until dark but I had a six mile bike ride ahead of me so I left with enough time to get home before dark. Rattlesnakes liked to warm themselves on the key's roads at night and riding a bike at night without a light wasn't a good idea. Dinner sure tasted good that evening.

In the following weeks, I made as many trips as I could and made friends with the pilots there. At least they not only tolerated me, they talked with me. I was genuinely interested in what they were doing and I knew airplanes and airplane talk. Wiping oil, washing an airplane sometimes, hawking tools and remaining silent at the right time put me in good stead with the gang. The best part of it, though, was finally getting know Tommy. He patiently taught me how an airplane worked mechanically and aerodynamically, the latter by actually taking me flying one afternoon in his "Sunday Plane."

Hot Dogs! I went up in an airplane and looked down on things. That's the way it would have been for any other kid who was simply curious, but to me it was opening the door to my dreams. Not only to be flying again, but also to have the joy of being accepted by a group that I looked at as being the nearest thing to the Knights of the Air about whom I read in "G8 and His Battle Aces." All were nice to me but not as patient and attentive as Tommy Livermore. He became a cross between a big brother and a father and he treated me accordingly. The only thing wrong was the infrequent times that we could meet at the airport. He was a busy crop duster and I couldn't always get to the field when he was there, but I enjoyed my visits with the other pilots and earned a few flights. One day much to my joy and surprise I was invited to go out to a celery farm nearby to help with the dusting operation. The ride in the old pick-up truck to the site took forever in my mind, but actually it was quite close and the truck was parked at the corner of a large flat meadow near the field that was to be dusted. I did what I could to help unload the sacks of dust but they were too heavy. I helped anyway.

It wasn't long before we heard the sound of an engine and a silver biplane appeared at the opposite corner slipped sharply down onto the pasture and rapidly taxied to our location. I could tell that it was Tommy as the Travel Air spun around, blowing chards of grass and dusty sand at us. He gave me a wave and a big smile as he sat in the plane, engine still running, while the load of dust was sack-by-sack emptied into the hopper. When he got the okay from the crew boss he opened the throttle and took off in the direction from whence he came. Just clearing the palmettos at the edge of the field, he banked to the right and disappeared behind the scrub. This operation was repeated several times until all the sacks of dust were empty. While we were busy putting the empty bags in the truck, Tommy unexpectedly returned, spun the airplane around and cut the engine.

He motioned me to the cockpit and thanked me for doing

such a good job and then asked, "Want a ride back to the field? You'll have to ride in the hopper." After I shook my head yes enough times to loosen it from my neck, he yelled for one of the guys to pull the hinge pins from the hopper lid and before I could think about it we were airborne in a matter of speaking, because if I had been riding on the lower wing I could have grabbed some tree leaves. I was scrunched up in the hopper and hanging on to a strut watching the scrub oaks and palmettos whizzing by as Tommy picked his way through the pine trees. Too soon we were landing at the field and after we taxied to the hangar deplaned he hosed the dust off of my head, face and arms.

"You take a good bath when you get home tonight," looking at me with a big grin. I promised, but who the hell was thinking about a bath after a ride like that! I relived the thrill over and over in a continuous closed loop of the event. Even if the flight was only 15 minutes long, it was the thrill of my life and I knew that my days of solitude on the beach would never be the same. I don't remember my bike ride home that afternoon.

My mind was in the Travel Air. I did remember to take a swim in the Gulf, clothes and all, to wash off the chemical dust. Many times I wondered what kind of dust they were dispersing, because whatever it was certainly covered me from head to foot as it swirled up out of the hopper. I don't think that it affected my mental health too much, but others may disagree.

I tried to get to Lowe's Field as often as I could, but family matters intervened too often and finally we had to move back to Washington, D.C for reasons now lost to me. I was now one half year behind in school and that would have some interesting consequences later on. School in the city, the absence of my flying friends and the beach was unbearable.

The kids that I knew were jitterbugging, listening to the latest Glenn Miller or Tommy Dorsey records and had no interest in aviation or anything outside the city so I had few friends and was living in an almost dispersed family. We were all under one roof but always apart doing something and I never saw them except at the dinner table. My older brother was in pre-med school, my sisters were either married or away working or in school. So I was beached, so to speak.

All was not lost, however, because my brother sometimes had a few moments of relaxation and he would take us to see some of the aviation happenings in the D.C. area. One day he told me to hop in his little 1931 Model A because a new helicopter was being demonstrated at Bolling Field. A helicopter? What the heck is a helicopter? Everybody knew what an autogyro was but this thing was really weird. I had to see it even if it wasn't an airplane. It was a cool windy day in early fall when we went to see this new machine and its inventor whose name was very familiar to me, Igor Sikorsky. I had drawn many pictures of his flying boats that flew for Pan American Airways.

As we drove past Anacostia Naval Air Station, that oddly enough was located next to Bolling Field, we were treated to the sound of a marvelously loud takeoff of three Grumman F3-F's resplendent in their bright navy colors. They looked like bumble bees with their stubby little bodies. Their props split the silence with a blaring crackle as they made a steep climb-out.

As if not to be outdone, an army air force Curtiss P-36 flashed its shiny aluminum finish with an equally loud takeoff from Bolling Field. Next to the area of the helicopter demonstration sat three blue and yellow Martin B-10 bombers with busy crews attending to them. I knew there was a good reason to be there! My brother and I walked to the large area between two hangars in time to see the helicopter start. It was an incredible sight to begin with but the thoughts of that blown down radio tower actually flying stretched our imagination.

Our dubiousness was soon dispelled when the maze of steel tubing with a huge propeller on top tentatively rose from the tarmac. The old gentleman flying it was not dressed in flying togs but in a business suit. He wasn't wearing the duty leather helmet and goggles, but he had a fedora perched square on his head with the brim turned up in the front. He was seriously concentrating on controlling the contraption that wasn't paying much attention to him because it was wandering all over the place at first.

Sikorsky's concentration won the fight and it settled down enough for him to hover five feet off the ground while an assistant placed a briefcase in a basket mounted on the front. Then it was a lifting and hovering demonstration with some carefully choreographed turns that seemed to be difficult to stop on a prescribed heading. He made a bouncy landing and concluded the exhibition.

I remember that there weren't many people watching the

display other than a group of army officers. Well, I could understand that. It was interesting and different, but who the heck would want some goofy thing like that? We left the helicopter to return to the Model A and our route took us behind the Martin B-10's when they were running them up and we got a thorough battering by the prop blast. Now those were REAL airplanes! They were huge powerful and exciting machines so we stopped and watched them and forgot the helicopter.

Unlike me, my brother was very studious and many Saturdays he would go to the University of Maryland to study. He would take me with him, but I was dropped off at the College Park Airport to spend the day "studying airplanes". College Park Airport was and still is the oldest airport in the country having been established by the Wright Brothers in 1909. I didn't know that then, all I knew was that I could spend the day watching airplanes and trains. The airport was across the road from the school and paralleling the road were the B&O railroad tracks, the main line running north out of Washington to Baltimore and New York. I had a nice lunch with me, lots of airplanes to watch, and if I got tired of that I could watch the trains go by. I couldn't have asked for anything better!

THE NEW AGE OF FLIGHT

Nineteen thirty-nine was an interesting year with some exciting airplanes making the news. Lockheed Aircraft rolled out the P-38, Bell Aircraft presented the P-39 and Curtiss started producing the P-40. Britain now had the Hawker Hurricane and another fighter built by Supermarine, the Spitfire. Germany was touting their new ME-109 but the magazine articles discounted it as being vastly inferior to anything that we had.

Of course, I believed every word but the military wasn't the only source of new designs, College Park had one. On my first visit there I saw the usual planes of which I was familiar: the Waco's, Fleets and Stinsons. But sitting in front of the hangar was a funny looking little plane with twin rudders and the little wheel in front instead of the back. It was made of aluminum. It had a wide fuselage with side-by-side seating and a big glass canopy over the cockpit. When I asked what it was, I was told that it was an experimental ERCOUPE. "Aircoupe?" I asked. "NO. ERcoupe. That stands for Engineering Research Corporation." So last year it was the Luscombe and now another funny little airplane that is supposed to drive/fly like a car. I didn't see it fly that day but I did later on. I sensed that aviation was changing pretty fast. I still preferred the big ol' biplanes so I made my way over to where they were parked in hopes that I could find a generous pilot who had an empty cockpit.

No luck that day so I decided to go watch the trains. I crossed the highway behind the airport, scrambled up the rock embankment and lay on my belly on the ballast just below the tracks. I didn't have to wait very long before I heard one of the crack specials sound its whistle at a crossing. And here it came, shaking the ground and looming huge! Wow! I could smell and FEEL the steam and oil as it thundered by at 70 miles per hour. This was more fun than watching airplanes so I stayed there until The Royal Blue and The President Washington came by with a freight train or two in between.

When mom asked me what I did during the day, the answer was always the same, "Oh, I watched airplanes and trains."

After school was out in 1941, mom, my sister and I moved back to Sarasota to the little cottage on Siesta Key. I cannot recall all of the moves and changes that occurred then but we bounced up and down the coast several times in several years to spend time in Florida.

This time dad drove us down there in the 1941 Ford that he was given in trade for a job that he did for a wealthy car dealer in Washington. So, we were left there to spend a summer that I will never forget. The "war" had erupted in 1939 in Europe and my juvenile excitement was directed not at the catastrophic consequences of the event, but at the aerial battles that were being fought over England. Hawker Hurricanes and Supermarine Spitfires were fighting the Messerschmit Me 109's, Ju 87 Stukas and Heinkle 111's of the German Air Force, now called the Luftwaffe. An odd name at first, but it soon became a household word.

MOM AT HER BEST

The two years of the war had drained the resources of the British and the French were humiliated by the Germans in an ignominious defeat. Britain was hanging on by the slimmest of margins and their future was in doubt.

Even as a pre-adolescent I realized the plight of the British, but when we were ensconced in our little beach house the only source of information was the little table radio on the shelf in the living room. The newspaper, The Sarasota Herald Tribune, was not delivered to our isolated little house so I listened to the radio to apprise myself of the latest news. Then once in a great while we went to the theater in town where we saw the latest films and the Movietone news that was interspersed between feature films.

I always looked forward to the dramatic scenes of the war in Europe narrated by Lowell Thomas but it was still a movie of events that weren't much different than those presented by Hollywood. Still exciting, though.

In spite of the fact that we weren't in the war yet, our little town began to stir from an unseen stimulus. More people were in town on Saturdays and we began to see military uniforms now and then. On one Saturday, we were presented the opportunity to become very familiar with not only the uniforms but with those who were wearing them.

Mom, my little sister, Janet and I had come into town one Saturday morning to buy groceries and to let mom get her favorite chocolate soda at Badger's drug store. Badger's was a typical old drugstore with a lunch counter and soda bar on the right side as one entered. When we entered the local hangout at "Five Points," the familiar aroma of chocolate and carbonated water greeted us: "Fizz water". That aroma greeted you like a siren of old. It drew you to the soda bar like an invisible lasso and FORCED you to order a chocolate soda. The only way to fight back was to order a banana split and that cost fifteen cents more than the soda. BUT you got a whole banana, three scoops of ice cream of your choice, two kinds of syrup, walnuts and whipped cream topped with a cherry: all for forty cents! I had one of those in mind as we approached the counter but there was a young soldier in front of us who was having great difficulty communicating with the girl behind the counter. She looked at him with an exasperated expression and said in perfect Southern-ese,

"May-un, Ah cain't unner-sta-un a thang yer say-un'."

The man in the uniform tried once more to make him understood then mom, characteristically, broke in.

"Young lady, this gentleman is asking for a vanilla ice cream cone!"

He turned quickly and said, "Ooh! Thank yew kindly, mum. I'm a'fred that oiv'e made a mess oov moiy English and caused a problem."

"No, the problem is behind the counter," mom answered. It was apparent that he was a "ferriner" and the little girl wasn't a whiz in American English much less a thick Scottish brogue. His blue-grey uniform made him stand out like a butler in a hunting camp and the emblem of a crown in his insignia identified him as an English soldier. We had seen more and more khaki uniforms appearing since the start of the war in Europe but this was the first time to see a blue–grey outfit. Mom asked him where he was from and he said Glasgow, Scotland.

"Well, that's obvious from your brogue but what are you doing in Sarasota, Florida?"

"We're on a weekend holiday from Clewiston where we are in flight training."

FLIGHT TRAINING!

That woke me up!

"Are there more of you?"

"Yes, mum. There are four of us. The others are looking for something to eat across the street."

"They won't find anything over there." My little sister chimed in.

The waitress shoved the cone at her customer and said, "Twenty-five cents!" The airman thanked her and turned to mom in time for her to ask him where they were staying.

"Ooh, we haven't figured that oot yet, mum."

'Well, I'm sure that you'll not find anything in town that you could afford even if there was a place available. This is a small town of just over 10,000 this time of year and rooms might be hard to get so I see no reason why you can't stay with us. We have plenty of room and you are certainly welcome to spend the weekend with us."

Sister Janet raised her eyebrows when mom mentioned, "plenty of room".

The young man stammered for a moment and said that he would have to check with the rest of the group.

"We had not planned to do much more than to see the town and we wouldn't want to be a bother."

"You've seen pretty much all of the town and I know that you would probably spend the night on the sidewalk and you will not be a bother."

Janet looked across the street and saw the rest of the group coming back and correctly observed that they hadn't found anything to eat. Here they came, carefully crossing the street, looking in the wrong direction for oncoming traffic, but they made it to our little group with smiling faces. There they stood all spit and polish in their natty blue uniforms, shiny black shoes, black neckties and hats cocked to the side of their heads.

Mother fired the first salvo.

"Now! You boys are going to spend the weekend at our house on the beach." The look on their faces was classic dumbfoundedness. They stuttered and stammered and looked at each other; then the older member of the group spoke.

"I dunno what to say, mum, we aren't prepared to..."

"Now I know that you boys don't know a soul in this town and you have no place to stay and there is no reason why you can't come home with us and spend a nice weekend swimming and playing on the beach."

Their eyes opened wide as they shot glances back and forth at each other. The "elder", a tall handsome David Niven look-alike, spoke again.

"That sounds wonderful, ma'am, but we don't have any swimming apparel and..."

"Never mind about that", mom interrupted as she opened her purse and handed me twenty dollars.

"Bobby, take these gentlemen over to Penney's and see that they get some swim trunks. Janet and I will go to the store and get some things and we will meet you here in twenty minutes."

Our master sergeant had spoken and we all hopped to our duties. The British aviation cadets looked as if they had been ambushed and they had been. Mother didn't mince words or hold back when she spotted the need to do something and she was determined to be a mother to these boys. The cadets and I reached Penney's and made our way to the rear of the store on old oil-soaked boards that somehow in spite of all the oil, emitted a chorus of pops and squeaks as we walked on them.

Our newly found friends silently chose their "swimming apparel" and gave them to the clerk who fascinated them when she put the payment into a capsule that was shot up to the cashier in the balcony via a vacuum tube. Purchases completed, we trooped back to meet mom and sister, Janet. Satisfied that we had done the right thing, mom herded us to the car like a hen with chicks, packed us into our 1940 Ford, and headed for Siesta Key. As we got underway for our six-mile drive, the older cadet made a proper introduction with a polite, "How do you do, my name is Bob Smith, age 26, from London." The others then followed with their introductions: "Collin, 20", "George, 19," and "Malcolm, 18".

I can remember their faces and first names, but the last names have slipped away in the 70 odd years that have passed. Collin was from Edinburgh, Malcolm was from Glasgow and George was from "the English countryside." Malcolm was the one who was struggling to order a vanilla ice cream cone with his thick Scottish brogue.

When we arrived at our little cottage, mom told "her boys" that they could do whatever they liked and that dinner would be ready at six o'clock sharp. We disembarked from the car like a clown act in the circus, a steady stream of bodies coming out of the car. Before my sister and I could get around to the walk leading to the front of the house, one of our guests did and strolled toward the front door. Half way there he exploded off the walk sideways and yelled, "Jaysus, Wude ye luke ot thot oogly beast!"

"Wot in God's name is that!"

"Oh. That's Blue Boy, our Indigo snake. He lives under the house.," said an unconcerned Janet.

"Gainsborough shood have a luke at this Blue Boy."

"Is he a friend at home?" Janet asked.

"Well, not exactly. He…"

"I'll explain later, Janet," mother interrupted.

The boys warily made their way around Blue Boy and found safety in the house.

"Now, you boys would certainly be more comfortable if you got out of those hot uniforms and enjoyed the beach." We showed them where they could change in our bedroom and they made a tenuous appearance with towels sheepishly draped over their shoulders. Mother reacted immediately to so much lily-white skin and produced a bottle of suntan lotion and admonished them to apply plenty of it before they went out in to the sun. Unlike the sun block that we use today, suntan lotion then did little to block the damaging rays, but it did make you oily and to smell good.

So it was off to the beach for a swim with suntan lotion, white skins, brand new "swimming apparel" and four apprehensive kids from the United Kingdom who still didn't know what had happened to them. They were cautious about entering the water at first, but Janet soon dispatched any of their timidity by vigorous splashing and taunting. It wasn't long before they had thrown their English conservatism to the wind and began to enjoy themselves. We had the use of a canoe and the boys began to paddle around close to shore, but they were soon subjected to irreverent treatment by Janet, who ambushed them from under water and tipped them over. We played and swam until mother appeared and announced "Tea Time".

"Tea Time?" one of the boys said in surprise. They stopped and looked at one another and quickly got to their towels and gathered on the screened porch where they were greeted by a table properly set for tea. A white lace table cloth made by mom, little cookies, made by mom, cups, saucers, cream and a pot of steaming tea. Their delight was impossible for them to hide as they stood at the table.

Bob Smith spoke, "Please, won't you join us, Mrs?"

"Oh, my goodness, no thanks. I have some things to finish for dinner and I wouldn't fit at that table anyway. It's for you boys, so enjoy it. Now, after your tea and a little rest, you might want to shower off all that salt water before dinner."

Mom had a way to soften instructions when she had to and the boys did respond to her "suggestions" without complaint but not until they had thoroughly enjoyed their tea. The sounds of their chatting and laughter mixed well with clatter of the cups and saucers.

Mom took a quick peek from the kitchen to see if they were enjoying themselves. She didn't have to. The crust of apprehension and reserve had cracked wide open and the boys relaxed for an hour and forgot that they were three thousand miles from their homes and in a strange home in a strange country.

At 6:00 PM straight up, they appeared at the dinner table in full uniform including tunics and they literally glowed. Not entirely from spit and polish, however, for their day in the sun had done the rest.

"You boys look wonderful in those crisp uniforms and I'm sure that your commanding officer would be pleased. But I'm sure that you would enjoy your dinner much more if you would get out of those warm coats and neckties. We want you to relax and enjoy yourselves while you're here. Besides, if you should spill something on those spotless suits I'm not sure that I could clean it properly and I wouldn't want to send you back like that." They complied without argument.

Her request couldn't have been more prophetic because once they got into dinner they encountered some things that could have been a disaster. They had quickly removed their coats and ties and gazed at the feast that mom had placed before them. They stood before the table looking alternately and at mother who invited them to be seated.

"We'll wait for you, mum." Bob, who stood at the end of the table, spoke with a firmness that even impressed mom.

"Alright, I guess that I'm through with everything." She wiped her hands and Collin attended her chair so that she could be seated.

When we were all seated and ready to dig in, Malcolm bowed his head in silence to say a blessing for himself, but the rest of us followed his lead and joined him in prayer. We never did that in our home so it was nice to see him show us the importance of blessing the food. After they sat staring at a table loaded with the typical Florence Parks Sunday dinner, even though it was Saturday. Mom knew that they had to leave at noon Sunday to return to their base at Clewiston so she made certain that they got the best that she could prepare while they were in her care. In the center of the table a platter of fried chicken awaited us. Fresh string beans, mashed potatoes, biscuits and gravy, and a gallon of fresh squeezed orange juice completed the setting. A dessert of chocolate cake was hidden in the kitchen.

Our guests tentatively began eating but soon they were digging in with enthusiasm. Collin, with typical English propriety, was trying to cut a drumstick with a knife and fork, chasing it all over his plate. Janet watched with the bemusement of a nine year old and finally said, "Collin, watch." She then picked up a drumstick and bit into it with a resounding crunch. Soon there was a chorus of crunches as the crew attacked their chicken "American Style". Malcolm was impressed with the "scones" and looked for some jam. Mother told him that they were for the gravy. She left the table for some more juice and when she returned she almost yelled,

"Malcolm, what are you doing!"?

Poor little Malcolm froze in fright with his left hand suspended above his plate holding a biscuit completely drenched in gravy that was beginning to run down his arm. Luckily, he had rolled up his sleeve, saving his shirt from a bath in gravy.

"You should put the biscuit on your plate and pour the gravy over it. I should have told you earlier so I'm at fault here."

"Very sorry if I caused a mess, I..."

"Now don't you fret! You didn't do anything wrong. I should have known that you don't have biscuits and gravy in Scotland the way we do. I'm just glad that you didn't soil your shirt."

Mom got a towel and cleaned up everything and we continued the meal with much crunching, chatter and laughter, assuring mother that the meal was a success. "Her boys" had left the war in England for a few moments and had a chance to be free of the heavy responsibilities they were carrying. They weren't giddy, but they loosened the tight control of English conservatism with which they conducted themselves.

After dinner we had dessert, mom's famous chocolate cake with vanilla ice cream and tea.

After that, we sat and talked with them about their homes and families. Each one related the details of their journey to Clewiston, but it all came down to the same thing; their country was in dire straits with a severe shortage of pilots and they had enlisted directly into the RAF or had transferred from another branch of service, like Bob Smith.

The Battle of Britain had seen heavy losses of pilots and planes. The capacity to train new pilots exceeded the capabilities of their homeland so there was an agreement with the U.S. to set up some civilian flight schools to train British aviation cadets. These English boys were being trained in the Civilian Pilots Training Program, so it had nothing to do with the military. We were not yet at war, so "strict" neutrality was observed. These men would not see their homes or family for at least another year. Some of them never would see their homes again.

Listening to this only strengthened mom's resolve to do everything that she could for them while they were near us.

There was enough light left to take a stroll on the beach and watch the glow of sunset. I took a football with me to toss around with the guys, but it generated so much confusion and humor amongst the "real futball players" that I ended up tucking it under my arm. Collin commented that it was puzzling how one could play football with something that wasn't a round ball and had points on both ends and was carried in one's hands. I couldn't argue with his humorous observation. Before darkness fell, which happens quickly on the beach, we returned to the house where our guests found books and magazines that occupied them for the rest of the evening. The latest issue of Saturday Evening Post had some articles about the war in Europe that evoked some lively discussions among them and Bob found one of dad's Charles Dickens classics that he read for a while. Soon the evening quieted down and there was an epidemic of yawns that heralded bedtime. One by one they bid us good night and retired. Mother soon followed for, as usual, she had worked very hard that day doing what she did best; that was her way.

Sunday morning breakfast was already cooking before any of us were awake. The smell of bacon and fresh coffee soon changed that and sounds of rustling and bumping came from the bedroom. The boys were up. Janet and I left our cozy cots on the porch and as we came into the living room mom was placing a platter of steaming biscuits next to the eggs, bacon, jam, and freshly squeezed orange juice. Mom had been up for quite a while to do all of this for us, but it was a powerful force in her personality to cook and do for people. It made her very happy to offer comfort and care to these young men so far from home. What she did made our guests happy, too, because Malcolm stood at the table and uttered in "Purrfect Scotch",

"Ach! Wude ye luke ot thot! And scones with jam, too!"

"Yes, Malcolm, they are not quite as good as your scones, but my biscuits are light and very good with jam."

"They will do, mum!"

"I see that you have your swim trunks on. Do you think you will have enough time for a swim and breakfast before you leave?"

"Yes, mum, I'll have to be quick about it, but I would like to have joost one more dip in the ocean. It's not something that we can do every day."

"Well, you can get started anytime you like."

"No Mum. We'll wait for you."

As he stood there, the rest of the group came out of the bedroom and assembled by the table dressed in their uniforms minus ties and tunics. Bob Smith stood at the end of the table, tall, handsome and reserved. To his right, Collin was his easy self, also tall and handsome and prone to joking around more than the others. He insisted on trying his "New Yoik" accent but with little success.

Then there was Malcolm, the shorter of the group but stocky, confident and unafraid to project his thoughts when he felt it was necessary. His face was square with a strong jaw. George was the quiet one and took his place across from Malcolm and waited with his head bowed as if in deep thought. He gave the impression of being preoccupied and a bit lonely. Perhaps he had reason to be. He was 18 years old, thousands of miles from home, and in a strange place for the first time. He admitted that he had not yet learned to drive a car.

We tried to talk to him more than the others and it helped a bit, but it was obvious that his thoughts were in England.

Mom, still busy in the kitchen, refused to sit down so everybody dug in and polished off the breakfast in time for Malcolm to run down to the Gulf and get wet once more. By noon the boys were clean and dressed to military perfection and ready for the trip to town. As they stood by the car Bob said,

"We'll not soon forget this time with you and your family."

"Is this the only time that you boys will have a weekend leave?"

"Uh, no mum."

"Well, I will expect you to call us when you have time off and we will meet you at the bus station. You boys and your friends are welcomed here any time."

The boys looked at in silence for a long moment and one of

them and Malcolm spoke,

"THAT we can do, mum, but we wish there was something that we could do to show our appreciation."

"You can do that by calling us when you can visit us again."

"Yes, thank you, mum."

Janet and I stayed home to make more room in the car so we waved them goodbye as they left.

We spent that summer on the beach and in the water as much as possible. We met some of the locals who lived nearby and that allowed us to expand our sphere of living on the key. It could get lonely and boring at times when all you had to talk to were the seagulls. Then, after that first weekend with the British cadets, we looked forward to the next one because they always came back.

Winston Churchill said that the Battle of Britain was their finest hour. I think that mom was having hers when "her boys" came to her house for mothering and R&R.

NOW IT WAS OUR TURN

In August of 1941, we again went back to Washington, D.C. and again, I don't know why. My parents rented an apartment in the N.W. section of the city and I was enrolled in high school. I was miserable and did not relish our new routine.

The concrete and stone of the city coupled with the attitudes of those who knew nothing else but the smells and noise of urban life was difficult to bear. I was locked into the life of an automaton on the treadmill of solitary confinement in the midst of thousands of people in the same boat. Then a break in the gloom! A telephone call from one of the British aviation cadets informing mom that they, two of them, would be in town for a few days and they wanted to see her.

Two of them? There were 12 boys who at different times spent weekends with us. Where were the rest of them? Never mind! They would be stopping in the city while they were en route to England and the war. Mom was beside herself and started to make preparations for their visit. The weather in the fall of 1941 was brisk and the month of December was on our doorstep so we couldn't depend on any extended outside activities like walking tours or picnics. Certainly mom was busy planning several dinners for the boys, but she was disappointed that they couldn't stay with us. They had military billets some other place and they would only be in Washington for three days.

Mom, the forever conniving politician, called an old high school friend who happened to be in the Secret Service and darned if she didn't arrange a tour of the White House for the next Saturday and dad came through with four tickets to the football game between the Washington Redskins and the Philadelphia Eagles on Sunday.

So, a great weekend was set. They could visit us on Saturday and Sunday.

Saturday morning, December 6th, was clear and crisp when we picked up the boys early enough to have a visit before our tour. As we ate lunch we learned that our group of aviation cadets had been decimated by washouts and fatal accidents. Six had survived and these two were the last of the bunch to head back to their homeland.

We drove the car right up to the entrance to the White House, arriving promptly at 2:30 and our special "agent" was waiting for us on the steps under the portico. Our British pilot guests were obviously awed and the elder of the group commented that it was like touring the Buckingham Palace of America.

We were given a tour of only the main floor but it was fascinating. We could look into the rooms as long as we wanted but no access was allowed. All of us had hoped to see President Roosevelt or the vice president or any official, but we were denied. We did see a number of support staffers scurrying about.

That evening mom cooked a fried chicken dinner just like the first one that she prepared for her boys in the cottage on Siesta Key. The coincidence wasn't lost on our guests and they spent several hours after dessert reminiscing about the wonderful times that they had at our little house on the beach. The drive to their hotel was quiet.

Luckily, Sunday was another clear and crisp day, perfect for a football game at Griffith Stadium. Our 40' Ford was crowded, but five of us made it to the game and took our seats in the east end bleachers. Bundled up in our overcoats and blankets, we watched an exciting game with two great quarterbacks literally slugging it out with each other.

The Redskins had Sammy Baugh and the Eagles had Davy O'Brien. Before they turned professional, both were stars at Texas Christian University. They were physical opposites. Baugh was a tall lanky triple threat because he did it all: pass, kick and run when he had to. O'Brien was short, stocky and fearless. He could pass and was a good running back, too, so the game in the first half was open war. Our British boys enjoyed it but had no idea what was going on except that it was "something like rugby."

About half way through the second quarter, the game was halted. The players stood on the field looking at each other in a confused state. The PA system came to life.

"Ladies and gentlemen. We have received word that the Japanese have attacked Pearl Harbor..." There were words that followed the initial announcement but they went unheard. We all stood up in shocked silence. One of the British cadets looked skyward and pumped a clenched fist and uttered an almost silent," Ahh". Then there were small voices rippling through the stands, "Where the hell is Pearl Harbor!" Then came many uneducated guesses. "It's in California." "It's somewhere near Alaska or the west coast someplace." No one seemed to know the location of Pearl Harbor and those few that did, said nothing.

The stadium emptied quickly as the grim faced fans rushed home to get more detailed news on their radios. Before we were halfway home there was an "extra" already being sold on the corners by the newsboys.

After a hurried farewell, our friends departed, never to be seen again.

The days that followed that Sunday were consumed by confused conjectures and too many what-ifs to process. Fear that we would be bombed soon triggered practice blackouts and the innocent complacent life that we had lead rapidly became a numb, but frantic search for some way to defend our country or to fight back somehow or to... Then when Pathe' News showed films of the attack on Pearl Harbor in the movie theaters and photos appeared in Life magazine and the newspapers, anger welled up in all of us. Almost immediately there was a rush of enlistments into the army and marines. Unbelievably, our Army Air Force had a few B-17 and

Douglas B-18's bombers and a smattering of, what we were soon to learn, second-rate fighters. Curtiss P-36's, new and untested P-38's and P-39's, early model P-40's and a very small cadre of pilots in the air force and the navy. The navy didn't have much of a fleet air arm either. The U.S. was in no condition to wage a global war.

But things began to happen fast at every level. Even in my high school the war effort came to me, a lowly freshman, when my wood shop teacher asked me if I wanted to build some Aircraft Identification models and I jumped at it. He knew that I was a model builder so he gave me a set of plans and some white pine, and turned me lose.

He was busy making beautiful wood casting patterns for the navy, the drawings for which had no title to identify what the part was, but we played a guessing game and figured that they were parts for a gun breech. By the time school was finished for the year, I had built six 1/72nd scale models painted with a mixture of shellac and lamp black. I got an A in wood shop on my report card. My wood shop teacher should have been given an A, too. After school he worked well into the night making patterns almost every day.

Unbeknownst to me, my dad had decided that half the family was going to move to Sarasota as soon as school was out. My little sister, mom, and I drove down the east coast with dad for the last time and that was fine with me to get back to what I considered home. On the way down, we saw quite a few convoys of army trucks full of troops.

The war was only seven months old and the buildup had rapidly taken hold. Uniforms and military vehicles were everywhere, everyone was rushing to do something, many young family men were gone, smiles were few and wasn't long before a phrase born of the conflict became the standard retort, "Don't you know there's a war on!"

As we approached the north end of Sarasota, a flight of five P-40's flew over! Then five more! Wow! Where did they come from? Two minutes later we found out. To the left and close to the highway was an Army Airbase teeming with fighter planes. I had gone to heaven and to convince me of it, I learned that within one hundred miles of our town there were no less than twelve military airfields in place. In a short burst of time the entire state of Florida had become one big army airbase ranging from primary, basic and advanced training bases up to tactical fighter and final bomber crew training.

After we got settled in our little house, it wasn't long before my daily private airshow began. The P-40's were flying over at all times of the day and night. Then P-47's appeared from another air base and Martin B-26's roared by at astonishingly low levels.

One sunny morning our peaceful breakfast was shattered by a roar that had everyone on their feet, startled beyond comprehension. I ran outside in time to see a flight of five B-17's at what I guessed at 300 feet altitude heading out into the Gulf. Mom asked, "What in God's name was that?" I told her that it was a flight of B-17's.

"Well! If they were that low, they must be lost!"

That incident set the stage for what we would experience for the next three years and sadly, my old haunt, Johnny Lowe's Field, was closed to all civilian flying except for the newly formed Civil Air Patrol. The pre-war biplanes and older monoplanes disappeared as if by magic and even though I was thrilled with all the heavy horsepower flying around I missed my old favorites.

The fighter planes and the daily aerial excitement wasn't the only change to our lives. Our relaxed evenings on the beach with the freedom to come and go as we pleased were quickly brought to a halt. All windows had to be blacked out and we weren't allowed to walk the beach at night.

When the attacks of the German submarine threat became better understood there were many changes to our life on the beach. We were living in a remote location on a key off the west coast of Florida. I have no idea how many people lived on this seven mile long stretch of sand and scrub palms but it couldn't have been more than one hundred people and one thousand rattlesnakes. A causeway at the northern end connected us with Sarasota that boasted a population of nine thousand. A causeway at the southern end of the island connected to Highway 41 that ran south to Fort Meyers. It was a perfect place to drop agents off on the beaches.

Spies were the first concern of the military and soon a contingent of Coast Guardsmen was installed in a big house down the beach from us. They patrolled the beach at night in Jeeps that roamed up and down the shore until daybreak. I supposed that it was up to us to spot treachery because we seldom saw them during the day. It was exciting to have an actual military operation right in our front yard, so to speak. Our lives were far from removed from the military operations in the rest of the country that had turned on all faucets of war preparations to full capacity. With the Coast Guard on Siesta Key we were now a part of it. Sailors in grey Jeeps were driving around with "Tommy Guns" slung on their shoulders and we were restricted to our homes at night.

As time went on that year things got more serious about security. Agents had been landed on the Atlantic side of Florida and near New York. The young men who were guarding our beach were no longer kids playing a role; they became serious hardened military men with a mission.

Many ships, silhouetted by lights from the shore, were being sunk off the coast of the U.S. by German submarines and now we had to observe blackout conditions at night. All the windows and doors had to be covered by heavy black cloth and nighttime activities outside the home were restricted. Offenders could be severely punished if they showed any light. So our nights were usually spent inside.

One quiet and boring evening when mom, my little sister, and I were engaged in our normal entertainment, which consisted of reading, or in my case, drawing and listening to the radio, we heard a Jeep roar up the beach road and skid to a stop in front of the house. Shouting erupted. Mother dropped her book and frightfully announced, "My God! They're here!" (Spies) We doused the lights and tried to peer out of the windows to see what was happening. Even though the moon was up, we couldn't see anything so I quietly sneaked out of the front door just as a long string of shouting and the unmistakable pop-pop-pop of a Thompson submachine gun burst the silence. Close after that, more shouting and the pops from several side arms.

Holding my breath I carefully made my way along a row of Australian Pines that lined the property line that stretched to the beach, being careful to keep a tree trunk between the commotion on the beach and me. I had one tree left before I would reach the beach when, suddenly, laughter erupted and took the place of the shouting. I could see a gathering of men near the water's edge and I walked down to them to ask what had happened. They knew me by now and invited me to look at the "spy" that they had challenged and put out of action.

There in her blood lay a poor turtle that had been naturally driven to come ashore to lay her eggs. She looked very much like a person crawling out of the water in the dim light of the moon and being a turtle, she didn't understand the command to halt and sadly became another casualty of the war. However, she made a good contribution to the war effort by becoming a huge pot of turtle soup for the Coast Guard station men.

As the year of 1942 matured, the war had taken control of every minute of everyone's life. It was like an avalanche accelerating down a steep chute, sweeping everything in its path. Soldiers and pilots were everywhere all day and all night. The sky was full of airplanes all the time. Every thought was related to something involving the war. Who was killed, who was wounded, where they were, gas rationing, food rationing, and the absence of able-bodied men who were older than 18.

Innocence was lost in every way. Grief and insecurity gripped families that lost husbands, brothers, and sons to the war. Before the war, the most that we had to worry about was bumps and bruises and maybe the flu. Certainly, we weren't getting the beating that Britain was getting but we poured thousands of our young men into the conflict when the allies were depleted of manpower. And the unending flood of airplanes, tanks, trucks, and related war equipment will go down in history as one of this nation's great achievements.

The entire country had tightened its gut, stiffened its back and became a nation with, as Yamamoto was supposed to have said, a nation with a terrible resolve.

As a teenager of 15 I had to do many things before my time simply because there was no one left to do them. My father was gone, working in Washington, D.C. on a war project. My brother was in an accelerated medical school program in Chicago Rush Medical Center, all of our older sisters were working in government jobs in Washington, D.C. That left mom, my younger sister, and me to make our way in the little house on the beach.

Everyone, no matter how old, tried to do their part and one late afternoon we would see some of the older citizens, probably in their late 40's or early 50's, giving what they could. The men we saw were two old pilots, or to be accurate, "Too old pilots."

Occasionally, we would see a little Stinson 105 flying out into the Gulf to search for submarines. The United States of America costal defense was a 90 horsepower fabric covered two-place light plane loaded with two 20-pound bombs. That was our lot in early 1942 and to emphasize how desperately ineffective our efforts were, the little Stinson appeared one late afternoon coming in low from the west with a "dead stick." Losing altitude fast, it made a forced landing in an Orange grove, ending up on its back. By the time we ran over to the demolished airplane, the two old pilots had extricated themselves and stood in stunned silence.

The nose was crumpled under the airplane, but there was little odor of fuel because they had run out of fuel over the Gulf and just managed to reach the shore in a long glide. We asked where the little bombs were and we were told that they thought that they had seen a submarine and had dropped them.

That little bit of excitement was to be repeated many times in the following years, but with far more impact as the pace of training accelerated at Sarasota Airbase. It soon became obvious that many of the young pilots lacked the skills or the depth of training required to fly the fighters that had been thrust upon them.

Hard partying at night didn't help to alleviate the problem either, so accidents and crashes seemed to be a daily occurrence as 1942 progressed. We learned to spot those who flew with hangovers by watching the "follow the leader" exercise where the instructor pilot led a long string of P-40's in a ballet of maneuvers. The pilots were to keep a short distance between each airplane, but the prescribed serpentine soon stretched out to a mile in length when some of the airplanes fell behind and opened large gaps in the string when they had to execute a hard pull-up. Occasionally one would even fall out of line. We watched this scene many times when we were on the beach in front of our house.

Flight training was conducted seven days a week, so my school buddy and I rode our bikes out to the airbase on Saturdays or Sundays to watch the show. We were never disappointed when we parked on the highway at the west end of the runway to watch the steady stream of P-40's taking off or landing after performing the classic "fighter pitchout" before circling to their final approach. Then the show switched from the air to the ground when there were many bounced landings and ground loops. The P-40 was not an easy airplane to land with its narrow spaced landing gear and intolerance for abuses in airspeed. One morning as we pedaled up the highway almost to the airbase, a flight was taking off and we were startled to see a P-40 blasting across the highway, still on the ground, with pieces filling the air after impacting the deep drainage ditch at the edge the field. I learned later that the pilot had neglected to set the friction lock on the throttle and it crept back to a power setting that was too low for takeoff.

To keep things interesting, the Air Force based a squadron of P-39's at Sarasota for a short time and we were presented with different sounds and incidents. The Bell P-39 had a distinctive whine and whistle at times and they were easily distinguished from the P-40's. They also had a seemingly disjointed and violent stall characteristic that my buddy and I witnessed one day when one of them had a fire and engine failure after takeoff.

With Sarasota Bay directly in front of him and the chance to make a survivable landing in the shallow water, he elected to try to turn back to the airfield. The airplane stalled and tumbled into the shoulder of the highway, spraying bits and pieces into the neighborhood there. I still can see the holes in a large billboard from the debris that shot through it.

In "normal" times, an airplane crash was shocking big news. But by the fall of 1942, it became epidemic to hear about or to see a crash and you didn't have to be near the airbase, as my schoolmates and I were one afternoon on our way home on the school bus.

We were about one mile from my stop on the road that paralleled the shore, when I spotted a P-40 on the deck coming right at the shoreline from the Gulf. He was low as he could get and had a full head of steam. He disappeared behind some Australian Pines that were ahead and to the right and then made a sharp pull up. Climbing steeply, he re-appeared -- in two pieces. His right hand wing had separated and we watched the gyrating P-40 still under full throttle hit the ground with a bang that shook the bus. A girl named Heidi who dated the flyboys lived in the house that he was buzzing. Of course, a couple of us went back to the scene of the crash after it was " cleaned up" and found many parts in the trees including a piece of pink skull bone stuck in the trunk of a scrub oak.

Enumerating the wild incidents that occurred then might strain credulity, but the times were just that: wild. The desperate headlong rush to assemble a fighting force left a trail of human and mechanical debris. They were boys 18 and 19 years old, rammed through flight school and with maybe 130 hours plopped into an airplane with 1500 horsepower that had no manners. And to assure that a high enough number managed to survive to meet the numbers required, it was programmed to accept a huge percentage of fatalities. The trainee pilots just out of advanced training in 600 horsepower AT-6's, were taught fighter tactics, air-to-ground gunnery, air-to-air gunnery and navigation.

In the middle of all that, they had to learn how to fly a hot fighter. If they survived, they shipped out with maybe 250-300 hours in their logbook. They had to face German and Japanese pilots who had perhaps 5 years of training and thousands of hours, a lot of it in combat.

The airbase was home to two squadrons of P-40's, the 98th and the 301st. If my memory serves me, the 98th had white spinners and displayed the letter "H" with a unit number on the nose. The 301st had a red spinner and displayed the letter "J" with a unit number. The new pilots were in the last step of their training syllabus and were going through O.T.U. (Operational Training Unit). As the beat went on with ground accidents, mid-air collisions and crashes, sometime in early 1943 the aerial demolition derby destroyed or demolished enough airplanes to wipe out one squadron.

This airbase was not the only game in the state. There was Mac Dill Field, a Martin B-26 training operation, garnered the descriptive shingle, "ONE A DAY IN TAMPA BAY", and there were others throughout the state and the country.

Official post war records show that almost 15,000 pilots and crew were killed in the 45 months of the war. Almost 14,000 airplanes were destroyed in 52,651 accidents -- all within the United States. Staggering figures.

MUSCLE

I can't recall the actual date, but I believe it was in the spring of 1943 that the government felt the need to impress the countries of South America with the might of the U.S.A.A.F. so an aerial parade was arranged for them.

The visitors were assembled on the beach on Longboat Key where they could witness the show without the interference of buildings or foliage. Then they viewed a never-ending stream of tactical and strategic aircraft that passed in front of them for at least an hour. I witnessed the parade from my own beach in front our home on Siesta Key, the next island south of Longboat.

I'll never forget the sight of successive formations of B-24's, B-17's, P-39's, P-40's, B-26's and P-47's flying by at a fairly low altitude. The altitude was low enough for me to recognize the same airplanes coming by more than once because of their large white squadron and unit identifications on the nose. There were hundreds of them flying in a huge circle, but never mind, it was an unforgettable sight and sound!

Later that afternoon at Sarasota Airbase, a high- ranking officer landed a P-39 wheels-up with the belly tank still attached. He somehow missed damaging any of the airplanes that lined the runways. The field was packed with airplanes staged there for the parade.

The northern tip of Longboat Key was virtually uninhabited then and the Air Force set up an air-to-ground gunnery range where the art of strafing was practiced. My buddy and I decided to ride our bikes 15 miles to the range one bright Saturday morning.

It took us over three hours to get there due to the heat and distance in a broiling sun, we had to rest in the shade of the pines that dotted our route. When we arrived at our destination, we were stopped by a black soldier guarding the road to stop anyone from proceeding onto the range and for good reason. Gunnery runs were already in progress. We were ordered to stay up-range and away from the target area so we parked our bikes under a stand of trees that was closer to the point of discharge of the fighter's guns.

To our left was the road, to the left of that was the row of targets, to the left of the targets was the Gulf of Mexico, so the airplanes were shooting west and out into the water. Shortly after our visual assessment of the layout, we saw our first airplane flying north, up the bay between the key and the mainland. It banked to the left and started a run-in on the target area. He was almost on top of us when we were shocked by the muzzle blast and the sound of six Cal. 50 machineguns firing.

Unlike the rhythmic "Rat-a-tat-tat" of the Hollywood films, it was a loud almost burping sound, "BRR-OPP!" We could see the trail of gun smoke behind the airplane and a stream of brass "empties" spewing out of the ejector chutes. He was good. Right on target and he had the point of convergence exactly at the target that was totally destroyed. A geyser of sand at least 20 feet high shot upward interspersed with debris from the wooden target frame and glowing tracers oddly looping about. Some were high enough that the fighter flew through them as it pulled up.

Shortly after our visit to the firing range, we were treated to the same gunnery exercises much closer -- right over our house. One morning I spotted a flight of P-40's, en trail, aimed right at us in a long dive. When the lead airplane was over the house, he fired a burst into the Gulf to produce a geyser of water. The following seven airplanes each took aim at the circle of foam and fired as they passed over the house. The racket was deafening and poor mom was thoroughly rattled along with the house that got a second dose of it when the spent brass and ammunition belt links rained down upon us. For weeks after, I picked up enough parts to assemble a belt of empty cartridges that was about 20 feet long.

So, we didn't have to pedal a round trip of thirty miles to visit the gunnery range anymore.

Mid-year of 1943, an advanced model of the P-40 arrived: the P-40N. It was considerably lighter and faster than earlier models but it brought a few problems with it. The much lighter sliding portion of the canopy had a habit of coming loose in flight.

This occurred infrequently, but one time it almost caused a fatality when it flew up and then down onto the pilot, pinning him to the instrument panel. He could only see out to his left through the side of the windshield; it was not good enough to land a P-40. He somehow radioed his predicament and another P-40 was sent up to fly him down to a safe landing. Flying very close and level to the stricken airplane, the "shepherd" guided the other in to a safe belly landing. Both the damaged airplane and pilot were back in the air in two days.

Nineteen forty-four saw fewer accidents and incidents. Better pilots were graduating from the flight schools, standards were raised and training was thorough, AND the shiny bare aluminum P-51 replaced the dull olive drab P-40. Trips to the airbase were less frequent now because at the ripe old age of 18, I was working and preparing to take my turn in the U.S.A.A.F. I had enlisted the year before at age 17 and in June of '44 I was gobbled up into the war machine, but not before I was treated to two memorable incidents, one good and one not so good.

I had just finished a walk and a swim one afternoon when I spotted a Douglas SBD dive bomber flying south parallel to the coastline at probably 5000 to 6000 feet and over the Gulf. Flying north and just about above me was a P-47 Thunderbolt.

As it passed my location it made a sharp turn in the direction of the SBD and aligned itself on the tail of the navy plane, closing fast. The SBD had garnered a nickname in the navy, "Slow But Deadly" to match its designation. This navy pilot was to demonstrate how it got its nickname. As the P-47 overtook the quarry to simulate a gunnery pass, the targeted SBD made a hard turn to his right as if to say, "Oh no you don't!" Then the dogfight started with the bigger faster Thunderbolt making wide circles and attempted gunnery passes on the nimble dive bomber but never achieving a "shot". The SBD was able to make what appeared to me as several good shooting positions on the army plane as it passed. The dive bomber, turning tighter, lined up on him.

This went on for possibly 10 minutes and the sound was marvelous! The roaring Thunderbolt and the chattering SBD were opposing sounds as they wheeled and turned in what could be termed as a muscular ballet.

The navy pilot terminated the melee by rolling his airplane over on its back and did a split –S as the P-47 almost over took him. The SBD went straight down with the P-47 trying to follow and getting closer.

The dive bomber, on the way down, made some side-stepping changes and some jinking maneuvers and the Thunderbolt roared past him on its way down. It was interesting to see that when the SBD was in its vertical dive, the tail was past the vertical as if the airplane would go over on its back. The noise was unbelievable as they pulled out of their dives and went on their way with the SBD, indeed, "Slow but Deadly."

My last visit to Sarasota Airbase reflected all that had happened for the past three years. I stood at the east end of the main runway to watch a flight of P-51's coming in for their fighter pitchout before landing.

The first plane pulled up in a sharp climbing bank, pulled some bright streamers from the wingtips and dropped his landing gear. The second plane made a tight bank, pulled up pulling some bright streamers, but he couldn't drop his gear before he went into a high-speed stall and tumbled down in a confused gyration of flashing aluminum to hit in the grass between the two runways. I drove away as the fire trucks raced to the burning wreckage. We were told that there was a standing competition to see who could pull the best streamers. I don't think this guy won.

Beach House 1943

Beach House Porch 1943

R.A.F. Guests 1940

The R.A.F. Boys Introduction to Life on the Beach

PART TWO
Chapter 3.

Into the USAAF.
Ft. Meade, Md. and Sheppard Field, Tex.

Robert Parks

MY TURN

For some reason that is lost to me, the entire family went back to Washington, D.C., leaving me to finish my last year of school in Sarasota. I lived with a sergeant and his wife in town and received much of my inside information from Andy, who was in base operations. I have no idea of how I traveled to Washington, but I left Sarasota in June 1944 and spent a few weeks with my family and then, into the service.

I was ordered to report on August 4th, 1944 to a bus station in the southeast part of the city. Dad drove me there and pulled up to the curb in front. We sat there for a few moments in uncomfortable silence and when I got out of the car he said, "Be a good boy and do what they tell you," and drove off to work. I felt an emotional tension and a cultural shock when I stood there with 35 kids that didn't look like anybody that I was accustomed to. Italians and other dark-haired European extractions were standing around outside the bus station. I was the only blonde dark-skinned kid there so I got the collective once-over.

Soon an army bus arrived with a sergeant who accounted for all of us and away we went to Ft. Meade, Maryland, a long established infantry and armor training base. During our trip up there we must have gone deaf, because the minute we got off the bus our welcoming non-com began yelling at the top of his lungs for us "to form a line of two rows and to put our 'little bags' in front of us and stand at attention. He addressed us to state our names and serial number loud and clear and remain standing at attention until told to do otherwise. "You're in the army now and you WILL move it when ordered."

It didn't take long to realize that we were not human beings, but nothing more than commodities like bullets, pieces of equipment, or some meat that had to be processed into the grinder. We were assumed to be deaf because orders were screamed at us from inches away. It was stupid because even the simplest command was repeated and detailed so we didn't screw it up, lazy and paralytic because we were pushed and shoved to start running wherever we were to go. The first place to which we were herded was the insurance building where we filled out forms stating who would get our vast fortunes if we should not come home, pay forms and many other army papers. From there we were rushed to a warehouse type of building that we entered single file.

We quickly passed a soldier behind a counter who was yelling numbers loud as he could. When I passed him he stared at me while shouting, "7, 15, 27 31, 10!" Then I shuffled past another glum-faced private who was throwing clothes at me as fast as I could catch them. I caught the clothes and caught on that the numbers the first guy was yelling out were my sizes: hat, neck, waist, pant length and shoe size. He was dead on except that he was an inch too big in the waist measurement. All of it was crammed into a barracks bag that we could barely carry back to our lovely abode.

"ALL RIGHT! GET THE GODDAM CIVIES OFF AND DRESS LIKE A SOLDIER! FALLOUT IN 5!" The first kind words we had heard so far were uttered by our jailer when we reached our barrack. After we dressed in our soldier suits and "fell-in" in front of our quarters we could now be recognized as government property and that was drilled into our little civy minds every minute of the day.

Then we were marched to the "mess hall" where we had to gulp down our "mess" or "chow" in 15 minutes. Some of the kids complained about the bad taste, but I don't see how they could when there wasn't enough time to chew it. I had no idea what it was other than a wad of something in my stomach.

Now for some fun! While we were still wiping our mouths, we were scrambled outside for a "march" to the dispensary. Marching wasn't our best talent at that time and our column resembled the movement of a spastic caterpillar much to the disgust of our non-com in charge. After all, we had been in the army for almost a day and we were the worst "new shoes" that had ever set foot at Ft. Meade. Upon entering the dispensary, we were ordered to strip bare -- everything. In two minutes the room was filled with naked boys and embarrassment. We were formed into two lines that were to proceed past two medics who stood between two tables each. The tables were filled with vials and syringes.

"ALL RIGHT! HANDS ON YOUR HIPS, ELBOWS SPREAD OUT AND DON'T MOVE EM! MOVE BETWEEN THOSE TWO MEN AT THE TABLES AND STOP, THEY'LL TELL YOU WHEN YOU CAN KEEP GOING!" I was well back in line and witnessed the mass production line of inoculations Army style. The corpsmen at the tables picked up a syringe in each hand and with a tennis player's backhand stroke, slammed it into the fleshy area in the back where the arm meets the body when each victim stopped. The medic didn't even look up when he was forcibly pumping the serum except to pick up another syringe and stab his quarry in the shoulder muscle and then yet another shot after that in the arm. "MOVE!"

Then we were poked, prodded, handled while coughing, measured, weighed, blood drawn, and again, "MOVE! GET DRESSED AND FALL OUT!" We were now "processed". All the paperwork was completed, uniforms issued, shots given, and dog tags issued. I was now, Parks, R.L. Pvt. 14189128--- P---O. Name, Rank, Serial Number,

Protestant (PROTESTER would have been more accurate), and Blood Type. O.

We were now government issue, GI's, therefore, we were eligible for that iconic birthright of the "new shoe", KP, and we were put on KP duty that night. With the infinite wisdom of the military, the kitchen police duty was ordered immediately after the shots and to show us how smart they were we were scheduled for our I.Q. tests the next morning. I was one of the group who had some serious reactions to the soup of serums that were injected into my body.

After the all-afternoon session with the tests I had a raging headache and nausea. Evening chow was not on the list of things to do that evening and I went to sickbay where I was given two large white tablets. I barely made it back to the barracks and needed the help of two of our group to get up the steps. I crashed on my bunk, out like a light.

The next morning we had the scheduled inspection by a captain. I was still unconscious on my bunk when the inspection took place and I was told that the captain flew into a rage. I paid heavily for that little episode with more KP and garbage duty. I never found out why, but the skin peeled on my forehead the next day.

ESCAPE

After six days of punishment for being "the wimpy little flyboy non-soldiers," we were told that we were going to be shipped out for basic training at Sheppard Field, Texas and we were moved to transient barracks near the railhead. The day after we moved, we could see some troops moving in to the barracks across the parade ground. They were quite noisy and we couldn't understand how or why they were getting away with it until a huge Nazi flag was hung from the second story and more German artifacts began to be displayed.

Then those who occupied the building began to roam around! Not in formation, not marching, AND no one was yelling at them. Before we could go over to talk to them we were ordered to stay away from them PERIOD. They had just returned from heavy combat in Africa and the ETO and they were simply "killing machines". We wisely obeyed and when we did see them in the mess hall, it was obvious that they were still living in a combat world and would turn on anyone who crossed them.

Even though we were soon to be shipped out, we still had lots of KP duty and I was on the line serving breakfast when the veterans came in. The first man through was unshaved, shirt open, blonde hair uncombed, and had the eyes of a lizard, completely devoid of expression. His mouth had a perpetual grimace and I could see the edge of a bandage near the edge of the open shirt. THEN I was subjected to a vicious and loud verbal attack because the toast that I served him was a bit stale. What the hell could I do when ALL of it was stale?

I saw him later that day on the parade ground with some of his friends carousing in an almost drunken euphoria. Forced and loud laughing at nothing was common for them and to see a bayonet slipped into the combat boot was warning enough to stay clear of them.

These men were the product of a military that didn't exist three years prior to 1944. Men of this type and caliber didn't exist either because they were farmers or clerks then, peaceful civilians. Now, three years later, here they were, hardened ruthless warriors who had no resemblance to their beginnings. They would kill without remorse.

Mid-August in Wichita Falls, Texas is not at all like the breezy beaches of Siesta Key this time of the year: searing sun, oppressive heat, dirt, dust and ugliness. It was the termination of a long boring train trip from Ft. Meade that wandered all over the country because there was an Infantile Paralysis (now called Polio) outbreak in Georgia. From Maryland we went north to Pittsburg where we had the only fun on the entire trip and that happened in the rail yards there during one of the many stops. We were told to stay on the train so we naturally got off to stretch our legs. While we were standing there close to our car, a trainload of Marines pulled alongside with their last car a short distance behind our last car. Ten minutes later a train pulled in on our other side with a load of sailors. Seeing us standing on the tracks I suppose encouraged the others to do the same. While troops from the Navy, Army, and Marines were sunning themselves in the "fresh" Pittsburg air, someone in our group yelled,

"What's worse than a dirty Sailor?" Then someone answered, "A clean Marine." It was like throwing a match in a pool of gasoline. We quickly scrambled back into our Pullman and watched a great fight.

Who said Air Force guys weren't smart?

From there we went to Chicago and then south through Illinois, Indiana, Nebraska, Oklahoma and finally Sheppard Field, Texas. I had been in the AAF for exactly two weeks and the train trip seemed much longer than that. Entertainment from card games and staring out the window grew old in a hurry. There was a lot of time to think. My thoughts went back to the first night at Ft. Meade when a kid on the second level started crying for his mother. The next morning he was absent from roll call and one of the guys asked the sergeant God where he went. "WHAT KID!"

"Well, that kid that was crying to go home."

"WHAT KID WHO WAS CRYING? I DIDN'T SEE NO KID WHO WAS CRYING!"

"Well, he was... Oh, yeah. I didn't see no kid who was crying, I guess."

That was the end of that and we never found out who or how the kid that wasn't there was removed without a trace. BUT we did find the source of what was producing a horrible stench in the barracks when we were preparing for an inspection. We thought something had died in the crawl space, but when I walked through the squad room at the end of the barrack to go outside, I discovered the source. To explain: every barrack had a permanent occupant whose duty was to care for the furnace and to be "fire watch." These people were the blank cards in the deck and it was all they could do to watch the furnace and be around all day.

This example was lying on his bunk in his little room with the door open and his bare feet hanging over the edge of his bunk. The odor was staggering. I contacted the non-com–in-control and asked him to check it out. When he walked to the other end of the room, there was another explosion of four letter words and threats of dire predictions if the fire watch didn't immediately take a shower. Not only just then, but TWICE A DAY. He was threatened with a "GI bath." Now, this was not a euphemism.

It was a serious threat for one to be stripped and put in the shower and bathed with Fels-Naptha soap and scrubbed with a stiff floor brush. The offender, an ex-Pennsylvania coal miner, was incensed that he would have to bath so much because he was sure to catch pneumonia.

"YOU ARE GOING TO CATCH SOMETHING WORSE THAN PNEUMONIA IF YOU DON'T GET YOUR FILTHY ASS IN THERE AND CLEAN UP -- EVERY GODDAM DAY!" the sergeant so gently stated. The next few days we didn't have to smell that ex-Pennsylvania coal miner and his feet because we were going to ship out.

When we were two days away from Sheppard Field, our troop train ran out of food. And we had some over-aged hot dogs and crushed pineapple with cheese twice a day. A captain at Sheppard Field welcomed us when we left the train and formed in the dock area. The first thing that occurred was a question by one of our group, a rather mincing Jewish boy. He asked if we could get something to eat since it was 1830 and dinnertime.

The captain mentioned that the mess hall was closed and wanted to know if we had evening chow on the train. When the answer came that we had not, he told us that we would have to wait until morning and then summoned the ex-train commander to present himself in the captain's office after we were dismissed. We could sense that things did not bode well for the 2nd Lt.

BASIC TRAINING

I can't recall the exact number, but I estimate that forty to fifty of us became Flight 314. That matched the barracks number on the base; a two-story cookie-cutter wooden building that, in the three years of war, had been built by the thousands at hundreds of military bases. At each end on the first floor were squad rooms for the non-coms and DI's (drill instructors).

Our DI was Sergeant Patin who was a short stocky little man from New Orleans and he occupied one of the squad rooms. At our first assembly in front of the barracks, we were made aware that "We WOULD rise at 0430 for roll call that was to take place at exactly 0433 in front of the barracks FULLY DRESSED!" We were then ordered to wash up, shave and march to morning chow. After chow we could "route step" back to the barracks where we were to assemble before beginning our morning training.

This became our morning routine five days per week with Sunday assigned to our personal needs: like cleaning and polishing everything except the sidewalk. So, our days were full from 0400 to 2130 when it was lights out. Our lights were about out too because we were running, marching in close order drill, physical training, learning to shoot with wooden rifles, and watching training films. The films were always shown right after lunch -- OOPS! -- noon chow.

We had just finished an 8-hour day, had consumed a good meal and you know what that does when you sit in a darkened air-conditioned theater. Sleep was as powerful as the 103-degree heat from which we had just been removed.

The instructors and DI's had a diabolical arrangement to expose those who slipped into unconsciousness. The instructor, in his normal tone, slipped in some instructions during his lecture that when he yelled attention we were to remain seated. There is no need to describe what happened when he yelled "TUUCH HUT!

When this ploy wasn't exercised, the DI's circulated around the audience with their billy clubs ready to deliver a sharp blow on top of the micarta helmet liner that we had to wear at all times. The resounding PONK reverberated through the cranium, almost blurring the vision of the dozing miscreant when he opened his eyes.

So, our training went on for four weeks in this hot, featureless, hard-baked garden spot of north Texas and our daily routine. It was seemingly harsh in the beginning and became the norm. Some mornings we were awake before the "morning messenger" came through at 0430 yelling, "314 CHOW!" He endeared himself to us by entering the barracks and banging his billy club on the heat ducts while he was yelling. One morning as he left to do the same damage in the next barracks, a voice broke the darkness, "One of these mornings I'm going to kill that sonavabitch!"

That didn't happen, but I thought that my DI was going to do me in one day when he spieled off some of his colorful four-letter-word laden military sentences. The cleverly devised descriptions painted by his profane prose struck my funny bone and I could not suppress my mirth. I had never heard them before and I started laughing while we were in a brace (attention) in formation.

While I struggled to contain my lack of military discipline, sergeant Patin, in his rage, helped me to completely lose it by unleashing a steady stream of his most colorful language while he was two inches from my face. I turned red in the face with laughter as he turned purple with anger. Both of us were out of control. It started when he was warning us about packing our warm clothing for our 20 mile hike to bivouac, "If you don't, yer' gonna' shiver like a dog sh---ing peach seeds -- sideways!" Then there were others in close order and just as colorful.

I spent that evening at chow time running around the parade ground, still giggling at times.

The evening before our march to bivouac, we finished rolling our packs and managed to slip away to the PX and got some beer to slake our thirst. I can't recall how we did it, but we had plenty and some of us got a bit looped. August evenings in Wichita Falls can be very warm and dry after a very hot and dry day.

The beer went down easy and quickly so we thought that we should take a practice hike to try out our full packs. It was still pretty hot and those packs were heavy so we figured that we could lighten up some other things and off we went smartly marching down the company street, all five of us in our helmets, full packs, and boots.

It was going very well with a formation of two by two and a right guide calling out cadence. It was dark and pretty late so there wasn't a problem of disturbing anyone, but we made the mistake of marching loudly enough and close enough to the post K-9 kennels and yard. Damn if the dogs weren't out and damn if they didn't start barking.

Just as we had made a beautiful sweeping maneuver to reverse direction, the MP's showed up with their Jeep and very bright spot lights. In the midst of their laughter one of them shouted, "Detail! Halt." And there we were, five bright (not because of our brains, but bright from the headlights and spotlights of the Jeep) young soldiers standing at attention. "What the hell are you guys up to? Where's your outfit!"

"Flight 314, we were just takin' a practice hike" we answered.

"NAKED?"

"Well, yeah. We thought it was a good idea at the time. Kinda' hot, ya' know."

"Okay, we got to get you nuts off the streets! Right face! Fo-wuhd Haw!"

It appeared that they were playing into our game and we

were playing into theirs, so off we went with the Jeep behind us with the headlights on high beam. I got to chuckling at the sight of the bobbing white buns of kid ahead of me. Instead of heading straight ahead and up the street to our abode, we were ordered to take a right turn. Okay, who cares, we weren't in too much trouble with the gendarmes but why the heck take a roundabout route. That question was answered when we realized that we were being paraded past the WACS barracks where we earned a few laughs and shouts of approval.

BIVOUAC

Dawn was driven out of the night and into the next day by a hot blast from the east. Our beer-fed episode the previous night said, "You'll be SORRY!" We were on our way at 0600 and started our 20-mile hike in a bright sun and an 80-degree temperature and we WERE sorry but we got sorrier when the temperature soon reached 108.

The sun baked hard packed clay road on which we were hiking must have been 120 degrees. Nobody died but we were wishing that we would as the hot miles slowly reeled by. We stopped every hour for water and salt tablets. At one rest stop a group of trainees returning to the base stopped on the other side of the road. One of the "old timers" sporting a bandage on his face sauntered across the road, pulled a plastic cigarette box out of his pocket, and showed us what was in it as he dropped the contents into his palm.

"This is what you guys are going to sleep with for the next week!"

It was a huge tarantula that had bitten him on his face when he tried to brush it off in his sleep.

We made it to the bivouac area just before evening chow. After visiting our assigned area where we dropped our gear, we went to the field kitchen to be fed. We formed a long line and each of us passed by a mess hand to have our mess kits filled with what appeared to be slop with a yellow hat.

I reached the man who was dispensing our evening meal and faced a mountainous snaggle-toothed behemoth that weighed possibly 100 pounds less than a B-17 and seemed to have great joy in sharing his cooking with us. I offered my containers and I could see that we were getting beef stew; that came first, PLOP! Then mashed potatoes and gravy, PLOP! Then dessert; crushed pineapple, raisins and cheese, PLOP! Everything went on top of the stew, potatoes and gravy and bread!

The 350-pound mess hand leaned down at me with an almost toothless grin and said, "Boy! If'n them raisins move, they ain't raisins!" He was correct. Some of them weren't raisins.

Flight 314 went through all of the shooting competitions, that we handily won, and excelled at the field maneuvers. Field maneuvers included sleeping in the mesquite several nights, two souls to a shelter half, a small piece of cloth supported by two poles and flaps at the end.

After weeks and weeks of hot bone dry weather our first night camping out in the bush was spent in the rain. Well never mind, we were protected by a sheet of the finest muslin the military could afford. Dawn sleepily awakened, as we did, to a gray sky. As the light grew brighter, I still felt the need to catch a few more winks. But my partner came to life with an explosion of movement coupled with a yell and he wiggled out of the shelter feet first.

Before I could ask what his problem was I looked up and had the answer. The entire inside of the little tent was covered by every known species of spiders, big and little, green, black, fuzzy, red and a mixture of all the colors in the spectrum. I ungracefully mimicked my partners exit from our quarters where the insects had sought shelter from the rain.

Now, fully awake, I started to put my boots on and remembered our DI warning us about scorpions moving into them during the night. Okay, go through the drill, turn the boots upside down and vigorously shake -- and out dropped an ugly scorpion!

Scorpions weren't the only critter problem we had to face. The rattlesnake had long since been chased out of this area, but the spiders weren't as smart and we were told to watch out for the black widow and the tarantula. My first visit to the large luxurious ditch latrine was a laugh as well as a warning.

"Don't slam the toilet seat! It makes the Black Widows Mad!"

"No need to stand on the toilet seat, the Crabs in here can jump ten feet!"

So, this was our life for a week in the field supposedly learning battlefield skills. Thank goodness we weren't sent overseas after our field training. We would have won the war, though, because the enemy would have died laughing at us. We did some things well, however. We got the highest scores on the firing range shooting the cal. 30 Carbine, M3 machine gun, Thomson sub machine, cal. 45 automatic and the cal.45 revolver. We all were southern boys who knew how to hunt and to shoot.

Since we won the shooting competition, we got a nice bus ride back to the base. We also were awarded a stop at a lake where we had an afternoon swim. The shower, cool water and an afternoon of playtime was completely offset when we had to dress in our stinking filthy clothes that hadn't been washed in a week of sweaty groveling in the Texas dirt.

The last days of our bivouac exercise were done on our own without our sergeant. He got orders to report for an interview prior to being sent to OCS to become a commissioned officer. Before he left, he gathered us in the field and informed us that he had convinced his superiors that we were capable of properly conducting ourselves for three days in his absence. Each one of us swore to uphold his confidence in us and in closing he said,"If you men screw up when I'm gone, you'd better send your heart to God because your ass is gonna' be mine!"

We did our job and kept his record, and ours, clean. He was a tough uncompromising drill instructor but somehow nurtured our respect and affection for him. We were always the lead flight in post parades and excelled in most everything that we had to do. On our last day there with him, we gave HIM an order and asked him to face us in formation from the steps of the barrack. One of our group stepped forward and gave a speech of thanks and presented him with wrist chronometer that we all pitched in to purchase.

Our tough little French/American DI, Sgt. Patin, stood there in tears as he received his gift.

Ready for
maneuvers on
bivouac with
carbine, heavy
marching order.
   Drawn from
memory.

This pack holds
2 wool blankets
mattress cover
tent half and pins, pole
rain coat
towel toilet articles
clothes
mess kit
field manuel.

Robert Parks

Chapter 4.

Hondo Army Airfield and San Antonio.
Troop train trip to new post.

FINALLY! AIRPLANES!

We passed all our tests. I qualified for pilot training, learned to shoot the Thompson sub-machine gun, cal. 45 "grease gun", cal. 30 Carbine, cal. 45 Colt revolver and the cal. 45 semi-automatic Colt pistol, getting expert in the carbine and revolver, sharpshooter in the pistol. We learned how to march and do a lot of stuff we would never use. Having been finally welcomed into the air force, we got a two-day train ride to Hondo Army Air Field, 45 miles west of San Antonio.

We were processed in the same way we were processed out of the previous post. Stabbed, poked, shot,

On Furlough 1944

handled and fingered. Then we were assigned to our outfit with the announcement that we were NOT going to flight school unless the war took a one hundred and eighty degree turn and the umpteen thousands of surplus pilots were used up and that was never going to happen. Okay, one week late and a dollar short again.

I was assigned to the 845th Navigation Training Squadron as an on-the-line–trainee. Oh Goody! I'm a glorified gas pump attendant. On second thought, I realized it was a helluva lot better than Ft. Meade. Hell would be better than that.

Hondo was a huge air base with a main ramp that was one mile long. At the north end of it, another half-mile long ramp angled to the right. From the air its configuration was an inverted "L ". It was the largest navigation training facility in the world. The ramps were crammed with two varieties of airplanes: three rows of Beechcraft AT-7's and Lockheed C-60's, 250 of them. All of them fitted out for training navigators.

I was assigned to a crew that maintained four AT-7's and two C-60's that operated twenty hours a day. While some of them were airborne we refueled, repaired and did the run-ups before it was their turn to fly. But before we were allowed to touch the airplanes, we had some very important "instructional training" to go through.

My first day on the line, I was told by an old timer to go to the PLM hangar at the far end of the ramp to get a bucket of prop wash. I obediently went on my search and darn if it didn't take ALL DAY. I walked all over that base looking at all the airplanes, operations in the Production Line Maintenance hangar and even had a bite to eat in the flight line cafeteria. Then I returned to my crew chief with the sad news that they were all out of prop wash and they told me to find some at the south end of the ramp. Well, they were out of it also so it looked like we would have to wait for a new shipment.

The next day I was put on a search for a generator paralleling bar and I got to see the rest of the base while I was looking for another non-existent item. Generators were paralleled with an ammeter. I never let on that I was not the dolt that my crew chief had assumed.

When we finally got down to serious work, our treatment by the non-coms and officers, was the complete antithesis of the crude brutality of our reception center at Ft. Meade. "RECEPTION?" Only the WW2 military could exercise such misappropriation of a word that is usually connected to something nice like a wedding or the introduction of a debutante.

Here at Hondo we were assumed to have a brain, good hearing and a sense of responsibility. We were shown how to do certain operations just once, then left to do our jobs under the supervision of a few old hands. The pace at times was hectic and we had to remain completely focused and aware of what was happening around us because the flight line had three rows of airplanes, wing tip to wing tip. When all of them were cranked up and ready to taxi out to the runway, it was roaring confusion and spinning props in every direction you looked.

We had to walk the wing tips as the planes moved out of the parking slot and on to the ramp to taxi to the runway. When the ramp was clear, we watched a steady stream of AT-7's taking off for their four-hour training mission.

If it was a morning mission, it launched at 0800 after three or more hours of preparation. The airplanes were serviced with fuel and oil, thoroughly checked for mechanical defects, then an engine run-up to check instruments and engine health. By the time the pilots and navigator cadets arrived, the airplane was warmed up and ready to go. After launch, we went to the mess hall for breakfast and we actually had time enough to eat and eat we did!

WHAT A MESS!

We had arrived at Hondo at night after a meal on the train, so we didn't have the experience of having chow in the mess hall. The next morning after roll call, we walked to the mess for breakfast. No marching and calling cadence, we just simply walked there. When we approached the food line, one of the kids stared at the food and turned wide-eyed and said, "We're in the wrong mess. This has got to be the officer's mess!"

The presence of many other enlisted men proved him wrong but the food service could have proved him to be right. There was an array of cereals and oatmeal to start with, next was a line cook who was cooking and serving FRESH EGGS, and to your order! There was fresh bacon and toast and the wonder of wonders, small individual steaks if you didn't like bacon. Then at the tail end of the line there were vats of juices: orange, grapefruit and grape. But the crown jewel was a rack of quart bottles of FRESH MILK. A mess sergeant told us that we could take the whole bottle but we had to drink it all, no waste. I colluded with my buddy to split one with me and, oh, how we relished that first long draught of it.

Most of us were used to good food when we were growing up and the fare at Ft. Meade and Sheppard Field was typical army. Watered down condensed milk or powdered milk, hard stale toast made from hard stale cardboard, stews, spam, spam, spam, tasteless cheese, tasteless baloney, rubber scrambled eggs and the forever crushed pineapple with cheese and raisins for dessert. Sometimes tasteless Jell-O was offered.

We couldn't believe our eyes that first morning at Hondo and we were equally impressed with the mid-day and evening meals -- no longer referred to as chow. All that good didn't come for free, however. We had to earn it. You were on duty until your duties were done, even if it took all night and that happened a few times. We had a minimum of one hour of physical training every day except Sunday, regardless of what your duties were the night before. So, we worked hard, trained pretty hard and were fed good healthy food.

A DAY IN PARADISE

One hundred octane fuel exhaust emits a unique odor and radial engines make a wonderful sound, so being able to participate in an environment where there were airplanes that produced all that, along with an exciting visual stimulus was better than any alternative to going to flight school. We saw and heard airplanes all day long and sometimes we worked on them all day and all night. That happened when we got a report that one of our airplanes had a serious accident at San Marcos when one of the landing gears collapsed on landing. They discovered a broken retraction chain link and several more that were cracked.

At mid-afternoon we got the order to run every single airplane through PLM (Production Line Maintenance) to check the retraction chains. We no sooner got started when a torrential downpour hit while we struggled with the airplanes on the ramp. But we got all those on the ramp lined up in a huge conga line that proceeded up to the maintenance hangar where they checked. I can't remember how many the hangar held, but there were quite a few lined up nose to tail on jacks. Those of us who weren't working the ramp at the time were up inside the wheel wells checking the retraction chains and we found many cracked links. The night was long, cold, wet and stretched in to the next morning and that stretched into the entire day -- and night. So did the rain.

With all the flying machines flying again, the routine returned to normal with the morning shift starting before dawn with a hearty breakfast and then out to the line in the dark. Normal mornings included a complete visual check of all the fluids even though the night crew was supposed to top everything off. Check the airplane for ramp rash or other damage, pull the props through to clear the oil out of the lower cylinders, check the chocks and climb aboard.

As I write this, my mind is dredging up visions from almost seventy years ago so if my recall isn't perfect, it's because my old head isn't either. Cranking up a cold Pratt and Whitney R985 in the winter requires some delicate procedures and a feel or understanding of how a radial engine behaves when it's awakened on a cold morning. There is a small syringe type of manual pump mounted on the instrument panel with which you prime the engine. A twist unlocks it and the plunger is pulled back to load it. Then you push it firmly in to inject raw fuel into the combustion chamber of the cylinders. This must be done as many as nine times to prime the engine. There is a fine line between too much prime and not enough. Too much will foul the spark plugs and not enough will defeat the purpose.

I had successfully started the left engine (number one) and was preparing to start number two when I heard the airplane next to me backfire a couple of times. I attended to my operations when I caught the glow of a fire that can quickly get your attention in the dark of the morning. The kid had not gotten a start due to over priming and the backfire ignited some fuel that had run out of the exhaust pipe and had a nice little fire burning not only under the wheel well but up into it. He should have kept cranking to get a start but froze and let the fire grow. Everybody shut down, grabbed fire extinguishers and attacked the fire but we were no match for it. Before we made a total retreat, the fire truck arrived in time to knock it down without too much damage but the airplane wouldn't fly for quite a while. We couldn't figure out how the guy got so much fuel spilled out in a simple start procedure.

This is where the wheat began to separate from the chaff. Some kids obviously lacked that innate quality to act quickly and correctly in an emerging threat. The inaction of the fireguard stationed a few feet away from the fire was a perfect example. He had backed away with the fire extinguisher instead of charging the fire in its early stage. Some could perform acceptably if they had a list to memorize. Some were just plain inept when it came to applying their education in an intelligent manner. We began to see those who would not make it through flight training. Then there were those who were miles ahead of the game and made it just that, a game.

Radio checks were part of the morning run up and sometimes the traffic was intense. Sometimes there were gaps in the chatter. During one of the brief interludes, some odd sounding static erupted and a typical British voice came on, "ello Amedica! This is BBC calling with the latest news from meddy 'Ol England. We are still at wah with the Jeddy and we seem to be winning but we have lost the bluudy wah to the Yanks who seem to be everywah! The Queen was rushed to hospital yestideah with a serious and painful HANG NAIL! Well, that is all the news. Cheerio."

This continued in spite of officially angry response from the tower that ordered an immediate cease to the illegal banter that flooded the radio airways. It went on every morning and some of it was hilarious. One that I will always remember was the "dullard" who tried to figure out how to start his airplane. "Let's see, now. You put your foot on lever A and then lever B." The double entendre was not lost on those who were listening -- leav'er be. In spite of frantic and diligent running up and down the ramp by MP's, the radio culprits were never caught. "I say, blokes, he's at the south end of the ramp now so fear not at the north end."

THE "COMEUPANCE"

Some of the pilots who flew the AT-7's were a bit above the normal bunch of 2nd Lt.'s who performed this rather ignominious task of flying trainees around and one of them was in our little flight. At something around five feet in height, he suffered from the little man syndrome and carried a swagger stick whenever he was seen on the ramp.

He was an instructor pilot who liked to hit the hands of a pilot with his swagger stick when they were performing an incorrect procedure in the cockpit. He was despised by all. One beautiful afternoon in broad daylight, an AT-7 made a wheels-up landing on the main north/south runway in front of the entire world. When the crew bailed out, the last one to emerge was the pilot with his swagger stick.

The ramp went wild with glee, "Look who's getting out! It's Little Napoleon. He did a wheels-up!" And sure enough, the landing gear switch was in the down position -- as always after an un-planned belly landing. When the airplane was jacked up, the landing gear switch worked amazingly well.

We never saw that swagger stick again.

NIGHT GAMES

Occasionally we were allowed to get off base to visit Hondo. After the first on-foot "trip" into town, we realized that the town of Hondo wasn't much better than finding something to do on the base. The population there was half that of the base and almost devoid of anything interesting or entertaining.

My buddy and I decided to walk through the town on our way back one Saturday evening and we went through the north end at the edge of town. We soon realized that it wasn't the high rent district when we passed a row of eight-foot diameter concrete sewer pipes left over from the construction of the air base, the ends of which were boarded up.

As we got closer we could see that they had crude doors through which people could pass. Then we could see little Mexican children and women gathered in front of these pipes. They were living in them. My partner and I were from middle class families and we had never been exposed to poverty at this level. As we walked by, we attempted to avoid staring at them but it was difficult.

We continued our walk to our destination, when we came upon a Mexican dance party that was being held in a barracks type of building in the middle of a dusty empty lot. Loud music poured out of the building while the occupants happily danced to the sounds performed by an ensemble composed of a trumpet, two guitars, a drummer and a saxophone. They were sometimes off key but they were blasting out the music that had everyone in their grasp.

We stood near the street and watched for a while and a young lady with a tray of goodies supported by a cord around her neck came up to us and asked if we would like to purchase something. We agreed and tried some "Mexican rollups" that quickly necessitated a bottle of Orange Crush to put out the fire in our mouths.

This delighted the little kids who had timidly gathered near us and we soon became a source of humor to them. So we bought some Mexican sweets and sat down in the dirt with them to share something more to our and their liking. We had a good time with them while trying to converse in their language and buying candy for them. We spent every penny we had on candy and goodies that they thoroughly enjoyed. They were beautiful and happy little kids.

We had to return to base by a certain hour and we had to leave our little friends with the promise that we would return. We had to check in with a sergeant on duty and he inquired about our dirty uniforms and asked if we had been "rolling around with someone." When we told him where we had been and what we had done, he exploded, "You WHAT!" We were in shock at his outburst.

"Do you know that we have had to pull our people out of there all cut up and beat up by those Greasers! That is an off limits area to you people! How the hell did you do that?"

We were dumbfounded. "All we did was to watch them dance and then played with the kids."

"Well, you mean that you didn't fool around with their young girls?"

"No. We just had something to eat and gave the kids some candy."

"You're Goddam lucky! I guess that as long as you didn't make a play for any of their women they let you go. You were most likely being watched the whole time by the men. You WILL stay away from there from now on, do you understand!"

So, that was one of our last visits to Hondo city.

Night duty on the line wasn't as dangerous as a trip through the north side of town, but it could get interesting if you were returning from a training mission at midnight. The flights departed at 2000 hours in the same kind of melee as they did during the day, but added to the roar and smoke were landing lights, navigation lights and exhaust flames. When the last plane made its take off and the navigation lights slowly disappeared into the night, you worked on whatever needed fixing and if you were lucky, you could relax in the line shack drinking an Orange Crush, eating a donut and listening to the jukebox playing something like "Don't Fence Me In" by Bing Crosby or The Andrews Sisters singing "Shoo Shoo Shoo Baby." Then five minutes before 2400 you went back to the flight line to watch the black sky suddenly erupt with hundreds of red and green lights as the AT-7's returned. They entered a 360-degree racetrack pattern that circled the field, providing those near a radio with a running stream of profanity as one after another got cut off by an impolite pilot breaking into the circle.

It was a beautiful sight to see them in that huge circle of lights rotating around the field. Then one-by-one, they banked into their final approach with landing lights piercing the darkness until their wheels chirped to announce their contact with Mother Earth. As they taxied in, the ramp became a dangerous seething mass of flashing lights, glistening propellers, orange and blue exhaust flames and shiny aluminum reflecting the movement of it all.

Men and airplanes seemed to move in all directions at once without choreography, but in a matter of minutes the airplanes were guided into their parking slots where the navigation students deplaned and the pilots filled out the form 1's and bitched to the ground crews about things that they had overlooked. Then we started our work to service and clean the airplanes. We were usually done by 0200-0300.

HAPPY HOLIDAYS

Operations continued unabated in the fall and winter of 1944. We were treated to a marvelous Thanksgiving dinner at the mess hall complete with all the trimmings that we would have received at home, turkey with gravy and dressing, sweet potatoes, pumpkin pie, fresh fruit AND a cigar at every place setting that was arranged on white table clothes. It was an unbelievable meal in a military establishment but our CO believed in hard work, hard exercise and good food.

Christmas came with a three-day pass for my buddies and me and we headed for San Antonio to see a real town. To see the town, one had to look through a million faces of all the military personnel that were crowding the streets. The place was packed. We bumped into every branch of the service plus some aviators from Brazil who emblazoned themselves with every aviation gimmick known to man at that time. Badges, patches, wings, 50-mission crush on their hats and buttons adorned their uniforms and there was no doubt that they were the hottest airmen to grace the skies. The most amazing thing about our immersion into the flood of military humanity was when we were walking down the main street in the most crowded section of downtown. The area was blazing with lights from the stores and theaters when I spotted a kid from my hometown coming my way, the quarterback of the football team on which I played! "What the hell are you doing here?"

"Same thing you are! Seeing the sights!"

After a brief conversation he went his way and I never saw him again.

When it came time to find a place to stay, we went to the USO west of town and the lady at the desk mentioned to us that a family would like to entertain two servicemen for the Christmas Holidays. We thought that would be nice so we accepted the offer but we didn't know that they would send a car to pick us up! Indeed, a chauffeur showed up in a big black car and drove us somewhere north of town to an estate complete with a curving driveway to the front door. We were greeted by a lovely lady and her husband who warmly invited us into a beautiful home that was decorated to the hilt with Christmas things.

We thought that we would maybe have dinner with them and

then return to a USO cot, but much to our surprise, we were shown to our separate bedrooms. I explained that we didn't have any luggage or sleepwear with us and we were told that there were pajamas and robes that we could use but before retiring, we were to have dinner and an evening with them.

We were invited to have a chat with them in the living room in front of a warming fireplace where they asked about our homes and our families. Their sincerity was a wonderfully refreshing change from the distant duty-fed queries from the military of which we were accustomed. The butler announced that dinner was served and we "retired" to the dining room. Dinner was a sumptuous Christmas meal complete with everything that one would envision, and served by a butler.

We could not believe what had happened to us. These people were obviously well to do. No, more than well to do. They were very rich but very generous. This was made apparent when after dinner we were guided into the living room by the Christmas tree and invited to open OUR Christmas presents. Indeed, there were presents for us under the tree!

Then after opening our presents and chatting and singing Christmas carols we went to our rooms to retire for the night. The soft, comfortable beds with smooth warm sheets were worth the entire year of being in the service. Sleeping in a soft bed with a big fluffy pillow was almost too much to handle. And it was deathly quiet. No engines running, no one yelling at you, no one snoring in the next bunk. It took all of three minutes to fall asleep.

We were allowed to sleep as long as we wanted, but we woke up early as usual, showered and dressed before the others. Then we looked at the things that decorated the halls and the living room and I noticed that there were many items of value that could have easily been taken, but the home was as if it were ours.

There were quite a few photos of two service men placed at noticeable places in the house. When our hosts appeared in the breakfast nook, we asked if the photos were those of their sons and said that they were: "one in Europe and one in the Pacific theater." After a nice breakfast of poached eggs and toast, we apologetically announced that we had to be back at the base by 1700 and that we should start our return.

One never knew how long it would take to travel 45 miles by

bus, hitch-hiking or a chance ride. So we had to leave. Our hosts wished us well and bid us a warm goodbye and we promised that we would honor their invitation to return as soon as we could. Their butler drove us to the USO where we could hopefully arrange for a ride back to the air base and we happened to mention where we had been to the lady at the desk. She shook her head and said, "Oh, you are so lucky. They are such lovely people and so good to the servicemen! They lost both of their sons last year."

That statement was like a load of bricks falling on us. Their warm and open treatment of us was certainly must have been difficult for them. That explained the ready availability of the pajamas and robes. The presents, singing Christmas carols and the free run of their huge home made more sense, but also drove home to us what outstanding and giving people they were when they were suffering the loss of their two sons.

Before we could respond to their invitation to return, we were told that we were being shipped out. We would never see them again but we would never forget them. Thus are the vagaries of war.

An AT-7 Morning Run-up | Robert Parks

Chapter 5.

Langley Field, Va. and new experiences with flight crews.

A B-24 Crew | Robert Parks

OUT OF TEXAS

The details of packing and being processed before our departure from Hondo have been lost in time, but the train trip to Langley Field has not. It took the best part of a week to get there but it was the most enjoyable and interesting trips of my life.

Again, we had the luxury of traveling in a posh Pullman car complete with flowered upholstery, pull down berths with sheets and blankets and leather appointments in the restrooms. We even had sitting areas with opposing seats and little mahogany tables between on which to play cards or write letters. Write letters? I tried a few but got few answers. Good food was served in the mess car too.

It took us a full day and a half to reach the border of Texas and Arkansas and a cheer went up when we did. I remember one kid saying that Texas wasn't a state, it was a condition. The other humorous memory was that of a big heavy Texas kid in our barrack at Hondo bemoaning the fact that he couldn't get home to his Texas residence and back on a three-day pass. We asked him where the hell he lived. "Mudaddy (one word) has a little spread in north Texas." When we asked what the name of it was he said with a nonchalant deadpan face, "Oklahoma." At least, he had a good sense of humor.

So, we had crossed most of Texas from the southwest to the northeast and saw a lot of nothing and realized that Hondo was in the prettiest part of the "condition", Hill Country. Indeed, when we crossed into Arkansas the small town through which we passed was barren and the soil blackened by oil spilled from the forest of bobbing stork-headed pumps. We never considered that these wells were helping us to keep our mechanized weapons fed.

Riding hour after hour, day after day on a troop train can be boring if the only activity is staring out of the window and playing cards. So spontaneously formed groups engaged in some interesting discussions. Our little group had a very bright young man from Washington, D.C. who claimed that his mother taught him how to hypnotize. Of course we doubted him and played along with his first attempt. That is, until his first attempt was obviously successful. That set the stage for a daily session of hypnotic parlor tricks that not only kept us entertained, but it gave us some education in the malleability of some human brains.

We learned that not everyone is a good subject for hypnotism and that a trained hypnotist can spot those who are. So there were five or six kids who offered their services without any concern. Our morning routine was quickly dispatched.

Roll call, berths made up and folded, breakfast after personal clean up, Pullman car policed (cleaned up) and we gathered in one of the compartments to see what our magician would do with his subjects. He used a medallion swinging on a chain in the light of one of the dim reading lamps in the wall and soon had one of his subjects entrapped as he spoke softly while swinging the lure in front of them. His first demonstration was a simple post-hypnotic suggestion that had his subject crawling the length of the car on his hands and knees after the hypnotist said a key word that had been implanted in the subjects mind.

We rocked gently in the Pullman and rolled along for five days through the southwest and every day we had the mentalist put on a show that was, at times, hilarious. He had two kids thinking that they were in an airplane climbing to 30,000 feet and freezing. And they were, shivering and hugging each other for warmth.

One boy was convinced that when he came out of the trance he was Harry James and the sight of his trying to play a trumpet when he had never touched one was a real HOOT. (I couldn't resist that one.) A Frank Sinatra appeared one morning and actually stood on the leather couch in the washroom and crooned with all the moves and inflections of the real singer. There couldn't have been any better entertainment than the variety show we were getting every day as we traveled through Arkansas, Mississippi, Tennessee, Kentucky, West Virginia and Virginia. Crossing the Mississippi River was a memorable sight on a dark and dreary day. We couldn't believe how wide and muddy it was as we slowly made our way across the bridge in the rain. There was snow on the famed pastures of the horse country.

Nearing the end of our journey, we stopped at a small town in West Virginia after evening chow. The train screeched and groaned to a stop with our car directly in front of the station platform that stair-stepped back and up from the tracks that were very close to the station. There was a lot of cast iron decorative bric-a-brac on the railings and posts of the structure covering the platform and some of the townspeople had gathered to see the train and we immediately made contact and struck up a conversation.

The Pullman cars in those days had windows that one could open and it didn't take long to get all of them up. And it didn't take long for many of the town's maidens to gather by the cars after we started singing our air force songs. Yeah, straight out of a Hollywood grade B movie. And to keep that scenario in place, one of the kids talked a pretty little girl into giving him a kiss. In order to reach her, he had to be lowered down to her level and that required us to hang onto his legs and ankles that just happened to be bare.

The heat had been turned up too high in the cars and some of the kids had stripped down to their shorts. This kid, Moody, was one of them and somehow he had been able to acquire some booze that not only diluted his discretion, but also numbed him to the winter temperature outside the train, it was January.

Never mind, he was bound to get a smooch so we did our duty for a lovesick soldier and managed to get him out of the window and lower him, but we did not manage to keep him from slipping from our grasp and he took a nose-dive, almost landing on the little girl. The crowd in the station had surged to what looked like the population of the town, brought there from our singing and commotion, I imagine, and they roared at Moody's mishap. He no sooner made his landing when the locomotive somewhere up ahead gave a long toot on the low-throated steamboat whistle signaling that it was moving out.

The scramble to get Moody back on the train was a Keystone Cops classic. We threw a blanket down to him in hopes that he could hold on while we pulled him up with his help. Much to our surprise, it worked, except that his shorts came off either in his dive or when he was being reeled in. His extraction and exit gave the town a first class mooning as the train gathered speed in its departure.

We made our way through a canyon in the dark and all that we could see were lonely lights off in the thick woods on either side of us through the thick rain soaked glass of the windows. Those lights were a weak orange in color that, to me, indicated that rural electrification had not reached this area yet. What we were seeing was the light of kerosene lanterns. I thought of one of our group who was from West Virginia, a little guy named Reeder who had become a big question mark among us. He had a sort of dumb bumpkin way about him but he always seemed to be out of reach by those who assigned onerous duties to us. He always had money, always had a smile for everybody, and could outshoot anybody including the range officer when we were on the gun range in basic training.

It seemed that he could charm even those in the security side of things since he returned from furlough carrying a gallon sized mayonnaise jar filled with some of his daddy's "squeezins". He explained, when challenged by the MP's, that he was carrying distilled liquids for his digestive problems. We found out why it was called "White Lightning" and I suspect that Moody had found out that he had some digestive problems earlier that evening.

We enjoyed our last night on the train as it wound its way through the darkness and rain. I snuggled into my berth where I would be lulled to sleep by the rocking of the train and the hypnotic sound of the rails clickity-clacking through the night. I still think that it is the best way to travel and I can only imagine how good it was on the luxury trains before the war.

REAL AIRPLANES -- BUT NO FLYING.
LANGLEY FIELD, VIRGINIA

We pulled into the rail siding that paralleled the flight line. In the darkness we could see the reflection of the rain on the shiny aluminum sides of the B-24's that were parked near the hangars lining the ramp. They looked like freight cars with wings with their slab-sided fuselages that were almost as large as freight cars.

They were parked all over the place and in the distance we could see some B-17's. What an exciting thing to see! Maybe we would be able to at least be line crew again. That would be a great way to be with the airplanes and perhaps get some flights like we did at Hondo.

Such are the dreams of the innocent.

After we were processed into the Langley Field installation, we were given the news that we were to be split up into various disciplines on the base and that none of them would involve flying. Some were sent to duties in the base hospital, some went into transportation and twenty of us were assigned to the Provost Marshall's office. Provost Marshall. That concerned jails and MP's and scary stuff and worst of all, ME. Here I was, standing at 5'-10" and weighing 150 pounds and I was going to be a base MP? Well, okay. I had always been good for laughs and this scenario should provide plenty when I try to collar a 220-pound ex-fullback who is half drunk and all strong. It also meant standing perimeter guard duty and special guard at sensitive installations. I could hardly wait.

We were put into an accelerated class to hone our shooting skills with the Colt revolver, basic "rules" of the base and hand–to-hand combat using the billy club, a 30" long piece of maple with a leather thong at the handle. Our instructor was a muscular Italian guy maybe 24 or 25 years of age. He was an old guy, who was fresh out of the OSS, Office of Strategic Services. His heavy frame was layered with hard bulging muscle and he had not one ounce of fat on his 190-pound body. Seeing him in a t-shirt and shorts convinced you that it would be very unwise to incur this guy's anger. His movements were such that he wasted no energy or motion to move from one point to another. But when he had to, he was quick as a snake. He got our attention in about 30 seconds.

Our first lecture was in the use of the Billy on larger adversaries and how this lightweight piece of wood could bring down the mighty. Anyone unfamiliar with this procedure would think that the Billy was to be used as a club and it could be at times, but its most effective use was to jab, jab in the correct place.

We were taught how to flex our arms and legs and to thrust at the solar plexus and when the adversary bent forward, a hard thrust under the chin to snap the head back and to disorient the recipient. If the opponent has turned away from you, a hard jab in the short ribs is very painful. A sharp rap in the side of the neck was a good way to disable someone, but the darkest of all things we were taught were the various uses of the everyday items at hand. Pencils and pens, ¼" dowels or plain old sticks can be jammed into the soft tissue under the chin or down into the shoulder just behind the clavicle. Lots of things to hit there like the sub-clavian artery or the sub-clavian vein.

We were taught too many dark and nasty ways to dispatch or to immobilize people and we questioned our instructor why we were being taught these things. We were unnerved by these gruesome applications, as they had absolutely nothing to do with our joining the air force.

Our complaints went duly unnoted and we were further instructed in the arts of emasculation and immobilization. After our intensive training for a couple of weeks we were given our side arms, white helmets and leggings and turned loose to protect the entire air force -- that is, the one at Langley Field, Virginia. There are enough stories here to fill another book so we won't delve into it except to say that in the next nine months I was given a crash course in the good, the bad and the ugly.

Perhaps to counter the ugliness of war, the American

serviceman had the unique ability to coat it with a bit of humor and one could find it in almost any venue as I found out on bivouac. Here at Langley, it lived as well. While visiting the latrine, I happened to read a poster placed conveniently in front of the urinal. "VD! Don't take a chance!" Penciled below, "Why not? Columbus did." Then next to it, "Yeah, but he was in virgin territory."

Then as I look up like so many men do when they are relieving themselves. "What the hell are you looking up here for? You're peeing on your shoe!"

In between the practical courses in daily and nightly human relations I managed to talk my way into flying on some of the training flights and got a taste of bomber operations in B-24's and B-17's. Langley Field was an old station, built in 1917. It saw the birth of the U. S. Army Air Service, then the U. S. Army Air Corps and finally the U. S. Army Air Forces during WW2. In 1944 there were two squadrons of bombers in the training operations, one each of B-24's and B-17's.

I suspect that there was more than the standard squadron strength because the flight line was full of airplanes and the action never stopped, day or night. The purpose of this mass of bombers was to train "Mickey" navigators and bombardiers who would and did use radar to do their job instead of the Norden bombsight, the E6B hand held computer and the stars. The ball turrets on these airplanes were replaced by a radar sweep and the navigator/bombardier operator used a six-inch diameter scope to read the image transmitted by the radar. He could then plot a course from what he saw or he could aim his bombs at the target below which was described by the radar through the clouds. One of these airplanes attached to a bomb squadron was called a pathfinder. The term "Mickey" was derived from the crews who called the radar image a "Mickey Mouse Movie."

Crews were being trained in HLPRB, High Level Precision Radar Bombing, and LLPRB, Low Level Precision Radar Bombing and Precision Radar Navigation. I was not privy to the training syllabus but it was not difficult to assess when you talked and flew with the crews. Mickey operations were already being used with success in the MTO and ETO so these crews were being trained for the assault on Japan where they would be doing things like low level skip bombing of ships and bombing strategic targets on land. To skip bomb a ship with a B-24 was to stretch the imagination, but they were planning and training to do just that.

Of greater interest, at least to me, was the array of NACA (National Advisory Committee on Aeronautics) wind tunnels dispersed around Langley Field and the flight test facility almost beside our barracks. This is where the NACA tested new military aircraft and conducted comparative tests on allied and enemy airplanes so we saw many unusual things in the air. They also experimented on new ideas for the existing military aircraft and we checked every day to see what weird and wonderful things popped up.

B-24 | Robert Parks

A BIT OF THE WILD BLUE

One month after we arrived at Langley, I managed to get approval from the colonel in charge of flight operations to go on a training mission with a B-24 crew. His last name happened to be the same as mine. Maybe that had something to do with my approval to take a ride in February.

It was 23 degrees at 0800 as I drew my equipment and donned everything that I was told to put on to keep from turning into a popsicle. Long johns, electrically heated suit, flight suit, electrically heated gloves, electrically heated booties, fleece lined pants, fleece lined boots, fleece lined jacket, fleece lined gloves, fleece lined helmet, oxygen mask, "May West", chute harness and parachute. And then you have to take a pee.

I waddled out to the airplane where I saw the pilot, a 25-year-old captain, out under the tail vomiting. I asked if he was going to fly when he was sick and I was told that he wasn't "sick" sick, it was just what he did before he flew. Too many tours in Europe. All four propellers were slowly "pulled through" several rotations to clear the oil that had drained into the lower cylinders of the engines. That done, we all climbed into the airplane through the bomb bay; the doors of which were like those on a roll-top desk.

The B-24 had an accommodating catwalk that was only about 24 inches from the ground. It was the lower attach point of the bomb racks and tied the forward and aft sections of the airplane together. I was instructed to go to the right waist position and remain there. There was no tail gunner, no waist gunners or ball turret gunner since the ball turret had been replaced by the radar sweep. So, it was just the radar operator/instructor, two trainees, crew chief/flight engineer, pilot, co-pilot, radioman and me.

I made my way aft and managed to get entangled twice on the bomb racks before I reached the well that led into the waist section. After I squirmed and wiggled my way into the right gunner's position I was able to take stock of what everybody assumed was a cavernous freight car of an airplane. It was not. Every inch of space had something jammed into it: boxes, panels, oxygen bottles and too much stuff to mention. There were no guns in the waist positions or any other station but the spaces were still minimized.

The flight engineer started the "putt-putt", the little two-cylinder engine that drove an electrical generator to start the big Pratt and Whitney radials on the B-24. I heard the bomb bay doors close and then the whine of the starter on number three. The airplane shook and shuddered when the engine finally kicked in and then in rapid succession, the airframe came to life with the pulses of the other three as they came to life.

Blue-ish white oil smoke enshrouded the back end of the airplane until it was burned off. There was a short period while the power systems were checked and the power came up to pull us away from the parking slot. The airplane became a living machine: vibrating, moving and undulating as it moved down the ramp to the taxiway for takeoff. I was told to watch for smoke on all engines and I obeyed by oscillating from the left window to the right. The run-up was a revelation in the power of a four-engine airplane. I had only experienced the twin-engine expressions of the AT-7 and C-60 'till then and the B-24 was a bit more than I expected.

The run-up was completed and we turned onto the active runway and started the takeoff and I watched for smoke as I was instructed: "white smoke not so bad -- black smoke, yell like hell". There was no black smoke. I watched the main gear wheel as we accelerated and saw it grow in diameter just before we lifted off and then it was braked to a stop and the strut rotated outward into the wheel well in the wing. We climbed out to the west and as we passed over Newport News shipyards, I looked down on a huge aircraft carrier under construction. I learned later that it was one of the new classes of super carriers that were being built and I realized that I didn't know much about the Navy. We climbed out to the north in a clear sunlit, but freezing cold day, and as we ascended it got colder and colder.

Half way to Richmond, I could see a finite line where the snow started changing the orange brown of the Virginia soil to a dirty white that soon changed to snow-white as we proceeded north at 20,000 feet. The radar sweep was cranked down and the training mission was in progress. As we climbed to 24,000, I felt a sense of helplessness as the cold crept through every tiny crack in my gear and there was no way that I could warm myself as I felt it sneaking in through the seams. I had plugged the electrically heated suit into the receptacle but it simply wasn't enough to do any good. No amount of movement or arm slapping had any effect.

Being a Florida boy, I soon realized what COLD was and it was frightening because there was no escape from this omnipotent force.

I asked permission to come forward to the flight deck to get some warmth and it was granted with a snicker. The catwalk seemed to be about thirty feet long as I went forward in the semi darkness. Nearing the forward end, I suddenly found myself floating and grabbing for something stabile as I floundered near the upper spaces of the bomb bay. I got a grip on a rope or a bomb rack and gradually found footing again on the catwalk.

I reached the flight deck well and struggled up into the space below the top turret. Ah yes! The Southwind gas heaters did make a difference -- but not much. At least there was no howling ice-cold wind to batter you here. I got some smiles, hidden by oxygen masks, and a comment or two about my "flight in the bomb bay", a sly trick played on new comers by pushing over at the right time to allow one to experience a bit of unscheduled weightlessness. The flight deck was as crowded as the rest of the airplane and gave me the impression that if the airplane were twice this size it would be just as crowded.

I watched the instructor at the PPI scope as we approached Washington, D.C. and I could easily recognize the dark Potomac River and some features of the lighter colored city. I watched in silence as they adjusted a calibrated ring on the perimeter of the scope for the course to the next city.

There were three dark splotches ahead in the whiter snow; the first was Baltimore, then Philadelphia and then New York. The Chesapeake Bay was black. We could see the Atlantic Ocean to the right as we reached New York and the features of the Hudson River and Manhattan were vivid. It was easy to see how the bomb groups in Europe were successfully bombing through solid undercasts with this equipment. We turned west and headed for Pittsburg, again on a heading set by the instructor and a student. Flying over Pennsylvania when it was covered by deep snow was a unique sight. The parallel mountains looked like a white wool blanket that had been pushed together into wrinkles. Leafless trees looked like they had fine black fuzz on them. When we reached Pittsburgh, the Susquehanna and Monongahela rivers were the color of coffee with two spoons full of cream and I could actually see the ice floes floating along in the current. The city was a huge black smudge.

We turned away and headed southwest for Indiana and eventually another turn southeast for Richmond and northeast for home. The instructor and students were navigating and bombing the cities along the round robin course by radar and by the end of the six-hour training session, I was ready to call it a day. The radar sweep was cranked up and I was ordered back to the waist to observe the landing gear and flaps during the landing.

The Chesapeake Bay appeared all of a sudden to the right and we started our approach to Langley Field. Soon the edge of the field flashed under us and the end of the runway was there as fast. The wheels impacted the runway and surprisingly jerked the oleo strut back in a cloud of smoke. The tire quickly spun up and increased diameter at an alarming rate but it had to go from zero to 125-130 mph in a split second. It kicked up dust and gravel as the airplane slowed down and the rolling–rocking motion returned.

Brakes moaned and howled during the runout and kept it up as we taxied back to the parking slot. I could smell fuel odors as we deplaned but no one else seemed to mind, so I waddled back to flight ops and turned in my gear. Stiff from the cold and with a cotton-dry mouth, I was looking for a hot shower and a drink of something and even though I was not treated as a crewmember, I would go aloft again as soon as I could.

Robert Parks

INTRO TO A CLASSIC

It took some time and a lot of talking to get my next flight and to my delight it was in a B-17. Already in only three years of action, it had wrapped itself in the aura of a gallant steed much like the warhorse of old, never flinching when wounded, and charging ahead until it could no longer carry on. It carried the beauty of line and the strength of a draught horse.

It wasn't as modern or as fast as the B-24, it didn't have as much range or carry as big a load, but it took good care of the crews with its reliability and toughness. It was designed in 1935 in a period of transition from the fabric covered machines to the all metal semi-monococque structures and it was over designed, much to its benefit.

It had good aerodynamics, stabile and forgiving, where the B-24, designed in 1940, was at the edge of the envelope and could, at times, turn on the unwary with fatal results.

It was the total opposite of the B-17, a boxy rather homely airplane with a high aspect ratio glider -type of wing that did not produce lift above 25,000 feet where the B-17 could operate at altitudes of 40,000 feet. But, the B-24 of simple modern construction was easier to produce and they were built literally by the thousands, 19,000 of them, and the U.S. and the British effectively used them in every theater of the war.

The B-24 had its aficionados and there were those who loved the B-17 and the arguments waged ad infinitum as to which airplane was better. They were both good but one was an apple and one was an orange.

I went through the dressing drill again and made my way to the airplane. As a supernumery/interloper/ extra, I was again instructed to take my position in the waist. No invitation to watch what was going on anywhere so I stayed where I was told. It was just as well because the B-17 was far less spacious than the B-24; in fact it was just plain small. It had one bomb bay instead of two, the fuselage was tight and circular and the pilot's compartment (as identified in the maintenance manual) was tight as well. The seats were high off the floor on stilt-like supports instead of being mounted on the flight deck.

A tunnel below the pilots gave access to the bombardier and navigator's position in the nose. Like the B-24, it was crammed with equipment and weapons, only worse, so I stayed where I was while everything was turned on, cranked up, and readied for flight.

Taxiing in a B-17 is like everything else between the B-24 and the B-17, totally different. There was no bouncing or rocking up and down in the waist, it was solidly on the ground but you could feel most of the irregularities in the ramp surface. The Fortress shook and rattled like the '-24 during the run-up before takeoff and it was a bit louder as it accelerated. The tail came up and swung a little bit, but soon we broke ground and climbed away, passing over the same aircraft carrier there in the Newport News shipyards. This mission was similar to the first one on which I flew but to different cities. Since there wasn't enough room for me to watch the radar I had to remain in the aft section of the airplane.

It can be pretty boring just staring down at the landscape below for hours so I looked around to check some things. First was the tail gunner's position. Getting there required squirming around the retracted tail wheel and the elevator controls and when you get there you're disappointed at the lack of accommodations.

A bicycle type of seat is what you had to sit on as you gazed out of three small windows to scan the sky for the dreaded enemy. The armor plate and twin "50's" were removed, making things a little roomier. I jumped at a spurt of white that shot back from the airplane. Enemy! No. Smoke! No. I then realized that it was a vapor trail from the exhaust and as I watched, all four began to produce streaks in spurts and finally settled down to a steady stream of white forming about 100 feet behind the airplane.

As I sat there watching the contrails, I couldn't help but think of my barracks buddy, Joe Frank Jones, an ex B17 tail gunner. Several months

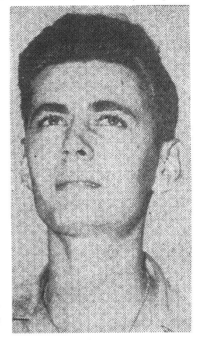

Joe Frank Jones

before, he arrived in the middle of the night and was there on the adjacent bunk in the morning, all moved in and sound asleep. It was a common occurrence to have "old hands" or veterans unfit for further combat to show up. We usually heard them when they arrived but not this guy, he was quiet most of the time.

When I was showering in the "public bath" he came in to clean up and I couldn't stop the urge to stare at the huge fresh scar on his abdomen. It ran from his pubic area to his rib cage and looked like a giant purple centipede that had him in its grip. He had other wounds healing on his arms and legs. I learned early that one did not pry into a soldier's private life unless you were invited so I jokingly said, "You must have gotten into a helluva knife fight," hoping that he would take it lightly.

"Yeah, with a British field surgeon, they opened me up like a chicken on the spit."

His speech was that of a southerner so that opened another door for conversation and we traded information about our civilian origins. Soon we became comfortable enough to go to breakfast where I got to know him and his story.

He and his crew were on a mission to bomb Ulm, Germany when another plane in the formation slid out of position and severed the tail of his airplane between the tail wheel and the ball turret. He quickly put on his chest pack and made his way to the aft entry door but it was jammed shut. He then tried to get through the jagged sheet metal where the fuselage had been severed but he couldn't. Moving in the gyrating, tumbling tail section was all but impossible. He was trapped.

He said that he returned to his position, strapped himself in and waited for the crash. It took forever to descend from 13,000 feet because the tail sometimes tried to fly. During that long fall, Joe lost consciousness and never realized that the tail section hit a large oak tree that cushioned the impact. That tree was in a Belgian farmer's field that at the time was being tended by the family.

They watched as the tail hit and rushed to the site to see if there was a survivor. They spotted Joe Jones in the wreckage and tried to extract him but he was impaled by some of the crumpled structure. The village blacksmith was called to cut the metal away to remove the tail gunner who was then taken to a British field hospital where his serious internal injuries were repaired.

Jones said that he regained consciousness several days later, unwashed, unshaven, and in pain. He shaved and washed himself the best he could and endured his situation until he was taken to an American hospital and eventually to England. After healing and a trip to his home in Fairfax, South Carolina, he was reassigned to Langley Field. When I met him he was nineteen years old.

I sat there in Joe Jones position for a long time trying to imagine how he folded up his tall lanky body and stayed in this cramped station for hours just to get shot at. The fuselage was a little over three feet in diameter at this point. Then riding it down from 13,000 feet was a frightening thought. Ironically, the name of his airplane was "Mr. Lucky."

We younger airmen found ourselves in the midst of many like Joe. Our bay was full of them and there were many veteran crews scattered throughout this base still flying as instructors for younger crews who would be bombing Japan. One of the guys in our bay was not in that category; he was a totally used up. I can't recall what his duty was but he was a waist gunner on a B-17 who suffered the burst of a rocket or flak, he didn't know. His back, buttocks and legs had been peppered by what looked like shotgun pellets.

I have to insert here how we had to shower when we cleaned up. Our facility was an open, tile faced rectangle of probably eight by sixteen feet with five or six showerheads and everybody showered together when we had to. No modesty here. Pat, the B-17 gunner, had numerous ugly pustules on his backside and legs that had to be lanced at least once a month to remove the pieces of shrapnel. He had a small box in which he kept them. His right heel had been shot off and an ugly purple "thing" was in its place after an early and unsuccessful attempt at plastic surgery.

He was bitter and in pain all the time and he took it out on us young guys whenever he could. He took it too far one night and after prodding and yelling at one of the kids, he got decked. The poor kid stood there with tears in his eyes saying, "I'm sorry, I'm sorry." Thus was the animosity felt by the old timers toward the dumb kids who had not "been there."

The worst case of what was called "battle fatigue" then occurred one Saturday night, or early Sunday morning, when another veteran gunner of the Eighth Air Force came in drunk. He ricocheted off the bunks and lockers as he made his way to his bunk at the end of the bay muttering to himself.

One of the old timers muttered in the dark, "Gonn'a be a bad night." An hour and a half later when everyone had fallen asleep a scream erupted. It was Roberts. The little guy from Georgia had lost it and he cut loose with a series of "Ahh! Ahh! Oh God, Ahh!" We could hear him thrashing around in his bunk and then a horrible splat when he bailed out and hit the concrete floor face first.

When we got to him, he was trying to break through the window to escape his bunk that, to him, was on fire. He had shredded his pillow, pulling the ripcord on his "chest pack". Two of us tried to restrain him and even at 140 pounds, was throwing us around like two rag dolls. Four more guys came to help and it was all we could do to hold him down.

During his struggle, someone called the ambulance and damned if he didn't hear it pull up to the court in the rear of the barrack three floors down. "Aha! You bastards called the meat wagon again!" Again? An incident from the past, no doubt. After he was strapped to a stretcher and taken out, we had a terrible mess to clean up. Broken teeth, snot, blood, vomit and urine was smeared all over the floor and us. The shower room was busy at 0230 that morning.

Some of us tried to visit Roberts the next day but he was restricted from visitations. He was listed as "Section 8."

All of those old timers were not affected the same way by their hard service. One in our bay seemed to be oblivious to the past, or the present for that matter. He walked around with a perpetual smile on his face that showed his bucked teeth. His frame was like a cadaver no matter what he ate, and he did plenty of that. He also did plenty of drinking and "Bones" came in one night so soused that he never made it to his bunk and slumped to the floor near the entry to our area. Bad timing. We had been warned that there was going to be a "surprise inspection" the next morning, Saturday. There was always a surprise inspection on Saturdays. In a stroke of rebellion or mischief (it was never really analyzed) we decided to fix up a proper setting on the spot for Bones to rest his weary body. Six or eight footlockers were stacked broadside in full view of the entry where it would greet anyone entering our floor.

We placed some blankets on them for padding and then carefully laid out Bones in peaceful repose with the requisite sheet draped over the funeral bier. We strapped him in place with some of our belts to keep him from rolling on to the floor.

It was early spring and someone ran downstairs to the front of the building and picked some yellow daffodils that we placed in his hands that were folded on his chest.

Saturday morning at 0730 we were busy on the finishing touches to get the place in order when the captain arrived. The captain was a man who should have been home slouched in an easy chair petting his cat. His hair was white and he had to have been in his fifty's but here he was, in charge of a bunch of guys for whom he was more of a father figure than a stern officer. But he could be tough when he had to be. We were holding our collective breaths.

"What the f---!" He stood there looking at Bones stretched so nice and peaceful and burst out laughing. He was still laughing as he walked out and down the hallway. He never did inspect our bay.

ODE TO THE GUNNERS
To the tune, "My Bonnie Lies Over The Ocean"

Take down your service flag, mother.
Put up your star of gold.
Your son is an aerial gunner.
He'll die when he's eighteen years old.

Chorus

TS...TS He'll die when he's eighteen years old.
TS...TS He'll die when he's eighteen years old.

He thought he would be a hot pilot.
And fly over Berlin and Rome.
But they made him an aerial gunner.
And they're shipping his dead body home.

Chorus

LIGHT AT THE END OF THE TUNNEL

The spring of 1945 broke warm and pleasant in Virginia. It matched the feeling that had sneaked into our psyche without our knowing it. Perhaps the war would end soon. Germany was about finished, but Japan had to be finally neutralized. We had the military machine to do it.

Strict intensity was loosening up some in spite of the continuing pace of training activity. The steady roar of engines filled the night, the ghostly moan and wailing brakes joined the chorus as B-17's and B-24's taxied by our barracks, and at night if they were launching to the east, we could see the four bright red "donuts" of the turbo superchargers as they passed over.

Our barrack building was adjacent to the east end of the main runway and we were on the third floor of a brick and concrete structure that was built in 1917. The architect was kind enough to provide huge windows for us to watch the airplanes.

The windows came into play one bright Sunday morning in April when we awoke to see a strange machine sitting in front of the barracks on the road that led to the NACA hangar. It was the most exotic and advanced thing we had ever seen -- dark blue all over and not one mark to indicate what it was other than a Navy fighter. It sat tall in a three-point attitude on a pair of long-legged landing gear struts attached to a pair of impossibly short wings. The nose cowl enclosed a huge radial engine equipped with a large four bladed prop. The fuselage carried a bubble canopy and it was just long enough to support a tail group.

We were all grouped at the window trying to guess what it was and as soon as we had a quick breakfast, it was out to examine the mysterious bird. What a wild looking beast! This was a serious fighter and unlike anything we had seen. Guesses ranged from a secret Vought, a new Curtiss and some other builders, but NONE identified it as a Grumman.

We finally found out that it was the first F8F Bearcat and soon we were to watch in awe as the NACA pilots began to fly this amazing airplane. The first P-51H happened to be at the NACA labs when the F8F showed up. It was predictable that the two would meet in the sky. When that day came, the vaunted P-51H announced as the ultimate P-51, was thoroughly thrashed but again, it was apples and oranges. The F8F would never be a good bomber escort unless the range was under a few hundred miles, but it was an interceptor par excellence.

It displayed this capability one day when the NACA pilot taxied out for takeoff and after run-up, roared down the runway in a three point attitude, hauled back on the stick and went into an almost vertical climb and continued out of sight. We had never seen anything like this and it was simply unbelievable. The F8F did have a few brake problems and they stood it on its nose a few times, but it was an exciting thing to watch as it was run through its tests.

One thing that it did to prove its mettle was a formation takeoff with the P-51H one sunny afternoon. As the P-51 was still on its takeoff run, the F8F leapt off the runway, pulled up and behind the Mustang, and started to make fighter passes on it as it was running down the runway. Other aircraft kept things interesting there, a two-bladed prop on a Bell P-63, a P-38L, a Mosquito and many others that came and went.

My first attempt to paint with watercolors.
An award winner in the army arts contest. | *Robert Parks*

With Granny 1944   *Robert Parks*

Robert Parks

Receiving Army Arts Awards. Two 1ˢᵗ Place and one Honorable Mention.

Chapter 6.

Virginia Beach, pretty little nurses, search for bodies, and VJ Day.

GOOD TIME ON A STRETCHED DIME

Four of us new guys managed to get a three-day pass at the same time and we decided to have a weekend at Virginia Beach. We didn't know anything about it except its location. So, on a bright and sunny Friday morning we piled into the 1937 Plymouth coup owned by one of them and headed for the ferry that would take us across the bay to the road that went to the coast. Being very short on cash, we brought blankets and some old sleeping bags just in case we couldn't find or buy any lodging.

We had made a wise decision and we made another smart move to avoid any extra costs when we approached the ferry tollbooth. Two of the guys crawled into the rumble seat and closed the lid so we had to pay just two fares for the crossing. This worked very well as long as they were quiet back there but as we approached the tollbooth the dingbats in the back started to make the noises of a catfight. The driver nervously explained to the gentleman in the booth that we were transporting some pets to my aunt. He nodded in an understanding way, gave us our ticket and said, "You boys have a good time in Virginia Beach and that includes the guys in the back too."

Virginia Beach was, from what we could see, a boardwalk on the beach and an amusement park. The town itself was about three or four blocks deep from the beach, a mixture of small cottages and small businesses. The first thing we did was to find something to eat and we managed to do that at the small local USO, eating everything in sight.

That night we tried to enter one or two of the clubs that lined the beach but predictably, we were turned away since we were still three years away from the "legal age". Legal age indeed! Eighteen year-old G.I's were being killed by the hundreds every day around the globe then but God forbid giving them a beer. So, it was back to the USO for a boring but restful night if you like sleeping on cots.

Saturday bloomed warm and clear and we headed for the beach after a meager breakfast and changing to swim trunks in the car. We sat on the seawall to make the acquaintances of many of the pretty little girls that were walking by but we didn't seem to have that magical touch.

The Atlantic Ocean wasn't so aloof so we succumbed to her beckoning and played in the water for several hours, body surfing the waves and trying to show off for the girls. The only female who showed any interest was a lovely brunette who let us borrow her air mattress to surf with. She was an older lady, perhaps in her early 30's. When the air mattress was returned she offered me a long lunch at her place but I had to decline.

Lunch again at the USO was more of the same, little sandwiches and pop. Then it was back to the boardwalk where we spied the Mystery House, a spooky place with Zombies and scary things. It cost 25 cents, so the four of us spent almost the last of our cash to see what was in the Spook House. It was completely dark inside and one was guided by a maze of narrow hallways that were predictably interrupted by displays of ghouls and cadavers that lit up when you approached.

Our youthful night vision allowed us to see the walls did not have a ceiling and it was a clear attic above them. Naturally we climbed up into the open area where we could roam freely through the entire complex.

We quickly realized that we were unseen by the newer patrons and if we were silent and moved carefully we could watch them, sometimes only feet below us. The four of us spread out and it wasn't long before more overt actions began to make the afternoon much more interesting.

"Geeze! This place is spooky! I could swear that somebody breathed on me!"

"Yeah! I felt like somebody touched my hair."

Then, several outbursts of laughter that were successfully

muffled almost exposed our secret but precarious position.

"GEORGE! CUT THAT OUT!

"Cut what out?"

"You know damn well what! You can wait until we get home!"

"Well, okay if you say so but I still don't know what I did."

We spent most of the afternoon in the FUN HOUSE.

Alas, it was time to make our exit down the chute that fired you out onto the boardwalk where we unsuccessfully tried to brush the dust from our uniforms. Then we concluded that it was time to start our journey back to Langley Field. It was almost 1600 hours and we had six hours before duty preparations. No problem, plenty of time, so, we hop into the car and cruise back to the base. The car didn't seem to have the same idea and two miles down the road one of the tires went flat. Okay, no problem, get the spare on. The spare was in cahoots with the flat tire because it also was flat. Now things were getting a bit tight and we had to get a tire somehow.

To find a tire that one could purchase, if one had enough money, was nearly impossible during the war, not impossible -- but nearly. Gasoline and tires were strictly rationed during the war and tires were run until the cords were visible. The cords were not only showing on this tire but there was a wide-open hole in it. One in our group of "Four Horsemen" remembered that there was a gas station ahead so we slowly drove north and did indeed find one. We hastily patched the tube and cut a section out of another carcass, put it inside the tire over the hole and went glumpity-glumping down the road.

Shortly thereafter, another tire disintegrated and there was no fixing this one. It was in shreds. The spare had been cut up to fix the first flat so we had to do something drastic. Three of the guys walked back to the gas station and somehow "out-flanked the operator trying to "buy" a tire out front while one kid borrowed a tire and tube from the back. They returned in 20 minutes, we had the tire and tube mounted and pumped up in 25 minutes.

"And away we went -- until we ran out of gas in North Norfolk. No problem. We borrowed some from a parked truck and made it to the ferry just in time to see it leave, so we had to wait another hour. Stealing gas or tires was a federal offense then but we, in a way, were federal employees so that made it okay -- to us.

We cleared the main gate at 2345, just enough time to put on a clean uniform and to stand inspection. Then with hair full of sand, sunburn, salt incrusted skin and hardly anything to eat for three days, we spent the longest duty night in history.

TOUGH HOSPITAL DUTY

On one of our sorties into Newport News we met three of the cutest little girls imaginable. They were from "Nawthcalina" and "Jaw-wid-ja" and it didn't take long to find out that they were nursing students at a hospital in the city. The three of us quickly struck a friendly note with them and had dates lined up for the next weekend.

Things happened fast during the war so we were immediately in love with these pretty little nurses and we could hardly wait for our next meeting. We found out that during the week, they had to stay at the hospital. But never mind! All was not lost! One of them told us about a ground level room that was unoccupied and accessible from the walkway on the south side of the hospital.

I can't recall the name of the hospital, but I do remember that it was in the north end of town and it was an old brick building, dark and foreboding at night. A bus ride and a short walk got us to our rendezvous and sure enough, a walk around to the back side of the hospital took us to a huge double hung window that we could open. The sill was at waist level so it was easy to slip inside where we awaited our hostesses. It didn't take long until they quietly slipped into the dark room and we got to know each other -- even in the dark.

This arrangement worked for several weeks and it sure beat Virginia Beach! Riding the bus to the hospital gave time to devise something to keep us occupied and it helped to lengthen our evening of fun. One of the trio sat apart from the other two who were also separated by one seat or two. One of the boys would pretend to notice the other and start a conversation. This was followed by a few questions of discovery.

"Say, aren't you the guy that used to live on Chestnut Street?'
"Well, yes, I did."
"And you used to have a little brown and white dog?"

"Yes! His name was Spot."

"I remember that your house was painted white and you had a cute little sister."

"Yes, I did."

"Her name was Suzy, wasn't it?"

"I remember the kitchen had a green table in it and your mom cooked wonderful cookies."

"Yer' right! She loved to do that."

By now everybody on the bus was into the play and the old ladies were gushing that two soldier boys had found each other. We kept the recognition-guessing game going for a good 15 minutes and had everyone on the bus feeling so good about our "chance meeting".

"Didn't yer' mom cook fish on Friday night, too?"

"Oh yeah and we had to eat it even if it smelled good."

"I remember that the living room had pink curtains and you used to play on the floor in front of the old Atwater-Kent radio, too."

"YES, YES!

Then the climax. The two raced to each other, grabbing each other by the shoulder and exclaimed.

"FATHER!"

"SON!"

We had to time it near our stop because sometimes it was prudent to get off the bus when our game had ruffled some sensitive feathers.

Our hospital visits were becoming a routine and we hardly gave it a thought when we arrived. We just opened the window and quietly slipped in and waited until our Southern Belles arrived. One sultry night our routine got a bit derailed. The first kid had entered the room with number two close behind, one foot on the floor and one still in the window opening. I was close behind to make a quick entry when the first kid burst out with an "Oh, SH" and frantically turned around to get back out of the window. Number two boy, still not completely through the window, was impacted by number one, who was hell bent to get out. Number two could see what was happening and tried to reverse course while he was still twisted up in the window. Number one, who was still bolting like a panicked cat, jammed himself into the window opening and the two of them in a melee' of flailing legs and arms somehow popped through the window with me under them.

How we did it is a mystery but we managed to scramble to our feet and make a strategic retreat. Safely to the bus stop, we asked number one what happened in the room.

"The minute I got in I saw something white move in the corner and the biggest damn nurse in the world came at me. She was an Amazon! She was worse than the time we found that dead body under the sheets in there!" To our dismay, the head nurse had caught on to the extracurricular activities in the secret classroom and put an end to our special classes. We never saw the pretty little nurses again and we hoped that they weren't kicked out of school.

So, it was true. Hospital duty was tough but we had to leave it for safer things, like running between spinning propellers.

A GLIMPSE AT AN OPEN LIFE

Sometime in May it was announced that there would be an air show to celebrate Armed Forces Day and that the public was invited into the base to witness it. You cannot imagine what a jolt that was to open the base for civilians to see an air show and did they come! Forty-five thousand of them packed the flight line to see the air force in action.

They weren't disappointed, the flight line was full of B-17's and B-24's and some additional planes were pulled in from other bases. P-47's, P-40's, a B-29, C-47's and some Waco cargo gliders were staged at the east end of the field. The bombers took off in an impressive 45-minute display of what they did in England and Italy when they were departing on a mission. The C-47's pulled several gliders off like they did for D-Day and several made aerial pick-ups of the gliders that were staged at the end of the runway.

The piece de resistance was the flight demonstration of America's first jet fighter, the Bell P-59. It made a long strenuous take-off on the main runway, turned around and made a low pass down the ramp. As it was making an anemic climb-out to the east, someone yelled, "LOOK LEFT!"

Coming down the ramp at no more than 20 feet altitude a

Vought Corsair made a dramatic and unscheduled appearance, kicking up dust off the ramp as it made its way past us with an uncharacteristic roar. We could see then that it wasn't an F4U, but an F2G, powered by an R4360 "corncob" housed under a checkerboard cowl. We howled as it caught the P-59 that was still in its climb, and passed it in a steeper climb that carried out of sight.

Shortly thereafter, the two squadrons of bombers came over in perfect formation with the flight of P-40's weaving above as "top cover". Then we picked out a dark speck above and began to hear an ominous howl and soon the F2G came hurtling down straight through the bomber formation and its "top cover". He made one more pass over the field and disappeared. Nobody knew who it was or where he had come from but he sure spiced up the air show.

Years later I learned from a navy pilot friend that it was a test pilot from Patuxtant River Naval Test Center who "crashed" our show.

ANOTHER RIDE

I had a furlough scheduled a few weeks after the show and when I was pulling main gate duty, a carload of airmen came up to the gate. I noticed that they were dressed in summer suntans and I asked the Colonel who was driving if they were from the south. An affirmative, "We are up here from Orlando." I mentioned that I was from Florida and had a furlough coming up in four days and asked if they were returning then. "Nope, we are leaving the day after tomorrow. If you want a flight home, you are welcome to come along. Our B-24 is parked in transient in front of the tower."

I had to do something quick to get a flight home so I approached our C.O. to see if I could get my orders re-cut. Our old dad of a C.O. heard my story and said, "Well, you've been a good boy and I don't see any reason why we can't change a few dates here. I'll just change this and sign it and that should be okay." I guess that he had forgotten about Bones and his "funeral."

I packed a small barracks bag and was ready the next day at 1400 beside the airplane but there was one big problem, I didn't have a parachute so I ran back to ops, checked out a chute and made it back to the airplane as they were cranking it up. It was a brand new B-24J being delivered to Pinecastle Air Base, near Orlando, Florida. My station was at the right waist window again and soon I was to be thankful for that.

Take-off over the shipyards again and I could see the aircraft carrier in the ways, slow progress. A hard left turn over Newport News took us out to the bay, but then we turned right and headed back toward the Norfolk area. What the heck was going on? Somewhere south of Norfolk we circled once and then heading west again the nose dropped and we started down at a good rate. I got a warning over the intercom that we were going to buzz the radioman's house on the river. Pretty soon "on the river" took on a literal description of what we were doing. We dropped down on the river and flew past a blur of people waving from the bank. We weren't very high because I could look directly out of the waist window at the houses and trees whizzing by.

Over the intercom: "Hang on." We started a pull-up that buckled my knees and I was pushed to the decking while hanging onto the gun mount. I looked out of the waist window down the trailing edge of the wing and saw nothing but the ground. We were in a hard climbing turn that terminated in a beautiful Chandelle, with us heading east again. A 180 turn and down we went again for a second pass ON THE RIVER and then a hard climbing turn to the left and we headed southeast toward the Atlantic, climbing slowly to 10,000 feet where we headed south.

I was still trying to process the adrenalin-pumping start of this flight when we approached a huge thunderhead over the Atlantic. We flew fairly close to it and almost under the "anvil" outcropping. I could see lightning flashing inside the cloud and occasionally running up the outer surface. Something one cannot see from the ground in daylight. Five minutes after we passed the cloud, we were jumped by a flight of P-47's out of Richmond Air Base and they began to practice gunnery runs on us. They formed a queue on our right with the sun behind them and pulled ahead before they peeled off to "rake" us from stem to stern, nothing but a silver-flashing blur as they went by. They tried it all and put on a marvelous show for us before they flew close in to give us a wing–wagging farewell.

In one hour I experienced enough to last a lifetime and it has. I can still vividly see those fighters sometimes as sparkling little dots of crystal against the dark blue of the ocean, or as ominous dark spots against the billowing white of the thunderhead behind us. Then the run on the river, the name of which I never learned, and the Chandelles was a once in a lifetime thrill never to be forgotten. The rest of the flight was boring as I watched the shoreline gradually disappear and I realized that I was getting cold at this altitude so I wrapped up in a tarp but it was almost as cold as everything else. I watched the fuselage skins wrinkle and buckle as we cruised along, something that you wouldn't see in a B-17. Also the bouncing around that the vertical fins did was interesting. I had to convince myself that they weren't loosely attached to the fuselage.

I must have drifted off for a little while as I huddled near the forward end of the waist deck because I realized that it was getting warmer. I looked out to see some coastline again as we were descending: Florida. Soon we were skimming over the pine trees and then flat terrain and a runway. I watched the main landing gear wheel do its thing at spin-up and we were down at 1730.

After we were parked and shut down, I gathered my gear and scrambled out of the airplane in time to see the crew preparing to board a "4x4" truck. There was no invitation to join them even though there was room so I didn't ask. As I shouldered my seat pack and my bag, I was able to take a look at the field and the equipment. The view to the south in the hot Florida haze showed a 2-mile long runway that seemed to stretch clear to Miami. Spindly Florida pines lined the confines of the field and there was absolutely no one in sight. The field had shut down for the day! Man! What a difference from Langley.

I made the long hot walk to the tower and flight ops and where one bored sergeant. Finally looked up and uttered a warm welcome, "Yeah?"

"Where do I check the chute in?"

"Did you check it out here?"

"No, from Langley Field."

"Then you can't check it here, it has to go back to Langley Field. Anything else?"

"Yes, where can I catch a bus for town?"

"Out front."

I was overcome by the flood of enthusiastic information, so I went out front to boil in the lowering sun and if I had to wait here for an hour it would be more comfortable than in flight ops. The rickety bus arrived in ten minutes and whisked me into town where he let me off at a Trailways bus station. Luckily a bus was leaving for Sarasota in about thirty minutes so things were working out pretty well.

I was one of the last passengers to enter the bus and as I was wrestling my bag and parachute down the aisle I passed two sweet old ladies. I overheard one of them say, "Look Maude! There's one of them Parachute Troopers!" The other one looked at me and the chute with a puzzled face and said,

"WELL! Fer' Christ sake, I didn't know they had to carry the goddam thing with 'em all the time!" Ah yes, two sweet little old ladies.

Old ladies and the war. When I was on a three-day pass to my home, we were talking about my brother-in-law when all the aunts and uncles were present. My sister mentioned that her husband was operations officer at Buckley Field and one of the old gals said, "Goodness! I didn't know that Bud was a doctor."

I rode that noisy stiff-legged clattering old bus for one hundred thirty miles and the next six and one half hours to get home -- at 0130.

My furlough was one of the most disappointing events in my young life. There was nobody there. I didn't have any of my old friends to visit. They were all serving somewhere. I didn't know any of the high school kids, and much to my dismay, my family had somehow gone to Washington, D.C. and I didn't know it. That was something that happened too many times in my life. Then reading the newspaper one day when I was roaming around town, I sadly saw an almost hidden notice that my old friend, Tommy Livermore, had been lost somewhere in the Caribbean on a flight while he was "deadheading" back from South America. He had been flying with the ATC delivering C-54's overseas. He always said that he would never die in an airplane if he were at the controls. I thought immediately of my returning the extra helmet to his Sunday Plane when he wasn't present. I wished that I could have kept it. My mother flew down at the last minute and she had a nice time visiting her old friends.

I spent some time wandering around town hoping that I would find someone that I knew but when I checked the old meeting sites all I found were ghosts. Bargreen's Drug store was nearest to the hotel at which we were staying and I went there first. Some strangers were sitting in the booth that our gang usually occupied when we came in for sodas on Saturdays and it was difficult not to tell them that they were in the wrong booth and they should leave.

As I stared at the booth I remembered some happy and funny times there. One of the last gatherings took place just before I left for the Air Force and six of us descended on our spot for lunch. With us was one of the class clowns, C.C. He was a short slender kid who had a bright purple birthmark that coursed from his cheek up through his left eye socket and he had lost that eye. But he had a glass eye that he always included in his personality. He was a born comedian and completely uninhibited.

He was sitting on the end of the booth and after the waitress had served us with large glasses of water and returned to her duties he called her over. "Miss, there is something in my water." When she looked in the glass she uttered an earsplitting scream when she saw an eye staring back at her and she ran back behind the counter.

C.C. was a heavy drinker and sometimes after a party night he had to change his glass eye to match the bloodshot eye on the other side and he always carried a case of spare eyes with him to make sure that everything looked even. He couldn't resist that glass of clear clean water to pull a "C.C. Joke".

Naturally, the manager came roaring out of the back room and ordered us out of his establishment. Well, okay, we'll leave, but not after a parting shot. All of us stretched paper napkins across the mouth of our glass and quickly turned them upside down on the table. There was perhaps a half- gallon of water that only one place to go.

Earlier that year, C.C. and I had been selected to speak for our favorite candidates in the school election for some kind of office during an all class assembly. I went first with a "speech" prepared on several rolls of window shade joined into one sheet. I opened with a statement that I had a few words to say on the behalf of my candidate whereupon I launched the roll that went from the stage to perhaps ten feet down the center aisle. I included some other gimmicks that thoroughly delighted the audience but caused the principal to approach the boiling point.

Then it was C.C.'s turn and he had adhered to every rule that the principal set for us, a sport jacket over a dress shirt and tie. We knew that something was coming because he was wearing a monocle---over his glass eye. He started his speech with passion and extolled his candidate with such energy that he had to remove his coat with great flourish. There he was, replete with the cuffs of the shirt around his wrists, the collar and tie around his neck and nothing else but a filthy moth-eaten undershirt with a hole that exposed his left nipple.

He didn't last long. The principal ended the proceedings and we got a lecture on the seriousness of the democratic processes of electing members of our government.

All of us except C.C. left for the service and when we came back he was no longer around. I always wondered what happened to him.

Hard as I tried I couldn't conjure up anything more than memorable images so I left the drugstore and walked east on Main Street to Smacks Drive-in where we all hung out and found the same thing---no one that I recognized. The parking lot was almost empty and the kids that were there were much younger than I and strangers to me. I went to the back corner of the parking area where we used to station the Model T and grass had grown up in what was a busy spot when we were there.

SUITED TO A T---model that is.

In the spring of 1943 my friend, Jimmy, and I heard that an elderly lady wanted to sell her late husband's Model T and we went to see what the car was like. It was a 1926 four- door convertible that had seen better times. It had been in her garage since her husband had died from an accident in the car ten years before. The back end was damaged but everything else was okay except the tires.

After two days of work we had it drivable except that it had only two inflatable tires so we simply drove it to Jimmy's house anyway, two tires on the left and two bare wheels on the right. We made it through town to Highway 41 and headed south. Highway 41, the Tamiami Trail(Tampa to Miami), at that time was a narrow two lane road with soft sand shoulders and that is where we placed the bare wire wheels. We must have looked like something out of a Buster Keaton movie as we careened down the road in a vehicle that was barely controllable. The top collapsed and we were peering out of a narrow gap, the tireless wheels were throwing a curtain of sand in the air but we pressed on, staggering and weaving down the road like a drunk. As we were making our way south of town a military convoy full of troops came the other way loudly cheering and laughing as they passed.

Several weeks of working on the car made it more drivable and we managed to find two more tires but each one had to have boots that were cut from other old tires inserted to patch the holes. Finding correct size inner tubes was impossible so we tried to use some larger sizes and stuffed them into the small Model T- type tires. That worked just fine until you turned the car. The inner tubes popped out of the rims and exposed themselves like huge bubble gum balloons that eventually completely removed the tire. A big problem!

Jimmy finally found two wheels off a 1937 Ford AND two matching tires that we had to modify to fit the Model T hub. The '37 Ford wheels bolt pattern was a unique configuration with the mounting bolts located near the circumference of the wheel. So, we welded a steel plate to the wheel and drilled holes for the Model T hub and mounting bolts. A piece of cake, right? Well, kind'a. We didn't get the hole for the hub on center and between that and the out of balance tires, the car ran down the road as if it had an itch in all the wrong places. Anything over 15 miles per hour would shake the fillings out of your teeth so we made some adjustments and cured some of it.

The rear part of the body was too far gone to repair to we removed it and made a flat bed onto which we bolted a lovely old wicker rocking chair. The girls loved it and it was seldom empty when we left the school to go to Smacks. We drove that old collection of junk for nine months without a license, a real license that is. That crossed our minds and before we could devise a work-around, it was solved one morning when we spotted a license plate that had fallen off a truck. So a coat hanger and some pliers was all that we needed to hang the license plate, but not in a conspicuous location.

The war was well into its second year and everything

important like tires, meat, and gasoline was rationed. We had sort of solved the tire problem but the gas took a bit of creativity and we found that the car would run on cleaning fluid, kerosene, and even real gas that we borrowed from some of the cars in town. The cops got used to our existence and bothered us only once when we drove past a church one Sunday morning and were stopped because we lacked a muffler. We were ordered to get one so we welded an empty paint can to the pipe. It didn't quiet things down much but it did change the tone. That is when the name was changed from the "Royal Rocket" to the "Royal Racket."

From the fall of 1943 to the spring of 1944 that old car was the center point of our gatherings at Smacks where we consumed great quantities of chocolate milk and ice cream, our favorite treat. Our spot was on the last row at the edge of the crushed shell parking lot and next to the street. It was our last few months, our last bright flare of freedom and fun before we went away to the service and we made the most of it. Jimmy went to the Navy, I went into the USAAF, and Eddy went to the Navy. I stood there and stared at the grass that had grown up in "our spot" and wondered if it had really happened. The Model T was gone and so were the kids. No reason to stand here any longer.

Our Model T, "The Royal Rocket."

NEARING THE END

When I returned to Langley, the attitude was definitely more relaxed and there was a Friday night party and dance. In spite of a violent summer storm in progress, pretty young ladies from town were in abundance. What a wonderful time we were having with them and I was sure that I would have some dates in the future. Then the PA system broke the magic with an announcement that all those attached to the provost marshal's office were to report with combat packs and rain gear. We couldn't imagine what had happened but we did what was ordered and assembled in front of the provost marshal's office building. We were loaded into 4 X 4's and driven north to someplace on the shores of the Chesapeake Bay south of Yorktown, Virginia. There we were to search for two crewmen who had bailed out of a B-17 without orders somewhere near our search area.

A raging thunderstorm was in progress with heavy rain, blinding lightning and earth shaking thunder. An hour earlier, a B-17 returning from a training mission had been struck by lightning and most of the instruments and electrical system had been burned out. The pilot masterfully landed his B-17 in the storm without mishap. The crew reported that the inside of the airplane turned into a ball of green fire and the number one engine had been knocked out. In the panic that followed, the bombardier and navigator bailed out unordered and we had to find them "somewhere south of Yorktown".

The countryside in that area in 1945 was mostly uninhabited and we were pushing through saw grass and open fields that were interspersed with marshes and inlets. We had orders to avoid any homes and we were not to knock on any doors. That was easy because there were maybe three lights that we could see, all with one half mile between them. We did, however, disturb some deer and bears while we were crashing through the underbrush. We were soaked in ten minutes either by the rain or the swamps that we were stumbling into. So, we thrashed around all night until we got to the shoreline where we were to see a most amazing display of weather and airmanship.

A Navy PBY-5 had been called to drop flares over the bay and river to aid in our search. The storm was still raging but that PBY cruised up and down the shore in and out of the mist and clouds dropping flares. It was the most bizarre thing that I had ever seen with the lightning illuminating the airplane sometimes and then when it was behind the sheets of rain, its image would be projected in silhouette by either the flares or bursts of lightning.

That guy flew up and down the bay all night dropping flares. He didn't leave until noon the next day after the storm had moved on. We searched for five days, most of the personnel had been sent back to the base and a few of us continued. The weather had turned hot, humid and calm. The bay was like glass and the beach exposed many dead fish and skates that smelled of the grand old sea.

Rounding a bend, the guy with me stopped and said that he thought that we had found somebody. The odor was far more powerful than the dead sea life and indeed there was something in the water ahead. One of the crew for whom we were searching was near the shore in the knee-deep water. One quick look was all that we needed to realize that we weren't cutout for recovery operations. The fish and crabs had been very busy.

After pulling the body ashore by the parachute, we called in and waited some distance away and were the butt of many derisive comments by the "gravediggers" who came to pick up the remains. Later that week when we were on main gate duty, a base ambulance came down the road with lights flashing to be passed through and as we waved them through we could see that they were wearing gas masks. They had found the second victim and we gave them a very loud dose of their own medicine since we didn't have gas masks when WE did our job.

Chapter 7.

Transfer to Keesler Field, Miss. Discharged at Drew Field, FLA.
Home again.

OUT OF LANGLEY FIELD

I was serving duty at the main gate one day in August when one of the guys yelled that a B-24 was going nuts and buzzing the base. I looked in time to see it pull up after making a run down the main street. THEN ANOTHER ONE came roaring across the field and made a pass at the base at 90 degrees from the first.

Then we figured it out. THE WAR WAS OVER!

The phone rang in the guardhouse. The base was shut down. Nobody gets out and only military personnel were to get in. The next three days were hell and the most fearful of my life but we won't cover it here except to say that I have never seen so much violence and bestial behavior. Soon I received orders that I was being transferred to Keesler Field in Biloxi, Mississippi and I left Langley near the end of August 1945. How I got to Keesler has been erased from my memory as have several other brief periods then. That will always be a mystery to me.

After walking what seemed to be 10 miles, I arrived at the base with everything I owned in my barracks bag and checked in with a bored corporal in a building that has almost escaped my memory, too. I have no idea where it was, but I was directed to a casuals area at the east end of the base bordering the town. My billet was in a row of tarpapered wooden barracks built in 1941 in the middle of a pecan grove.

I looked up and down the row to get the sight of someone but it was soon clear to me that I was alone. It was late, I was sick with a sore throat, and I was tired, so I entered the nearest "hotel", unrolled one of the mattresses and stretched out. I was awakened in the middle of the night by a strange noise and bolted upright to hear something scrambling around inside and on ME. The scratching and scurrying sound was soon interrupted by a loud buzzing near my face. After swatting a two pounder away from my nose, I realized they were flying cockroaches. They sounded like a squadron of B-29's.

The light switch didn't work any better than the screen-less windows so I got up and moved to another building that was secure. It even had one light bulb that functioned. There were a couple of the cockroaches in residence there that I quickly dispatched with my boot, they were about two inches long and should have had NC numbers on their wings.

Since there wasn't any bedding, I covered myself with my overcoat and slept until morning. I awoke to the sounds of someone coming into the building. It was another casual and soon there were several more. None of us had an assignment or knew where we were to go, but after a couple of days we decided that we had been forgotten and to avoid things like KP and other onerous duties, we made certain that it would continue to be so.

The mess hall was a mile away and once a day we would go there for dinner. The rest of the time we ate pecan nuts that we shook from the trees every morning. At night we would wander around to the beer gardens near the PX's and have a few suds. I had noticed odd lights rising up from the base into the sky on clear calm nights and I mentioned them to some of the old hands as being something that the weather guys were sending up to measure something in the atmosphere. They laughed their heads off.

"You're new here, aren't you?"

"Well, yeah."

"There aren't any weather people here. Those lights are rubbers out of the pro kits (prophylactic) that we fill up with gas from the heaters then tie them off and tie toilet paper onto them, let them go up, and light the last piece of paper. Then when the fire gets to the condom: BOOM."

So much for the mysterious Keesler Field Lights.

This went on for a month and in that span of time we found "GATE NUMBER 3½", a break in the fence hidden by underbrush that gave access to town anytime we needed it. We used Gate 3½ almost every night to go into Biloxi to partake of the free delicious seafood at the bars that lined almost every street downtown. There were platters of hard-boiled eggs, shrimp, oysters and a pitcher of beer for 50 cents.

Sometime near the end of September, somebody finally found us and wondered, "Where the hell we had been!" I was soon processed out to go to Drew Field, Tampa Florida for honorable discharge. Again, how I got there is a mystery to me. I cannot recall my travel there, but I do recall signing some papers after a short stay and making a long walk out to the main gate with my barracks bag.

The wheels had come off the war wagon and I was hiking for home.

SHIFTING GEARS WITH A BAD CLUTCH

After hitch hiking home from Tampa, my last ride dropped me off near my house and I excitedly entered to what I thought would be a wonderful welcoming event. But everybody was involved in a loud Halloween party conducted by my little sister. No one had the desire to do anything but keep the party going. I said hi to mom and got out of there as fast as I could and went into town.

There wasn't anyone that I knew, so I sort of roamed around trying to revisit my old high school haunts. Bad idea. I could have been on Mars. So I ended up in the Flamingo Bar and Grill. It was just as I remembered it from my high school days, decorated in chartreuse and cherry red junk. Fake palm trees and bamboo furniture from 1939 and from the looks of them, the windows and mirrors hadn't been cleaned since then. Years of cigarette smoke and cooking grease had left a film of grime that could have been carved with a knife.

I hadn't been there more than ten minutes when I felt a hand on my shoulder and smelled stale cigarette breath, body odor, booze, and cheap perfume. I turned to see an old fixture of the wartime party-scene of Sarasota, Ginny Howard. "Old" is a sad term to lay on Ginny because she wasn't more than twenty four or twenty five but she looked like she had been "rode hard and put away wet." What was once a vivacious and beautiful blonde was now a seedy, fat, sloppy bar fly -- an alcoholic lush. What I saw when I turned to see who had their hand on my shoulder was a shocking remnant of one of the town beauties.

She still used her old trick of sidling up close enough to lay one of her breasts on the forearm of a potential mark. Her proximity was repulsive. Her breath smelled of a brew of cigarette smoke, booze, and halitosis. Her body odor and dirty clothes put the finishing touches to the noxious mixture. I looked into vacant eyes, still a beautiful blue but glazed and empty.

"Buy a girl a drink, soldier?"

Girl? Well she was once but she had spent the last four years rushing to her end, burning her candle at both ends and the middle at the same time. I remembered her from 1942 when I was a sophomore in high school. She had already graduated and took wing, so to speak, with most of the pilots who had descended on our quiet little town. Nineteen forty-two saw an explosion of wartime activity in Florida. Every small town had an airbase pop up next to it and all of a sudden there were thousands of pilots and aircrew all over the place but most of them were dashing young fighter pilots living a fast life. That's what they had to be because a conservative "Milquetoast Maury" would not have survived in a P-40 or P-39. One had to be aggressive, and not the least bit concerned with longevity. However, they were very interested in living big and now.

This was the flame that too many young "female moths" fluttered to. Our innocent little town was no different than hundreds of others when thousands of young men appeared in a matter of months to bring excitement and a sense of urgency to young and old alike.

Ginny was the Queen Moth in our town with her long wavy blonde hair, lovely and well-endowed figure, plus a confident outgoing personality…well, it was more than that, it was a "Come-hither-inviting-I'm available-let's have some fun" personality. And she did have fun almost 24 hours a day with an endless supply of fliers had the money and the desire to partake of her favors. On weekends she could be seen at any time of the day or night with one or two dashing young officers in the bars or at the beach.

Oh yes, there was a bar at the Lido Casino right on the beach and when she wasn't in the bar she was stretched out on the sand sleeping off the previous night getting the dark tan that made her so striking. She was blessed with natural blonde hair, dark tan, knockout figure, and a face that matched everything else. Yep, perfectly equipped for the task and the pace never let up. Nighttime during the week was as busy as the weekends because the flyboys came to town to party after a hard day's flying and the ladies were there to help them. So, it was a seven days a week job but somebody had to do it.

Back to the Flamingo. "Okay, what's your pleasure?" I asked.

"Oh, just some bourbon in a glass…a double." She smiled as she answered and then I could see the cause of the scar on her upper lip. One of her front teeth was broken. I thought to myself that girls don't get broken teeth, by kissing too hard. I had seen plenty abuse when I was an MP at Langley Field and I knew how she lost that tooth. It was sad to see her dishevelment. Her low-necked-too-tight tee shirt was stained with food spills, her dark slacks had dog hair all over them, and her shoes were run down and dirty. Her hair, once shimmering and bright, was a dirty tangled mass that smelled of all the bars in town.

She was drawn to the glass of bourbon as if it was a magnet and drank half of it like one would take a drink of water. After staring down at the glass for a moment she looked up and said, "You up for a party tonight?"

"Nope, I've had enough partying, I'm just relaxing."

She sat there staring at me with a vacant half smile as if I were transparent. I could see that her lipstick was melting and running into the cracks and wrinkles around her lips. Her skin, that was once smooth and golden, was tough like saddle leather and splotched with sunspots from too much hot sun.

"You don't remember me, do you Ginny?"

"Sure, honey, you're from out at the airbase."

I had the feeling that I could have been George Washington and she would have said the same thing. At that moment I realized that the human face is a marvelous instrument with its ability to display a person's inner emotions or the lack of them. Ginny stared at me, or rather stared through me, with an empty smile and had absolutely no idea who I was other than an airman and that meant "from out at the airbase". For all she knew she had gotten drunk and slept with me sometime, maybe yesterday.

"No, not Sarasota Airbase, a lot of others, but not Sarasota. Do you remember the life guard at Lido Beach?"

She stared at me with a vacuous look. There was no body home.

"Yeah, I went to Lido a lot."

A lot! She lived there for almost 4 years, day and night … mostly night. I lived there, too, for one summer when I was hired as one of the lifeguards and I saw her with her friends almost every day in the bar. By 1943 the number of adult males in the town had sunk to almost zero and the song that was popular then, "They're Either Too Young or Too Old" told the story. White haired old men were the police and 16 year olds were lifeguards. The old men had no training and neither did we. We read the Red Cross book on life saving and went to work watching over hundreds of people on the beach and the fresh water swimming pool. Lido Beach and the art deco casino was a beautiful place for servicemen on weekends who descended on the area by the hundreds. Many of them came from airbases in Venice, Ft. Meyers, Sebring, and Tampa, all of which had beaches but this was THE fun place. Beautiful white sand, a bar on the beach, a fresh water pool fed by an Artesian Well, and plenty of pretty girls, made it an attractive destination for soldiers looking for fun.

It wasn't much fun for us, however, when we had to watch over hundreds of bathers on the beach and to control those in the swimming pool. The bar was adjacent to the pool and you can imagine the temptation that it held for the drunks to jump into the pool to cool themselves. That added to our workload because some of them were too far gone to be in the water but there was little that we could do to stop them.

One Saturday when it was quite crowded I watched a big raw-boned guy go off the high diving board, dropping straight into the water feet first after missing the front of the board after the first spring. Ah! Another clown that drew some giggles from those in the pool. The "clown" tried another dive but this time he was too close to the end and he hit the end of the board in the small of his back and pitched forward, hitting the water with a loud belly flop. By the time I got to him he was half way to the bottom and out cold.

I had to get help to pull him out of the pool and get him stretched out fearing that I had a potential drowning victim on my hands but the impact had knocked the wind out of him and he hadn't ingested any water. He came to his senses but he was in a lot of pain.

There was a huge abrasion on his back and he had lost most of the flesh on the "knobs" of his spine so the next few days weren't going to be very comfortable for him. We covered him with blankets and kept him there until the ambulance arrived.

Drunken soldiers weren't the only hazard when Ginny was around and she had a snoot full. The lifeguards were allowed to enter the lounge to get some juice or non-alcoholic drinks. The two of us were a long way from the legal age of 21 but oddly enough, neither were most of the pilots. It was nice and cool in the lounge and the never-ending music was always nice to hear inside. We could always hear it in the guard's chair at the pool, too.

"Frenesi", "I'll Be Seeing You", "Begin the Beguine", "Wait for Me Mary", and many more that Frank Sinatra, Dick Haymes, Tommy Dorsey, and Harry James played and made the war a little more bearable.

Of course, Ginny was there, sitting on a stool at the end of the bar next to the bartender's station. As I stood there waiting for my cold drink, Ginny jumped off her stool and planted a wet sloppy kiss on me and made sure her crowd saw her crudely groping me. My gyrations to extricate myself from her grip gave everybody a big laugh...except me.

I knew all about Ginny. Looking at her approaching another soldier, I could see how terrible she looked. She was war casualty as much as some of the soldiers.

I stayed in town late enough to make certain that everyone was asleep and I came home to a quiet house.

I had a cot on a screened porch with the gentle sounds of the surf lapping the shore and it was not easy to adapt to such a quiet and peaceful environment. Drifting off to sleep and hearing the engines to which I had been so addicted would lull me to sleep. Then, sometime later my sleep would be interrupted. I would jump the track into a semi-conscious state of silence and bolt upright because all the engines had stopped and all I could hear was the lapping of the waves. It was a weird phenomenon that took months to erase. Many walks on the beach at 0200 and a glass of milk sometimes did the trick to relax me enough to sleep.

PART THREE
Chapter 8.

A tossed fish and a day in court.

THE CLOSEST CALL

Several days after I got home I drove into town and noticed a large Kingfish lying at the foot of the Five Points intersection in the middle of town. It was still there when I went home later in the day. It was a puzzle why someone would waste a good fish like that. That night I decided to go into town to see if I could locate anyone that I knew and one of the wonders of the world blossomed. My old high school buddies in crime appeared as if they popped out of the ground. They had been recently discharged from the Navy and mysteriously all of us came together at the same instant. Excitement joyfully bubbled forth and it didn't take long before the creative juices started to flow. I remembered the fish at the 5 Points flagpole and went to see if it was still there and unbelievably no one had removed it. It soon made us a foursome and we proceeded to make our rounds to the bars with the fish as a thirsty companion.

We soon realized that we weren't making many friends even after making a few jokes that we thought were funny, like " We saw on the menu that you served fish so I'll have a beer and the fish would like a scotch." After incurring the wrath of several bartenders we decided that there was something else that we could do so we went to Smacks for something to eat and in two minutes we saw what we had to do. We parked in the back of the drive-in instead of near front to wash the fish off our hands in the men's room.

The ladies and men's restrooms were side by side and each had a little garden area in front of it since both were entered from the outside. A lattice fence separated the two. A transom over the doors provided ventilation and that got our attention. In less than a minute we knew what we had to do and we waited for the first customer to use the ladies room.

We took turns at introducing the Kingfish to the ladies by slowly shoving it up and through the transom so that it looked down at the occupant with its wide-eyed stare and partially opened mouth that was full of large sharp teeth. The Kingfish resembled a Barracuda with a long sharp nose, large eyes, and a menacing mouth so when it visited its captive audience the result was almost always the same.

It was hilarious to see the escapees exiting the restroom in various stages of disrepair trying to run when they were not quite all put together. We retrieved the "monster" after each incident and retreated to the car so we could welcome the next visitor. This went on for perhaps an hour or more and after numerous inspections by the owner who was diligently trying to figure out what or who was causing the disruption, we decide that it was time to go. It was late and we had to dispose of the fish and we made the mistake of passing a saloon in Newtown, the black section of town. Without giving a thought to where we were, we threw the fish into the saloon. Bad idea!

Someone was quick enough to get the license number of the car and shortly we became guests of the police department for the night. In keeping within the law, we were allowed one phone call to get bail or to get sprung. The other two in the group made their calls and were quickly taken home. My call went like this.

'Dad, this is Bob, I need some assistance"

"What kind of assistance?"

" I'm in jail and I need some bail."

"Why the hell are you in jail?"

"Well, I threw a fish."

"You what?"

"I threw a fish into a saloon." Silence hung on the other end of the line for 10 seconds.

"If you are that stupid you can spend the night where you are!"

Our light-hearted antics had earned us a rather serious charge of trying to incite a race riot by throwing a fish into a saloon owned by a Negro and we had crossed the line. We were looking at possible long jail terms, possibly in federal prison. We quickly had a court date before a judge. The games were over.

COURT

The three of us arrived early to make certain that we were there when our names came up on the docket. The only parent to sit with us was my mother who was worried about her son, and rightly so. We didn't realize it but we were in big trouble. There were two cases ahead of us that gave us a chance to see how the judge handled things as far as being fair and devoid of biases. Just before the hearings started, we realized that Judge Early was the father of one of our high school buddies, Charley, with whom we played on the football team. A glimmer of hope showed, not much of one, but a bit of light. The judge wore a hearing aid and as proceedings progressed we noticed that turned the device off when he had heard all that he wanted to hear of a defendants testimony. Then he turned it back on when he pronounced his decision. It was hilarious to see him sit in silence when the miscreant was droning on about his innocence and then flatly announce, " Thirty dollars, thirty days."

The case before ours involved a white man who was mixed up with a colored woman who was charged with soliciting, but there were some gray areas as to who was soliciting whom. The black woman was first to state her case. She gracefully strode to the front of the room and faced the judge with self-confidence but without displaying arrogance or disrespect for the court. She was un-ruffled in the presence of officialdom and stood erect in her Sunday best. Her Sunday best was a thin dark blue dress of cotton with rose-colored flowers in the field. Her short hair supported a little black pillbox hat that sat squarely on top of her head that added to her height because she was well over six feet tall and skinny as a rail. She couldn't have weighed more than 130 pounds and was as flat-chested as a 12 year old boy. I had to admire her, though. She was alone and at the mercy of a room full of white people who could send her away just to speed up the proceedings if they had a mind to do so. She bravely stood there as she held her little black purse in front of her.

" State your name and place of residence please," the bailiff ordered.

" Daisy Johnson an Ah lives in the 'partment in Newtown."

" State your age, please"

" Ah'm thirty", she answered.

The judge questioned her as he was reading the charges.

"Now Miss Johnson, you are charged with soliciting from that gentleman in the room here, is that true?" The judge looked up and pointed at the gentleman.

"Nawsuh, Yon'ah. Ah jes git off'n the bus from Jacksonville lookin' fo' work down heah' an' dat man ax me if'n Ah could do laundry fo' him an' Ah said no. How am I gonna' do laundry when Ah jes' git off'n the bus?"

"I see. But you were seen to enter the hotel with him, now why was that if you refused his request to do his laundry?"

'Well, he ax me if Ah would like some gin an Ah said Ah didn't want no gin."

"Good." The judge commented a bit too quickly.

"But I wouldn't mind some whiskey an' watah."

At this point she had taken two steps forward and two steps back but she was completely candid in her responses.

"So, he asked you to go up to his room?"

"Yasuh, I could'a used a nice drink aftah dat hot bus ride, it gits pretty hot in de' back."

"What transpired then?"

"What?"

"What happened after you had your drink?"

"Well, he wanted me to do some stuff an Ah tole him dat Ah wasn't inta' any funny business an Ah started to git outa' dere' when de po-lees come in an' arrest me."

"I see. Now Miss Johnson, have you ever been arrested before?"

"Yasuh."

"And what was your infraction?"

"What?"

"Why did they arrest you?"

"Ah poked mah' boy fren' inna' eye when git nasty wif' me an Ah beat on him some."

"So, that's the only time that you have been arrested?"

"Yasuh, dat happen up in Jacksonville some time back. You can ax em' up dere."

The judge thought for several minutes and looked at the man

who was apprehended with Daisy. The judge looked back at Daisy and asked her what kind of work she could do if she was steadily employed.

"Ah do cleanin' cookin', arnin' an Ahm real good wif little chillins'. Ah kin take care of babies, Ah like babies. Jedge, Ah come here lookin fo' work but not the stuff dat' man wanted me to do." She pointed to the man sitting in the gallery behind her. The judge shuffled a few papers and looked at the black woman and told her that he could find no reason to hold her because she had not committed any of the offenses for which she had been arrested. He finished by ordering her to report to the court when she had gainful employment.

"Yasuh, Ah kin do dat an Ah'm tryin' to git a good job. Thank y'all."

She turned and gracefully glided down the aisle on her way to the door. I didn't know it then, but mother slipped a note into her hand with the address and phone number of a friend who needed a housemaid.

The gentleman who was apprehended with her tried in vain to wiggle out of his arrest. His ploy of seeking someone to do his laundry was quickly exposed when the arresting officer stated that there was no laundry in his convertible and his recent arrest record was no help to him either. He ended up in jail for a series of soliciting offenses that followed him from another county.

Now it was our turn.

The three of us presented ourselves before the judge where we went through the "state-yours" routine. The judge furrowed his brow and turned up his hearing aid when we stated our names.

"Now, I'm not sure of what I'm reading here. You boys threw a FISH into a saloon down there in New Town?"

The colored section of town was seldom visited by white boys and that was the way it was. It was a "We don't go down there and they don't go up here" type of situation. Remember, this happened in 1946 and the times were different. So, the judge's question was steeped in age old southern mores but showed evidence of changes a-foot…" Those nice colored folks."

"Well, we were just on our way home from having some fun and just passed by this place with swinging doors and it was a spur of the moment idea to toss the fish through them. We weren't trying to rile up anybody. It was just the tail end of the evening."

I was trying to get out as many words as possible in the shortest time possible to state our case as one of innocent horseplay, which it was.

"Now, you say that you were having an evening of fun, were you drinking?"

" Yes sir, but not much. We were almost broke."

The judge was getting interested in what else we had done and he turned up his hearing aid.

" A good time. What else did you do?" We surmised that he was suspicious of other nefarious acts that we had committed.

The three of us took turns describing our forays into three nighttime establishments with the fish and finally ending our long session at Smacks shoving the fish through the transom into the ladies restroom. To our amazement, we could see that the judge was having trouble keeping a straight face and some of the officers in the courtroom were squinching their lips to stifle smiles. We laid it on thick and gave him vivid descriptions of the girls running out of the restroom in various stages of disarray. The colored sheriff who arrested us showed no signs of mirth.

"Now, you boys did all this before you threw the fish into the establishment in Newtown?"

"Yes sir, it had been a long nightand we just wanted to unload the fish someplace. We didn't target anybody on purpose."

Judge early looked down at us with furrowed brow and said, "You know, if you boys had served any time in the service like my son, Charles, you wouldn't be doing silly things like this."

Ed spoke first," I just got out of the Navy two days ago and Jimmy got of the Navy last week."

The judge looked at me, " And what about you?"

"I got out of the Air Force two weeks ago. That's why we were celebrating, I guess."

The judge looked at us with sharp concentration.

"You must be about the same age as my son, he was in the Marines."

" Yes sir, we know Charley. We were on the football team with him," we answered. Somehow the answer had been phrased to subtly imply that Charley was an active player in the games. That we were on the football team WITH Charley sounded much better than to say that Charley was a substitute. He tried hard but he just wasn't an athlete. However, he pleased his father by playing a bit in some games.

The judge sat back in his chair and frowned some more, looking at us and finally said , "Humm. Now I recognize your names! I can't believe that you boys would be doing this kind Tomfoolery after being in the service. You should be ashamed for causing so much trouble with the colored folks, but it appears that you spread your mischief around pretty evenly between the white people and the colored folks and I'm convinced that you weren't trying to incite any racial trouble by what you did with that fish.

Relief crept slowly into our minds and it looked like we weren't going to prison. We listened intently as the judge let the other shoe drop.

"I'm fining each of you one hundred seventy five dollars and each one of you will go down to that establishment in Newtown and personally apologize to the owner for what you did.

Okay, that will be easy, I thought. Then the other shoe dropped. A good judge has three shoes, I guess.

"The three of you will report to the owner every Saturday morning at eight o'clock for four consecutive weeks and do whatever cleaning and other work that he has for you to do in the eight hours that you will be there. He will report to me every Monday until you have completed your service to him. Any absence from your assignment will result in immediate incarceration. I don't want to see you boys in my court again. UNDERSTOOD!

"Yes sir." We answered meekly and simultaneously.

We left the courtroom with relief and the realization that we were no longer the three high school goof balls and that maybe we should grow up. In the last three years, the town had grown up too. There were new faces on the police force and they didn't look the other way as they had done before.

We obeyed the judge and did our penance at the saloon under the strained jurisdiction of the owner and we couldn't get out of there fast enough.

We never got together again after that and went our separate ways.

We never went back to Newtown again.

Smack's Drive-In | Courtesy of Sarasota History Alive

Chapter 9.

Working in construction with Levy Green, who was actually black.

LEVY GREEN

He stood silently as the boss issued instructions to the crew. He stood literally head and shoulders above the rest. He stood erect and tall, staring into the distance and at times looking down at the ground as if he wasn't listening to the directions being given to us before we went to work. The boss, Mr. Abbott, could hardly be seen as he gave his orders while standing in the middle of the crew. He couldn't have been more than five feet three or four inches in height but had the authority in his manner and tone to erase any doubt that he was in charge-----all one hundred and forty pounds of him. I was hired as a common laborer who would be in the company of some hard and tough men who, in their most taciturn manner, offered me nothing on that first morning; Not even a look, much less some kind of greeting. Never mind. I was a white boy who could quit any time I felt like it and it wouldn't bother them one way or another so I watched them as they listened and tried to assess their demeanor. It was obvious that they had already measured me and gave the impression that they would have to put up with "the white boy" for a little while.

The tall black man who towered over all of us was almost a perfect example of what was then called a "buck nigger." He had a body that was built from good genes and years of hard labor. His wide shoulders and bowling ball sized shoulder muscles would fill a doorway and his upper arms were muscled with huge biceps that never seemed to relax. A tiny waist that seemed to be far too small supported his bulging chest and thigh-sized neck. He was wearing an old chambray shirt that was losing the battle to cover his torso. A tattered remnant of cloth that was once a sleeve, hung from the seam of each shoulder, but it was properly buttoned and spotlessly clean. The tails were tucked into the waistband of his faded black pants, the cuffs of which had been worn away like the sleeves of his shirt. This served to show much of his lower leg and his run down work shoes that he wore without the luxury of socks. His head was covered by a sweat-stained dark brown dirty fedora that long ago had lost its hatband. It was pulled down so low that one could hardly see much more than a fairly prominent nose and a classic Negro mouth.

As he turned away when the group dispersed I confirmed what I thought that I could see at first glance. His left arm and left leg were smaller than those on the right side of his body and he walked with a slight limp. I could think of only one thing that would cause that kind of atrophy, Infantile Paralysis as it was called then. Those limbs that were shrunken were still larger than mine, but his stature was unaffected because he was at least six feet five or six inches tall and stood erect and proud, not arrogant or haughty, but with a quiet self respect. Even with the shuffling limp, his movements were fluid and graceful as he went to the truck to pick the tools that he would use that morning. He spoke to no one and went about his work silently as if he were in another place unto himself. The rest of the crew addressed their tasks with the same stoic resignation but soon they were chatting briefly as they worked and at times they stopped to rest on their picks or shovels or to light a cigarette. The big black man kept digging like a machine, never slowing, never noticing, or at least giving the indication that those near him were lagging. He kept at his pace until lunchtime because there were no scheduled rest breaks on this job.

The crew was a colorless group of men ranging from their early twenties to their fifties; colorless in that they exhibited no outstanding features or stature. They wore grey or tan shirts, faded black pants or worn out dungarees, sweat stained baseball caps or straw farmer-type hats that produced a neutral color when they were in a group. Their personalities were no different. They said little and when they did, their talk was superficial and usually concerned their latest weekend drinking binge. Other than that, they worked and smoked. They were all career laborers with little education or the desire to achieve one so they put in their time everyday for five days, took their pay on Friday, and laid around or drank for two days; then started the process all over on Monday. I had previously seen some of them in town with their wives or girlfriends and I knew the type.

I was told to "pair-up" with Meeker who was another white man. He would show me some of the things that I had to do on my first day operating a pick and shovel. Meeker was an old man, probably fifty or fifty-two years old and showed signs of many years in the sun, many years of rough labor, and the deterioration that comes with it. His tanned face was creased with the coarse wrinkles that sun toughened skin exhibits. His dry and cracked lips were devoid of color from long exposure to the hot sun and traces of tobacco juice resided in the corners of his mouth. Everybody either smoked, chewed, or had a wad of snuff stuffed in front of his lower lip. I thought that they must have felt that it was their sworn duty to hasten their demise by adding to the effects of the hard life that they were already living.

"Name's Addy, "he said without looking up or offering a hand.

"My name's Bob, glad to meet you." I didn't offer a hand either.

"We's supposed ta' level out this patch so's the slabs ken be put down. Dig out all the grass an' weeds an' we level it. Gotta be done by enda' the day."

"Man! That's a lot do in eight hours!"

"Yup."

I looked at the patch of ground with dismay. It was half the size of a football field and thick with short grass and a few palmettos. We would never make it, but Addy had already started with his pick and he was tearing up big chunks along the string line that marked the edges of the area to be cleared so I fell in behind him and kept up with him for a while but old as he was, I couldn't maintain his pace. It was obvious after the first hour that this was going to be a long day, because fatigue became more of an adversary than the plot of ground we had to clear. It was a good thing it was February when the weather was cooler than it would be in a couple of months. Then the temperature would be up in the 80's and the word "hard" in front of the word "labor" would take on its full meaning.

February 1946. I had been out of the service for three months. I had tried three jobs and simply could not settle down enough to achieve the required mental attachment. All of them were so boring; sedentary, uninteresting, unimportant and dead-ended, that I simply couldn't face the entrapment. The people, as nice as they were, seemed to be out of touch with what had just happened in the world outside of this little town; but then, they couldn't be expected to be. Their minds were totally occupied with business and making money while the war was going on and they still were. Empty talk about inane and empty things were aggravating as hell, but it wasn't their fault. Yet, it was difficult to listen to their babbling about nothing without feeling the anger rising in me. Never mind, I was with people now who said so little that none of it was offensive or enlightening and a few of them looked like they had seen action in the war, but said nothing about it and that was fine with me. So many war stories were being told now that one learned how to sift the real from the imagined. I looked at the crew spread out on the construction site. Their heads were down while they picked, shoveled, pounded stakes for markers and kept a steady and busy pace to complete their work. The big black man was alone at the end of the property breaking up old concrete slabs that were walkways and foundations for motel cottages that were once here. I heard that they were built in the early 20's and the owner was going to modernize and enlarge the operation to take care of the surge of tourists that were sure to come after the war was over. Now how the hell would he know that! Nobody had ever heard of Sarasota, Florida. Well, maybe a few of the airman who were stationed out at the airbase might want to live here, but a "SURGE?" I don't think so. Okay, if those dreams provided work, so be it.

This was a "one lung outfit". What it lacked in powered equipment it made up for with the right number of men with muscle and a boss who knew how to get the most out of them. It appeared that Mr. Abbott had the clue to the plot, because the ten or twelve men who were changing this patch of ground were getting the desired results pretty quick this morning and they worked smoothly and efficiently. I wondered how much nicer it would have been if there was a small bulldozer in the outfit. The scraping and leveling that would take Addy and me all day would have been done in a couple of hours. There was an occasional banter between those men who worked close to each other but the big black man worked apart from the group, saying nothing while he pounded the concrete into dust and fragments. I watched him for a short time as methodically went about his work, never slowing, never looking at anything but the slab in front of him as he attacked it with relentless blows of the sledge hammer. Mr. Abbott also watched the work with the countenance of a hawk and he had the face to match. Intense beady dark eyes peered from under a heavy dark brow, darting here and there to see every item of the work and issuing orders to some of the crew to adjust what they were doing to assist someone else or to speed up or to do whatever he thought was necessary to keep the work coordinated and efficient. It was interesting to see this diminutive man moving about with total authority and respect from men who towered over him. His face looked as if it had been chipped from a piece of flint as there wasn't an ounce of fat under the tan and wrinkled skin. His mouth was a thin gash between his nose and chin, devoid of shape and sensitivity, it was held tightly shut until he uttered a command that was usually short and concise.

So the day wore on as I wore down, unable to make my young but soft body keep pace with my cohorts, many of whom were much older than I. I wondered why the hell I was doing this. The pay wasn't half what I was getting on the other jobs that I had tried, but I was outside in the fresh air and sunshine doing something productive and working with simple men whose ambition was to make enough money for some food and shelter. For most of them there were no thoughts of the future. The future was next Friday night and drinking beer with their friends; and that would last until they could no longer swing a pick. Then what? Retirement? Well, that was something that the rich did when they came to Florida and besides, that was too far into the future for them to even think about. Keep working, stay out of jail (if you could), and pray that you didn't get hurt. That was more important than everything else because if you couldn't work you couldn't eat. It was that simple for these men, just as it was in the nineteenth century there was no company insurance, no worker's compensation, no vacation, no sick leave, and there was no on-the-job first aid that I could see. The dangers were obvious with axes, sledge hammers, picks, and enumerable sharp objects about. Injuries were quickly and quietly wrapped with a rag and the injured party kept working. If it was serious enough to require a doctor's attention, like hemorrhaging, the injured man was taken to a doctor's office or the hospital and he was responsible for the payment. You can imagine that only the most serious injury was given that kind of treatment.

The next day was tough. I was stiff and thought that maybe I should do something a bit easier; but, again, it was outside and healthy for me and money wasn't the sole object at this point. It was the pick and me for the second day and, like the rest of the crew, I put my head down and scratched at the earth. The day was long and boring but I looked at it as something that improved my body and gave me time to think. What were those other guys thinking? Where they thinking at all? I soon came to the conclusion that they weren't. They chopped and dug and wacked away at their tasks without a word or a thought and I was supposed to do the same. This was a hell of a way to make a living and so many men were doing it.

The big black man was still off on his own, sort of. He was finished with the destruction of the concrete slabs and turned his efforts to the clearing of the patch of ground to receive the new slabs for the motel units. I didn't see anyone tell him to what to do, but there he was, working with us and like the little bulldozer that I mentioned before. He churned through the weeds and soil at twice the pace that we managed and he made up the deficit that I perceived that morning with his power and persistence. Thanks to him, we made our objective that evening. The patch was ready to stake out the slabs the next morning.

As I mentioned before, this was a one-lung outfit. We did everything that other larger outfits did with machines. When I reported for work the next day I was given the task of running the cement mixer because the pads, approximately twelve by fourteen feet, were ready to be poured as soon as they were staked out. I can't remember how many there were, but it was probably eighteen to twenty and there was a huge pile of cement sacks, gravel, and sand that I had to turn into a mixture of slurry that could be poured into the forms that outlined the pads for the motel units. Have you ever heard the song "Cement Mixer, Put-tee-put-tee"? No? Well it described the machine that I was charged with. Of course, it had the barrel into which the sand, gravel, water, and cement were put, but it was turned by a one cylinder put-put engine that came out of the twenty's. I remembered them as a kid, a large horizontal piston, driving a flywheel around which a belt was wrapped that in turn was wrapped onto another wheel driving the gears that turned the barrel that mixed the cement mix. It ran with an interesting intermittent pulse of power that happened only when the rotation of the barrel fell below a certain speed. It then kicked in with a putt-putt-putt-putt and then coasted with a chuck-chuk-chuk until the speed dropped again. An ancient little "hit and miss" engine that was reliable, powerful, and today, worth a great deal of money. Anyway, in nineteen forty six, there weren't many cement trucks for little outfits like Abbott Construction so the Putti-Putti was how they mixed cement and to make enough cement mix to keep the crew pouring the slabs. Putti-put and I worked at flank speed and by ten o'clock in the morning, I was reeling from the pace of shoveling sand and gravel into that ravenous maw and frantically ripping open sacks of cement to pour into the ever hungry mouth that faced me. The line of men with wheelbarrows waiting for the product of this diabolic little machine grew as the morning wore on. I felt that I was not only splitting in half, but being looked at as a wimpy white boy who should be home with his mommy. I thought of that a few times myself.

The week wore on and we finished the slabs at the motel job and we all agreed that the guy was wasting his money building a twelve- unit motel on Highway 41 on the south edge of town. Oh well, to each his own. We were off on another job, but I was shunted off on a side job to fill some lady's old swimming pool with sand. No problem, right? Just back a dump truck up to it and dump the sand into it. Not when the pool is in the usual location in her back yard and there is no access for the truck so that meant a pile of sand in the driveway, a wheelbarrow, a shovel, and me. You have no idea how much sand an empty swimming pool can hold. I was given three days to do it and that meant fast work for eight hours or more. I was learning the value of an education at this point, and also the value of color; my color. On the second day of this assignment, the owner of the property stood on her lawn watching me struggling to keep up with the deliveries of sand while I tried to fill the vacant pool.

"How come they have a white boy doing nigger work?" she asked as she stood there with her hands on her hips.

"Jobs are assigned to whoever is available. It has nothing to do with who you are in this outfit," I told her.

She made some comments about my being improperly used and wanted assurance that the work would be done as promised and walked back to the house.

The next day I had some help in the person of a black man, the big guy that I had watched with interest on the motel job. Obviously the lady had complained about my progress or something else, and he sent his biggest and best "human machine" to please her. "My help" was dropped off shortly after I arrived on the site without comment of any kind, but it wasn't difficult to figure out. I had no illusion that he was my helper. He was the heavy hitter in the group and believe me, I welcomed him! I would be the help in this case. The old Ford pick-up truck had pulled up in front of the house with the black man sitting in the back amongst sacks, concrete blocks, and other supplies. The front was unoccupied. He lifted himself out of the truck box, reached in and retrieved a shovel and a sack, then without a word, he walked to the pile of sand and quietly stood there. The driver was one of the crew and curtly told me that Levy had been put on the job and that they would check on the progress the next morning.

"I thought that your name was Levi, that's what everybody calls you, don't they?"

"Ma'mumma called me Levy an' you can call me Levy," he said as he looked at the ground.

"Okay, LEE-VI, I'll call you Levy if you want."

He worked up the smallest of grins but stared at the ground.

"My name's Bob."

"Ah knows dat. I hear'ed dem talkin' to you."

"Sure glad you're here because that hole in the ground is bigger than I thought and I know that I'm not going to get it filled by tomorrow."

"I know'd dat when dey put you on de job. Gonna' take two of us an we might not git it done by tomorrow, but we kin sho try."

"Okay, Lee-vi, you pay attention to what I do and we might get it done. Really, I'm sure glad you're here."

He grinned again as he looked at the ground, "Yas'uh, I'll look close while you work."

We put in a good morning with him shoveling the sand into the pool cavity while I tried my best to keep up with him. I accused him of cheating because he had equipped himself with a large square-ended shovel instead of the smaller oval shaped tool that I was using. It was obvious why I couldn't keep up with him; his shovel carried more and he worked twice as fast as I could. We made great progress that morning and mid-way through it the owner called me over to the screened porch and said that she had a pitcher of ice water for me when I got thirsty. I could see the set up on a table through the screens, a pitcher of water and one glass. I thanked her and said that we were doing fine with the water hose.

"Well! I never!" She stomped back into the house.

I hadn't made any points with this woman and what few were left were certainly gone now.

Noontime finally got a notice from my empty stomach and I asked Levy if he thought that we should stop to eat.

"I thought you would never say somethin' 'bout dat."

We found a shady place under a huge magnolia tree in the lower backyard and sat down in the cool grass to open our lunches and rest a bit while we ate. On other jobs he usually ate his lunch apart from the crew for some reason. It didn't bother anyone. In fact it appeared that they didn't really care. They grouped together, ate, chatted and smoked a few cigarettes, and took a short nap if there was some shade. Here at the swimming pool job it was just Levy and me. He seemed a little self-conscious and hesitant without a place to go eat as he usually did, and sat for a while trying to adjust to the different situation in which he found himself.

"Levy, I'm sure glad that we have this big magnolia and cool grass to have a nice lunch on, aren't you?"

"Yassuh, it's nice."

"I think it's nice to be able to chat with someone. Get to know people that way and besides, I'm a talker. Hope you don't mind because we never get the chance to talk on the other jobs."

"Nawsuh, that's fine."

I opened my lunch bag to see what my mother had fixed for me this day. Not much different than the other days, two sandwiches neatly wrapped in waxed paper, one meat and one cheese, cookies, an orange and a thermos of milk. It was always a good meal that I thoroughly enjoyed after four hours of hard work. As I ate, I watched Levy remove his meal from the grease stained paper sack and place it on his lap. He looked into a gray porcelain bowl heaping with fried fish, greens and hushpuppies. I could smell the aroma and knew that I would enjoy it as much as he. After a moment with his head bowed, he looked into the distance briefly and addressed his meal. He then deftly dismembered the fish with his huge hands, putting the pieces daintily into his mouth, all the while looking away from me. I sneaked glances in his direction as he ate his lunch and I was struck by the graceful manner in which he consumed everything, barehanded. The bowl was wiped clean with his forefinger, scoured with sand to remove the grease, and carefully placed back into the greasy sack.

After we had finished a silent meal I felt determined to establish some sort of relaxed association with this man. I could sense tension and uneasiness in Levy at having the inability to put his customary space between himself and someone else on the crew, especially a white boy. I let it go for that day.

The next day was somewhat the same. We worked hard and gained on the job of filling the pool and sat under the tree for our noontime meal. We both had the same lunches as before but we sat a little closer and he was less secretive and aloof. Black men or niggers, as most called them, were cautious in their relationships with white people and to be placed in a rather personal situation with a white man, or boy in my case, was cause to be subservient. All I had to do was to say one word that he was uppity or disrespectful and he could be fired and in the worst case, arrested. That atmosphere made me uncomfortable, too, and I was determined that, at least between us, I would change it. He was a good man. He worked hard and long and, never complained about anything, and helped everyone, white or black.

"Where are you from, Levy, are you a Florida boy?" I asked as we were lying back against the magnolia.

"Nawsuh, Ah's born somewhere in South'Calinah."

Further conversation established that he didn't know where or when he came into the world. He didn't have any idea how old he was and neither did I. One couldn't tell his age from the condition of his body as it was upright, erect, and free of any sign of aging. There were no wrinkles or other age defining evidence that told his age. His hat covered enough of his head to keep his hair, or the lack of it, from giving one a clue as to his age. I guessed at 40 to 45 years

"Have you always worked in construction?"

"Nawsuh, I worked at the Chas'un Navy yard all durin' the war."

"Oh, the Charleston Navy yard. What did you do there?"

"Ah jes hep out."

"You must have helped out a lot because they put out quite a few ships. I'll bet that you moved the ships around for them, didn't you?"

"Aw nahsuh, but ah did carry a lot of stuff." That exchange actually produced a smile, a small one but it broke the ice.

"Well, do you think we should get back to the pool and finish it today?"

"Yasuh, I reckon we can."

And we did.

Our next job was to build a dock and seawall at a location on Big Pass. I couldn't believe it when the boss told us that the job was at the Out-Of-Door School on Siesta Key, about half a mile from our house on the beach. Our little house faced the gulf and the school was around the point and east of us. Big Pass was a deep water-dividing cut between Siesta Key and Longboat Key to the north. The sides of the channel were steep and the current swift during a tide change. In fact, the pass ran like a river and several times my brother and I swam out into the current when the tide was coming in to ride it down the beach a mile or so instead of walking. Thinking about that now gives me chills when I think of the sharks that could have been riding the current in with us. The deep channel went out to an entrance buoy in deep water about a mile off shore.

I hadn't been to the beach in front of the school for four years. It seemed a lifetime since I went there to swim and play with the children of a writer and his wife. At the time I didn't have the slightest idea who MacKinlay Kantor was. I could see him sometimes dictating to his secretary while he wrote his books, pacing back and forth in his studio verbally writing while she sat and recorded it in shorthand. Mrs. Kantor was a lovely generous lady who was very nice to us kids and I enjoyed going down there to visit and to swim with Layne and Timothy, their children. We swam in an enclosure that was supposed to keep out the sharks, but I soon found out that the screen didn't go all the way down to the sides of the channel due to the steep slope of the bottom. It was reassuring to the parents, anyway.

The beach was almost non-existent at that point in the shore along the channel, maybe fifteen feet wide at the most. Then it dropped rapidly down into deep water. One day when I was swimming on the beach, I continued out, contouring the bottom as it dropped away. I came upon a large out-cropping that appeared to be a rock so I swam up to it to push off into deeper water and in the moss that was waving off the "rock" I saw a large eye staring at me. The "rock" was a huge Jew fish, a giant sea bass that had to have been at least six to seven feet long. Before it could make a move toward me or do anything else, I rocketed out of there as fast as I could move which wasn't fast enough for me. Jew Fish haven't been known to attack swimmers, but this guy was large enough to try and if he had grabbed me there would have been no escape.

I screamed to the other kids and Mrs. Kantor what I had seen and they said, "Oh, that's Giles, he's down there all the time." Well, ol' Giles had it made sitting down there amongst the pilings of the dock gulping up mullet and snapper as they swam by in the current and I wasn't going to bother him.

By March 1946, the seawall that kept the beach from encroaching on the lawn had begun to rot and had to be replaced. The dock had reached that point too so it was a major rebuilding project and I looked forward to the task and possibly re-visiting some old friends. My aspirations of seeing old friends were not to be because the work kept us on the beach and those who I had hoped to see were not there. Four years is a long time and too many changes had taken place. I was still learning how to realize that. Soon after we reported to the location Levy started to work without any instructions or directions. He knew what to do and attacked the wooden wall with an axe and wrecking bar. It wasn't long before he had a pile of rotten wood on the narrow beach. The rest of the crew pitched in and started to remove the debris and trim back the bank so we could start constructing the new wooden wall. A stack of cypress lumber was delivered later that day by one of the senior members of the crew who had taken the old dump truck into town to pick up the materials.

Levy busied himself by digging deep holes for the posts with a posthole digger and a chipping bar, making certain that they were properly spaced. He didn't know how to read, he didn't know how to "cipher,"but he had the holes right where they should have been and they were aligned with a string so that they were straight. He worked with a series of wooden poles cut to several lengths; six- footers, eight-footers, etc. and he always knew which one to use. As I watched the gang working, I realized that I got exactly what I wanted when I thought that I had to have an active job outside. I got my wish on both accounts even with a lot of machinery, made use of a great deal of muscle. This little outfit didn't have a lot of machinery, but it had a lot of muscle and it used it in everything it did. Slabs and foundations are poured by calling in a cement truck, right? Not with this outfit. When that little gas-powered concrete mixer started chugging along, the guy feeding it better chug along right with it; shoveling sand and gravel and dumping in 100 pound sacks of cement as fast as you could until the job was done. I was learning what hard work was all about. More importantly, I was learning about those whose only offering was their manual skills and their endurance with the pick and shovel, or how long their back would last and, more often than not, how long they could go without being seriously hurt.

There was little energy available for talk during the day, but during lunch I was able to chat with my partners and I got to know several of them fairly well. Addy, the man that I met on my first day, was about forty-five or fifty years old and completely worn out; but he forged ahead as best he could. I chatted with him at lunch one day, but he had little knowledge of anything about which to talk. It didn't matter, really, because all he wanted to do was to nap and rest so that he could make it through the day. By noontime his face was flushed and he was shuffling and panting like an old horse. That's what he was, sadly. He liked to lie on his back in the cool shaded sand beneath one of the Australian pines to take a nap after his meager lunch; snoring and snorting as he slept. One day he gave us all a good laugh when a fly explored the cavern of his gapping mouth and got sucked in when he inhaled. Snorting, cussing, coughing and flailing around, he gave us quite a show. I don't think that he owned anything but one pair of faded blue bibbed overalls, a tee shirt, and a tattered straw hat, because that was his apparel every day and it matched his life; same thing, day in and day out.

The other crew-members were white men, typical of the laborers that construction outfits have. Non-descript, non-conversant, shallow and had nothing to do with me. They resented my presence and from some of their comments they expected me to quit when the work got too tough for "the little white boy." So I was almost on my own for a while.

There was one other black man on the crew, but he spoke only in grunts and didn't like me much. I didn't work with him. The other black man, Levy, was cautious at first, but he welcomed my approach and chatted with me showing me the required respect and constraint. The Civil War ended eighty-two years before and here this fine black man who routinely out-worked me, who knew much more than I about the work, and out-weighed me by at least one hundred pounds HAD to show me that he was subservient and inferior. Inferior indeed. My first day on the job was tough and I was burdened not only by my diminutive size, but by my lack of know how when it came to moving heavy objects. When I was trying to move a large chunk of concrete slab nearer to the dump truck, I was gently, but firmly pushed aside and Levy picked up the slab and stood there looking at it.

"Where you want 'dis ?"

"Oh, I was going to get it over to the truck."

"You ax' me next time," he said as he lifted the slab up into the truck and let it fall with a crash. That slab had to have weighed 200 pounds, but it wasn't a problem to Levy. He had just verified why the boss had a barrel of axe handles, sledge hammer handles, and shovel handles in the back of the pickup. When I asked him about it, he told me that they were for Levy because he broke so many of them everyday.

"Good night! Doesn't that get expensive?" I asked.

"You do as much work as Levy and I'll buy you a barrel of handles." He didn't have to say anymore.

MAKING A CONNECTION

"Mom, would you please put my lunch in a brown paper bag tomorrow?"

She didn't understand my answer to her questioning my request, but the next morning I left with my lunch in a brown paper bag; two sandwiches; one beef, one ham and cheese. Homemade cookies, an orange from our tree, and a thermos jug of milk completed my noon meal. When I arrived that morning I made sure that I put my bag next to Levy's brown paper bag in the box of the pickup. That morning was a heavy one with a lot of pick and shovel work chipping back the embankment to clear our way for the new seawall. Lunchtime was a welcomed relief and each of us found a shady and cool place to rest and replenish. For several days I had noticed Levy looking at my lunch as I ate, just as I had been eyeing his lunch as he ate. I went to the truck first and picked up a brown bag and quickly made my way to a cool patch of grass under a tree and low and behold, I had picked Levy's bag! Well, too late to change, I had already opened it and I wasn't going to give it up!

Levy knew immediately that he had the wrong bag when he opened it up. I could hardly contain my laughter when I saw the concern and confusion on his face. He looked around until our eyes met and started to get up to exchange bags but I shook my head "no" and gave him a sign inviting him to eat my lunch. He balked and had a grim look on his face until I gave him a smile and a "thumbs-up." I ate a marvelous lunch of fresh snapper, hush puppies and collard greens. I wiped the bowl clean with sand and rinsed it in the gulf just like Levy would do. Levy had a lunch with white bread, cookies, and fruit. We didn't mention it that afternoon, but I could tell that he was pleased as I was. Funny, the same thing happened the next day.

When we broke for lunch on the third day, Levy sat a little apart from us and set up his own little banquet starting with a red and white gingham napkin that he spread on his lap. He then carefully arranged his sandwiches and cookies on his lap, and said his prayer before he slowly ate his meal that had a third sandwich added to it. I was certain that I got the best of the switch but Levy would have argued that point.

While the work was progressing on the seawall, preparations for building the dock were put in place and the demolition of the rotten pieces began. The boss found it necessary to hire two more men. Both of them were young black men from North Carolina and they immediately took a disliking to me for some reason. I caught hard looks and in the process of working, unnecessary bumps and comments. I made sure that I steered clear of them as much as possible. One day the boss showed up with a derrick on the back of the dump truck and put it in place where the dock would start on the beach. It was obvious that it was a homemade affair composed of heavy timbers, cables, and a one-lung horizontal gas engine powered winch connected to an assembly of gears. A Rube Goldberg machine that had an aire of authority about it because it showed signs of work and usefulness sat on the sand near the water.

Levy busied himself nearby putting some long wooden open-topped boxes together that were aligned with the direction of the dock. When I asked the boss what the plan was with the boxes, he told me that they were forms for the concrete pilings for the dock. Well, that was a departure! Most docks had treated wooden pilings so it was going to be interesting to see how we did this one. It didn't take long after all the lumber was delivered. Piles of decking and beams were added to the seawall lumber so the pace of the work accelerated and the small crew put in some very demanding days. Spring had arrived and temperatures rose, but there were no more breaks than usual; just a short one in the morning and one in the afternoon. Addy was showing signs of wearing down and I felt a bit sorry for him. He was way too old to be doing heavy work in the heat and his face showed signs of stress; flushed cheeks, heavy breathing even when he wasn't working, and longer effort to return to work after lunch. I began to realize that there was a heavy price to pay for a lack of education.

The arrival of the putt-putt concrete mixer one morning signaled the start of the important work, making and setting the pilings. Along with the mixer came a gas-engine powered pump and a hose with a long pipe attached to the end. Things were getting quite interesting and it appeared that the boredom of the never-ending pick and shovel labor was about to end. Wooden dock pilings near the seawall were quickly set in place and the dock decking was laid so we had a base to start extending the structure out into the water. As soon as enough decking was completed, the derrick was moved onto it and placed at the end of the decking. Part of the crew that wasn't working on the dock was building the boxes that would be the forms for the concrete pilings. The forms were aligned with the dock and I began to see the picture and sure enough as soon as the first piling was cured a cable from the derrick was routed under the dock and attached to an eyebolt on the piling which was then pulled under the dock and out to end of the structure.

With a series of ropes and booms, the piling was pulled upright and moved into place to hold the dock frame. The pump was primed and started and one of the old crew placed the long pipe next to the piling and started to "blow" away the sand at the foot of the piling with a powerful jet of water. The piling rapidly sank into the emulsified sand. When it was determined that it was aligned and plumb, the jet of water was stopped and the sand quickly returned to its original compacted form, trapping the piling in an unbreakable grip of sand and water pressure. And so it went. Pilings were set in a procession slowly marching out into the gulf and the dock was built right behind them.

Then the "Carefully Laid Plans of Mice and" fell apart, or at least hit a snag. The steep slope of the channel made it necessary to attach another line with a choker to the pilings as they were drawn into deeper water. Deep water; that was the problem. No one in the crew would go into water over their head, much less water that was way over their head. The pilings were now extremely long to reach the bottom and to have at least eight to ten feet in the sand.

Since I was a swimmer and comfortable in deep water, I volunteered to do the choker resetting. The water wasn't "summertime warm," but I could stand it for short periods. But the short periods turned into long periods and I spent a lot of time in the water. As we neared the end of the dock I was having trouble with the last of the pilings and due to the strong current and the cold water I had to wait until the tide was slack so that we could quickly get the pilings manipulated into place. One day when I was resting and warming up, Levy for the first time looked me in the eye and said, "Mistah' Bob, I can see you way down there in the wahta. I sho couldn't do dat."

"Well, Levy, what would you do if you fell in?"

"I sho don't know how to swim, but I got it all figured out."

"Yeah? What would you do?"

"I reckon that I would jes sink to the bottom and walk out!"

One more piling to go and it looked like an easy one. I had finished setting the choker and was on my way up when I was almost hit by a large chipping bar on its way down to the bottom. How could anyone be so damn careless when everybody knew that I was right under them! I was going to cuss somebody out when I got to the top! When I surfaced I was almost hit again, but this time by a body, spread-eagled and flying over me, crashing into the water just past where I had surfaced.

"What the hell is going on?" I yelled up to the dock.

"Somebody better grab him, he can't swim!" one of the crew yelled down at me.

I turned to see one of the black kids struggling to stay afloat and I grabbed his collar while I held on to one of the pilings. Eventually we got to shore where the boy sat gasping and shaking. His friend stood by in total silence and was obviously shaken by the accidental tumble taken by his buddy. Before I could grasp what was transpiring, Levy came striding off the dock straight for the two boys, grabbing the "dry one" by the arm and pulled him up close to his face. In a quiet even tone of voice he said, "You mess wif mistah Bob again, I break you like a stick!"

He went back to his work as if nothing had happened. The black boy stood there rubbing his arm where Levy's iron grip had made an impression. I was slowly putting things together and realized that the two kids had colluded in trying to do something to me. The bar had not been accidently dropped off the dock but probably kicked. And Levy saw it.

I got dried off and took a break in the sun so that I could warm up. When I had the chance, I asked Levy about the incident and he told me that he had been watching the two kids from day one because he had them pegged as troublemakers. I thought about it and I could recall some of their comments and "accidental bumpings" when we were working. I'm certain that if the boss had been on the job when this happened, he would have fired the two kids, but as it turned out, he didn't have to. They didn't show up for work the next day, or any day thereafter.

With fifty feet of dock to finish, we pitched in with what and who we had. Having two less on the crew didn't bother us and the pace remained steady. Heavy timbers were bolted to the pilings and decking was nailed into place by Levy. "Nails" were really dock spikes that were one quarter inch in diameter and some eight to ten inches long. If I were to pound them in, it would be with a sledgehammer and I would probably bend half of them. Levy, being the human machine that he was, simply nailed them in with a two pound hand sledge like any normal person would if they were building a little box.

Watching this giant doing his work was a lesson in personal integrity and reliability. Never once was he reprimanded for not doing something correctly or on time. He was punctual every day, started his task immediately without hanging around for half an hour smoking and chatting. He never criticized anyone or had a bad word about anyone. Always a gentleman, he never uttered a swear word and would, without being asked, help anyone who was having trouble with something. Without directions or detailed instructions, he just plodded ahead in silence like a big ol' work horse, which is exactly what he was. Thank the Lord, he had a gentle disposition. We saw him angry, but under control. If he truly lost his temper and flew into a rage, there weren't enough of us there to do anything about it. It would take a shot from a cannon to stop him.

As the work progressed and the crew congealed somewhat, Levy and I got more relaxed with each other and we chatted every day after lunch about what we were doing. Soon the conversations got to things that he was curious about.

"Mistah Bob, I looks out at the wadah and I knows they's something out there on the other side. What's out dere?"

Here was a man who had no schooling at all; he couldn't write anything other than crudely printing his name, and he couldn't read, yet he had questions about the world around him. The others on the crew concentrated their interests on what they were going to do on Friday night or problems they were having at home. Blah blah blah. No interest in anything beyond what their arms could reach.

"Well, technically, Levy, we are facing north and we went in that direction we would hit the panhandle of Florida."

"Panhandle?"

"Yes, that is what they call the land that sticks out from the top of the state."

"What do it look like?"

I smoothed a patch of sand and drew a map of the state and labeled cities and put directional arrows to indicate how we were situated in relation to the map.

"How far is that handle?"

"About 250 miles."

"What's over here?" He pointed to the sand that would be west of Florida.

"That would be Mexico." I drew a rough facsimile of the east coast of Mexico and the questions flew. What's up here, what's out there, how far is that from that? Where's South Carolina?

The next day I brought a map of the United States to work and we had intense sessions every day after that as we identified states and cities. At the end of the week, he recited names and places, pointing to them without prompting. Soon eating lunch was done a little quicker so he could get down to the maps and pictures much to the disgust and derision of the other workers. We didn't stop our " classes". How could I deny this man his yearning to learn something, questions that were burning in his mind for answers? When I brought an entire atlas for him to take home, he argued that it was too much for him to take. I won the argument. He carried that book back to the truck as if it were the crown jewels of England.

Every night someone had to take him home since he didn't drive and someone had to pick him up in the morning. Lucky for him there was always a car or a truck coming by to either get him to work or to get him home. Nobody complained because without Levy, their work load would double. I had my old car handy so I opted to take Levy home at the end of the day. He and his wife lived in the "black bottom" section of town, Newtown. It was an area of run down houses and shacks so typical of the Negro sections of small southern towns. Their little house was situated in the front center of the lot without a shred of vegetation around it, just a one room unpainted shack set on concrete blocks with a porch in the front. It had a tin sheathed roof set at a forty-five degree pitch. An old brick chimney clung to the side of the house that seemed a bit odd for Florida, but it was there. Behind the house, however, was a large and verdant vegetable garden with pole beans, Swiss chard, lettuce and everything else you could want in a garden. A good distance in the rear of the lot I could see an outhouse almost completely camouflaged by a Bougainvilla. After a quick scan, it was difficult not to notice how clean and neat their little place was.

"See you in the morning, Levy." I said as he unfolded himself and struggled out of the car. No wonder he preferred to ride in the back of the trucks; it was the only place that his body would comfortably fit.

"Yasuh, see you in the mownin." He still avoided a direct eye contact with me (or anyone else) and looked at the ground as he got out. His wife appeared at the door as he neared the house and I could see that she was a tall full woman, but not obese. She wore the classic head cloth; the word "bandanna" could not be used here because she was typical Negro lady. She wore a red and white flowered head wrap tied in the front. Her dress was typical also; cotton, flowered, long, and clean. She stood there bare-foot with a big smile and waved to me. She was a perfect match for Levy. They made a handsome couple as both were over six feet tall and moved with equal grace. He approached her without greeting and just put his hand on her shoulder as he stepped up on the porch and he turned to wave goodbye. This routine was repeated almost the same for several days until his wife came to the truck and addressed me one night.

"Mistah Bob, we would be proud if'n you would come in for a spell."

From the look on Levy's face, the word "we" was not appropriate at the time.

"I would be pleased, Mrs. Green"

"People call me Rose," she answered.

"Yasuh, dis here's my wife, Rose" as Levy quickly caught up to the pace of things. He was caught unprepared by his wife's invitation and showed it.

"I would like to take a load off my feet, and besides, Levy and I might have some work stuff to talk about, huh, Levy?"

"Huh. I reckon we could." He wasn't at all convinced that we had anything to talk about regarding work but he went along with the emerging situation in which he was visibly uncomfortable.

I waited a short time and shut the truck down and went into their little house. I felt that they might need a little time to maybe smooth things out before I went in. Keep in mind, white people hardly ever went inside a Negro's house unless they were picking up the rent or had to check something. I wasn't uneasy about it but Levy was obviously uncomfortable so I kept talking about everything I could think of. It worked and Levy was distracted enough to forget his discomfort. When I walked in the first thing that I noticed was the absolute cleanliness of the sparse interior. It smelled of bacon grease and lye soap and, indeed, the pine floors were almost white from successive washings.

Levy and his wife lived in a one- room structure that wasn't much bigger than the average living room; maybe it was 16x20. On the right side to the rear was the kitchen area that consisted of a crude wooden sink and small counter/ drain board. On the back of the sink, sure enough, there was a caramel-colored block of "Fel's Naptha Soap" just like that which we used in the service to wash everything. I hate the smell of lye soap to this day. To the left side of the room, a bedspread was hung from a rope to hide the bed. In the "front room" there was a wooden table and several chairs, one of which was an overstuffed easy chair that so much of the stuffing had departed that it had become simply a stuffed chair, maybe even an under-stuffed chair. A picture of Jesus hung from a nail driven into one of the framing studs, all of which were exposed as there was no interior wall covering.

There was nothing else in their little home but the bright clean floors and walls and the bare necessities. The outhouse was way behind the house and I had to assume that they bathed in the house or the back yard in the dark. That was not unheard of. Never mind, it was none of my business but I couldn't help thinking about how they managed. They managed as well as the rest of us and better than some of the crew with which we worked. Both of them were clean and wore impeccably clean clothes; ragged but clean. I would have bet that there was a washtub hanging on the back of the house and a clothesline stretched out to the garden.

Rose had dinner cooking on the little wood-fired stove next to the sink in the rear of the kitchen space and it smelled wonderful. Like most of the housewives then, meat was fried in Crisco or bacon grease. It smelled like Crisco.

"Ah catched me a mess of feesh today, Mistah Bob. It would'a been wrong to waste 'em."

"I don't believe they would be wasted with both Levy and me eating them every day, Rose"

"Yasuh, you right, Mistah Bob. Levy been tellin' me how you been eatin' his lunch now and he been eatin' yours."

I felt that I had to "cover" Levy's appearing to have betrayed Rose by switching to my lunch instead eating his own and told Rose that it was all my doing because I purposely mixed up the bags.

"Ah knows about dat, Mistah Bob. I know he might get tard of eatin feesh every day so dats why Ah goes to our neighbor sometimes to trade him some feesh for a chicken or two. Levy likes chicken but we has to eat a lot of feesh."

"Rose fishes every day and she does good at it." Levy said as a looked at Rose with open pride and affection. The two of them told me how she fished from the bridges and causeways every day and usually caught their dinner and enough fish for Levy's lunches. He told me how she arose before he did in the morning to cook his fish so that it would be fresh for him.

Rose finished setting the table with gingham napkins placed next to the blue porcelain plates. A fork and knife were in their proper places and a porcelain cup sat to the right of the place setting. The old pine table was bare of any other decor except for salt and pepper shakers that one would find in a restaurant. The aroma of dinner and coffee cooking on the stove filled the little house with a wonderful invitation to a delightful meal and we were certainly ready for that after a long day of hard work. Levy motioned for me to sit in the old chair to his left. Rose would sit to his right so that she could tend to the stove and the food when she had to. Before I could get seated Rose stepped to the side of the sink and said, "Maybe you men would like to wash your hands befo' we eat."

"Oh, yasuh, dat's sompin ah always do. Ah jes fogot dis tahm."

"Me too, Levy. I guess we were too anxious to dig into Rose's good cooking."

"Yasuh, Ah suppose so."

Levy was completely unraveled and ill at ease so I started jabbering about work things and tried to get his opinion on some things that I thought he would be interested in, but it was only partially effective in calming him. It was apparent that he was a shy man as well as being subservient in the company of whites. He still avoided direct eye contact with me and I assumed that would never be changed in a man who had lived in the shadow of white supremacy all his life but I would keep trying. He was such a good man and had so little for his hard work that it amazed me that he was so acquiescent in the face of his life.

I stood behind my chair and waited for Levy and Rose, but she invited us to be seated so that she could serve the meal that was beginning to tantalize us with its wonderful aroma. She placed a platter of fried fish, hush puppies and onions in the center of the table. This was followed by a large porcelain bowl of grits and a bowl of greens. To the side was a plate of corn bread. As simple as it was, it was a meal fit for royalty. After Rose was seated, Levy paused for a moment and bowed his head and gave a silent prayer, just as he did every day before he ate his lunch. When he lifted his head, Rose began to serve us and things relaxed somewhat as we started to eat her dinner. Levy and Rose weren't fancy people and they lived way down on the socio-economical scale but they displayed an innate grace in the way they approached everything they did and their manners at the table were no different. Of course, Levy had two large pieces of fish and a heap of grits, but he was a huge man who did huge work and he deserved and required everything he could get. I couldn't complain. I had a very large fillet of fish myself and an ample serving of grits and greens that I savored.

"Rose, this is Mullet, isn't it?"

"Yasuh, I got a nice one today along wid ' de' snappah."

"Snatch hooking, huh?" (Mullet are bottom feeders and don't bite hooks.)

"Dat's right, I thought I'd try it today offin' de' end of de' causeway near de' channel. Dey was a bunch in dere' doin' de' tide change."

"That's my favorite fish, Rose. They aren't so fishy tasting and nice and tender even when they are big. Do you ever have them smoked?"

"Nahsuh, we ain't had em' dat way, but I heared day is good dat way."

Levy said little as he ate. I could tell that he was hungry because his serving of fish had disappeared long before we were halfway through ours but he started to work on the grits and greens so he was happy.

The rest of the meal was dispatched in silence, mostly, and Rose put fresh coffee on the table to have with dessert. Dessert at most homes would have been ice cream or some kind of cookies, maybe fruit, but these folks only had a small icebox to keep things cool not frozen. I imagine that the fish and butter that we put on the grits and cornbread were kept cool in there but not ice cream. Rose placed a cup of warmed syrup on the table along with some warmed cornbread. Levy was first and he buttered a piece and poured the syrup over it and we followed suit. That was a nice finish to a fine meal.

"Rose, you cook the same way and as good as my mom or maybe my mom cooks almost as good as you."

Her smile was as generous as she was and it showed her bright white teeth with a bright gold incisor in front. "Lawz, Mistah Bob, Ah knows you used to bettah things dan dis."

"Rose, I'm used to different things, maybe, but we were raised in the south and, honest, my mother cooks like this. We aren't rich and we are used to good home cooking, so that's why I enjoyed this dinner so much. It was perfect and I can see that you have totally spoiled Levy." She smiled and agreed with me. Levy looked down, mumbled and shuffled his feet in embarrassment. I know that he agreed too.

I told Rose and Levy of our life on the farm during the depression when our mother cooked on a much larger wood range like the one in their kitchen area. They listened intently as I described the vegetable garden and the chickens and their eggs that kept us alive for the first year.

This struck a sensitive spot with them and they listened intently as I described our life there.

"How did you come to be on that farm if'n you all weren't country people?" Levy asked. He was beginning to make eye contact with me since he was becoming involved in the subject of conversation.

I told them how dad was an architect in Washington, D.C. And lost everything in the depression and we had to move to the farm.

"Ah remembers dem's tahms when ah was a boy. Dey was be'fo' de woah an' dey was bad." Levy stared at the floor for a while and the conversation came to a slow halt.

"I've been here long enough and I should get home," I said as I got up. I thanked Rose and Levy for a nice dinner and a lovely evening. Everyone was tired and I had been there for several hours, but I felt that it was enjoyed by all of us. Certainly the meal was delightful for someone who had grown up with that kind of southern cooking and my "story telling" had given Rose and Levy a window to look into the lives of some other people. They couldn't read so their only contact with the outer world was by means of the spoken word, someone telling them their stories, contrived or not. It was their books, their films, and they relished it. I remembered as a child of seven on the farm telling the Russell family about the movie that I had seen and they listened raptly to every word and laughed at the funny things that sometimes I made up.

I thought that Levy and Rose had enjoyed the evening as much as I.

As I drove home, I thought about the Russell family and their close association with our family and the farm on which we lived during the depression. I remember seeing Mr. Russell coming up the road with his horses to ask mother if there was any work that he could do with his horses and plow. I don't know what transpired between our parents, but Mr. Russell did come back and plowed the field in front of the house and planted potatoes in it. Then he plowed the field south of the house and planted corn. I worried about one of his horses, the white and brown one named Zoots. He was hobbling and had enlarged joints in his legs, but he still worked as best he could. The other horse was black. His name was Snowball and soon he was doing most of the work because his partner was having too much pain to pull the plow.

I recall how it came about that the Russell family moved into the log cabin near the barn. They had been evicted from their place down near the river and Mr. Russell happened to mention it to mother one day. She told him that they could move into the old cabin and that they could help us in return. The Russells had a little grandson named Tommy who was my age and a daughter who was much older. I can't remember her name but it didn't matter, she was not as friendly as the rest and she had work somewhere else so we didn't see her very much.

The cabin had been built during the Civil War to house slaves, long before the farmhouse and it had been used recently to store empty liquor bottles during prohibition. For that matter, so had the house. Even the yard was full of empties when we arrived there and it took days to clean out the bottles alone. The cabin was a classic log structure with the typical locking logs, shingled roof, and crude translucent windows. The "floor" was smooth hard packed dirt, worn smooth and shiny by many bare feet. We had been told that it housed slaves seventy years before this black family occupied it. I could almost imagine seeing them gathered around the wide stone fireplace cooking or trying to keep warm in the winter. To the rear of the cabin a ladder made of skinned saplings gave access to the sleeping loft. When I visited the Russells I could see the hay-filled cotton bags that served as mattresses for Tommy and his sister and I didn't think anything about it since we played in the hayloft and that seemed comfortable enough.

Tommy and I spent a lot of time together working a little bit and playing a lot. We were close buddies, I ate lunch in the cabin with him and many times he ate with me in our kitchen. Mrs. Russell was in the house every day helping mom to clean and to cook and my fifteen-year old brother, Joe, worked with Mr. Russell sometimes to plow or to split wood. It was always busy during the summer but not too busy to go down to the creek with Tommy for a swim once in a while. It was a good life but I didn't realize it at the time. I did when it was time to go to school, though. Tommy couldn't go to the same school as I did. To this day I have no idea where he went or if he went to school. I have a hunch that he didn't attend school because there were no "black schools" nearby. Wintertime caused us to drift apart and we seldom saw each other during the week and even our Saturdays and Sundays were intermittent. Soon our relationship just died. However, the Russells continued to live in the cabin and were still a part of the farm until we left to go back to the suburbs of Washington, D.C.

I was invited to the Green's many times after that first dinner. I accepted the invitations, too, because I felt comfortable there and thoroughly enjoyed their hospitality. They wanted me to tell them more and more stories of what I had done in my life in areas unknown to them and activities that were foreign to their way of living. Again, their rapt attention was reminiscent of the Russells and they reveled in the stories. At work, Levy and I spent every lunch period studying maps and connecting our experiences to geographical entities. His concentration and memory was amazing, he absorbed knowledge like the proverbial sponge and thirsted for more every time we met.

"Dat farm you was on. Where's dat Murland place from here? I knows dat its nawth from here." I showed him on the map and he recorded it in a retrievable place in his memory. And so it went, every day he demanded a study session to learn more about places and things and after one explanation, he remembered it precisely. His quest for information was insatiable and he absorbed everything quickly and went on to something else. It was obvious that he was not the "dumb nigger" that almost anybody would call him then.

He was anything but dumb. He figured out many things that the crew did without crediting him for devising them. The adjustable forms for casting the concrete pilings, the method to get them winched out to the end of the dock, and measuring rods that we used to space the seawall pilings and dock pilings were his ideas, but they were accepted without rewarding him. I asked him one day if that bothered him. His answer, "Dats de way it is, Mistah Bob." That seemed to be his answer to everything.

"Levy, don't you get tired of people getting paid more than you do?"

"Dats de way it is."

I thought about that for a minute and considered some other inequities in his life.

"Doesn't upset you that you and Rose have to ride in the back of the bus or drink from a separate fountain?"

"Dats de way it is."

Again, we both knew that we had formed a bond of friendship and mutual trust and I asked him,

"Why can't you call me Bob instead of always Mistah Bob? I'm just Bob, Levy."

"Ah knows dat, but ah growed up for a long time doin' an' speakin' jes one way 'cause ah'd git whipped if'n ah showed disrespeck an ah cain't change ol' ways."

"We are friends, Levy, and I respect you as much as you respect me so we're even, okay? So I'm just Bob."

"Okay, Mistah Bob."

"You're not only big, but you are stubborn."

"Yasuh, Mistah Bob."

My next visit to Levy and Rose's was a pleasant surprise because all the lunch time lessons that we had done for the past month burst forth visually when I entered their home. The walls had maps tacked up like a grade school classroom and places were circled with names that Levy had penciled in himself, copying them from those printed on the map.

"Levy done that hiself," Rose said with a huge smile. "Ah sho proud of him an' so is he."

We studied them together in silence until Rose announced that dinner was ready. After dinner, we addressed the display and traced what he had done in identifying states and cities. He had done them correctly.

We went over the places that we had discussed and then I answered his questions about it, I showed him where I had been stationed when I was in the Air Force and that opened up a whole new vista for him to explore. The entire United States to the west was opened to him like those who did the same thing one hundred years before.

"Now how far is dat place? Is dat near Chas' ton? "And so on. Question after question. Intense concentration to file the information coming to him removed his presence from the others in the room and he was on a journey until we brought him back to reality and his little house in Sarasota when I announced that I had to leave.

"We'll go to some more places tomorrow, Levy." As said as I left.

"Yasuh, dat be fine."

On my way home, I felt that I had a tiger by the tail or a runaway boulder rolling down a mountainside with my friend Levy virtually inhaling everything that I could show him. Knowledge that was so basic to me, facts that I learned years ago in grade school were opening up a new world for someone who had lived all his life in a smothering closed circle of back-breaking work and neglect. His life. How old was he? I really had difficulty in figuring that one out. He didn't have any wrinkles, his body was a monumental display of physical perfection in spite of the disparity in size between his left side and his right, but when he took his hat off for dinner that first night, he was bald as a bowling ball. His age showed for the first time but I still couldn't nail it down. He couldn't either. When I asked him, he said that he didn't rightly know. "Ah's jes bone on a farm in South Cahlina some time back." Based on some of the things that he recalled, I figured that he would have to be near fifty years old. One thing that I could figure for certain was the cause of his atrophied left arm and leg. He admitted to having "the fevers" when he was a little boy, so his affliction was most certainly infantile paralysis, as it was called then. His "bad" limbs were still twice the size and strength of mine and only slowed him slightly in his work.

Work on the dock came to an end after several weeks and we started on another project in town, interfering with the school sessions because of the heat and strenuous nature of what we were doing. We still got together a few times for dinner but Levy seemed preoccupied and a little distant at times. He went back to sitting under a tree and gazing out at the world in deep thought. What a regal figure he was even at rest, back straight, chin up, his ancient fedora set low on his head, and he was mentally removed from the rest of us as he pondered his private mysteries. Rising to get back to work his movements were like those of a male lion; graceful, slow but with purpose and potentially powerful. He even had the patina of hard life that male lions usually displayed, instead of the dark marks of battle, his were white scars on dark flesh, medals bestowed by the work he had done for past masters. Masters? He was mastered by no one. Oh, he did what he was told or sometimes asked to do but he never relinquished that indefinable strength of character, that undefeatable spirit that always lay beneath the surface of his acquiescent demeanor. I asked him many times about his life of doing for others and being used. The answer was always the same.

"Dats de way it is, Mistah Bob."

His was a strength; not only of a physical nature, but one much deeper and more durable. He knew that he was somehow above his place in life, not better than others, but for some reason he had managed to accept his current existence with stoicism and knew that there was going to be something better. I could never see him as just another "big nigger" and I had a feeling that if he were back in his country of ancestral origin, he would be a tribal chief. Looking at him sitting under the tree, aloof, private, virtually imperturbable, and modest about it all, I knew that he was truly apart from his kind. Apart from me, too.

It was well into spring, the weather was warming to the point where the work was getting more physically demanding, and fatigue was cutting into my performance. I was forced to take more rest breaks at times and drinking water was crucial to keeping the body going. That, I learned in the service. This job was becoming a strain on my body and I began to realize that I really didn't have to do this kind of back- breaking labor. My enthusiasm had waned to the point of possibly quitting pretty soon. The white boy was getting "wore down."

I was still taking Levy home in the truck even though it meant driving into Newtown and back out to Siesta Key, I didn't mind because it gave some time to talk. He wasn't riding in the back in the box anymore. This day he wasn't saying much and appeared to be disturbed and tense. As we reached his house he turned and looked at me with a serious pall on his face (he had finally learned how to look at me eye-to-eye) and I didn't like the way his eyes looked this time.

"Mistah Bob, you cain't come into mah house no mo."

"Well, what did I do, Levy?" I couldn't believe that something had gone wrong with our friendship.

"Nothin you did Mistah Bob. Theys talk that ah's gittin to be a uppity niggah havin a white boy in mah house."

"I can understand that, I guess. You don't see that very often, but we are friends and we aren't doing anything wrong."

"Ah knows dat but they's talk at work and around and it has to be. Ah cain't see nobody gittin hurt on account of me an' you bein' too friendly so best you not come in no mo."

I was saddened but I probably shouldn't have been because I had sense enough to know how things were in the deep South. I agreed with him but I said that we would still talk at work if it was okay with him.

"Yasuh, I reckon so."

As I walked to the truck Levy said, "Mistah Bob, Rose an' me know who left dat ham on Easter day. Thank you an' thank yo' momma."

That did it. There was no need to stay with the Abbott Construction Company. I was tired and bored with the work and worst of all, I was causing a problem for my friend. Time to go.

Some of the whites on the crew had never been too friendly. And now Levy's neighbors had said some things to him and I figured that there would be some friction on the crew, also. It angered me that such an innocent friendship would cause such a dire and potentially dangerous situation for him. Levy was so obviously worried about something or somebody, so the next day I gave notice and removed myself from the mix.

I said a sad goodbye to Levy but he has never left my mind and after 70 years we visit every day.

Chapter 10.

Working at the airport.
Getting my flying license.

My flight instructors: Buck Criddlebaugh, Bob Ahern, Ed Denham,
Robert Parks | 1946

BACK TO THE SWEET SPOT AND A 4000 POUND LADY

I learned to fly, finally! I took flying lessons at Johnny Lowe's Field east of town. I soloed in a 1937 Piper Cub and received my Private Pilot's License in 1945 while flying a Cessna 120. I flew every chance I could when money was available. Sarasota Airbase was turned over to Sarasota County and it became Sarasota-Bradenton Airport sometime in 1946.

The long concrete runways and more advanced facilities attracted most of the pilots and their airplanes, but Johnny hung on, still giving flight lessons and was supported by old fans. I split my flying between Sarasota-Bradenton and Lowe's because there was just too much history there going back to when I was welcomed as a little kid 10 years earlier.

One day when I was shooting landings at the old short grass strip, I engaged in a conversation with and older visitor who told me about an elephant at the Ringling Brother's Circus training grounds, across the road from Johnny's field. The elephant would place her foot on your nose as you lay on the ground in front of her. Well. I had to check that one out.

I knew a lot of circus people since I went to school with one of the high wire performers who eventually ran away to escape the life of putting your life on the line. They had training equipment set up in their back yard and many times when I would go by the house, I could see the kids walking a high wire or working out on the trapeze. So, I went over to the training quarters where I met the elephant trainer and he did have a sweet little elephant named Minyak. And sure enough, she would gently place her foot on your nose as you lay on your back, face up.

A stinky dirty black foot but she wouldn't lower it any lower after it touched your nose. I gave her some fruit and a hug -- on her trunk. I'm sure glad that she liked me. Some of the lady high wire performers liked me too but have you ever seen the biceps and shoulders on those women?

I soloed at Johnny Lowe's in an old Cub that had no brakes and a spring leaf tailskid, no radio and operated off the grass. I trained with a basic down to the minimums machine that had no more amenities than a WW1 airplane. Landing and taxiing required some planning if you didn't want to hit the hangar, especially if you were taxiing in a downwind. I got my first hours out there but did my training at Sarasota Airport in Cessna 120' and 140's.

My instructor, Bob Ahern, was excellent and used a Socratic technique in his lessons. You were not just told that "such and so" would happen if you did or didn't do something correctly. He would work you into a situation and let you come close to disaster and then get you out of it all the while explaining what you did wrong. The examples were set in my mind like concrete after the "awakening".

My first flight with him in the Cub was certainly a wakeup call. As soon as we were at a safe altitude, he did a loop and asked if I liked it. With a positive answer from the student he forged ahead with a strenuous routine after that. I took it that if the student didn't like the loop he would start out with an easier routine. A future student, who went to school with me, a pretty little blonde girl, loved the loops when she took lessons from Bob. She was such a good student that they were married soon after she soloed.

The training in the Cub included a variety of stalls, steep turns and accuracy landings. One interesting lesson in the Cub came just before I soloed. We were on the downwind and coming up on the turn to the base leg when he took the airplane and asked, "Does it look like we have enough airspeed for our turn onto base?" I answered that it looked like we were scooting right along. He then made a steep turn to enter the base leg and the airplane stalled and entered a spin. Briefly, I could see the pointy ends of the trees spinning around and getting damn close. It made one turn and he pulled it out nicely and as he did so he said," Now that is how many students kill themselves by looking at the ground instead of the airspeed indicator!" We then made a nice flat turn to base and landed whereupon I got a talk about relative airspeed.

After soloing and getting checked out in the Cessna 120 and 140, I started getting the dual to prepare for my private license. Rectangular patterns in a crosswind, 720's left and right without loss of altitude, spins left and right with precision recovery on a point, deep "rudder exercise stalls", falling leaf, pylon eights, eights on pylon, rolling on a point and accuracy landings. Then a dual cross country and a solo cross country.

The rudder exercise stalls were one of the more difficult maneuvers to learn the use of the rudder when the airplane was near or in a stall. The procedure was to leave cruise power on the airplane, pull the stick all the way back into the gut, let it stall. Walk the nose down in a straight line, keeping it from falling off on a wing with the rudder, the only effective control left. If you failed to catch it quick enough, it quickly broke into a spin. After all, you had the stick all the way back and the airplane was stalled.

My instructor wanted five full stalls in a row without falling off. Mistakes produced a spin many times and spins became an inconvenience at times but I had fun doing them. I soon got to the point where I did stall after stall without a spin. These exercises gave the pilot a good feel for the airplane and quick and effective rudder control.

My solo cross-country consisted of three legs of one hundred miles in length. I had planned to go from Sarasota to Ft. Meyers, then to Plant City and west to Drew Field, Tampa and back to Sarasota. The first leg to Ft. Meyers was easy with plenty of landmarks. But the leg north to Plant City traveled over terrain that had features like millions of trees, uncounted acres of grass, thousands of lakes and swamps, no structures, no roads, and a bunch of alligators and bad snakes. Climbing away from Ft. Meyers, I soon noticed the compass deviations and swings so I wasn't totally sure that I was on the heading that I had laid out on the sectional. Check marks every ten miles are great if you have something to check on the ground other than swamp grass and trees.

Okay, we'll keep on an estimated heading and hope for the best. Oh, is that a thunderhead up ahead? I believe it is, right on my course. Okay, I will have to exercise the storm avoidance course deviation that I learned. A 45-degree turn to the left and time it, then a 90-degree turn to the right and time it, then a 45-degree turn to the left and go on my way. Simple. I droned on for an hour and failed to pick up the landmarks that I was supposed to, but I did find a small road wandering off into the haze. Hmm. Time to make a course change to see if I can find a big road, one with a big town on it. Nothing. So I turned to a heading of 270 and waited to see what I could see and soon a town appeared on my left. I could recognize it from the sectional as Plant City. From then on it was a piece of cake: Tampa and Drew Field, then a run south over Tampa Bay to Sarasota. My landing at Drew Field didn't go unnoticed to me that one year earlier it was the Air Force base from which I was discharged.

My check ride for my private pilot's license came soon thereafter and I was run through all the requirements that my instructor trained me for, except for a thunder storm at the far end of the active runway that put me in a bit of a sticky wicket on my last accuracy landing. On short final we got an extreme 180-degree wind shift and I felt the bottom drop out just as I was preparing to flare. The airplane stalled and I had to walk it down with rudder. We hit in a semi three-point attitude with the sound of a tin garbage can falling off the back end of a truck.

The airplane veered to the right onto the grass shoulder but under control and I straightened it out. Damn! I thought. There goes my entire check ride. Not a word from the examiner except one brief, "You should have stayed on the runway." Runway? I thought that I was lucky to get it on the ground right side up.

We taxied in under a torrential downpour typical of a Florida summer and ran into the office where he filled out a bunch of paperwork and much to my surprise handed me my temporary private license. My instructor mentioned several weeks later that the examiner told him that I did a damn good job of getting the airplane down.

It always amazed me that during that desperate landing he sat there with his arms folded. He was one cool guy and he did the same thing when he pulled the throttle back for a forced landing in the middle of a pylon-eight when I was coming out of one of the eights.

I had to kick left rudder to get lined up with the rows in the stubble field that I had picked before the maneuver and then pop it into a hard left slip with right aileron to get it down to the end of the field. With the airplane low enough, I straightened out and fully expected the tail wheel to clip the barbed wire fence as we scooted over it. I was coming back on the wheel to flare because we were that low and the examiner reached over and slowly opened the throttle to climb power and we climbed away.

He gave me a "forced landing" on takeoff, and to make it more interesting I had to do a 2½ turn spin with recovery on a predetermined point, not the three turn spin. He was very certain that I hit the prop wash from my previous turns in the 720's. It was a sweaty day but I was signed off for my Private Pilot's Certificate.

Chapter 11.

A stormy boat adventure on Tampa Bay.

ABOUT BOATS AND WATER

I had met an attractive young lady who knew a boy who was the son of a mullet fisherman and one weekend he asked me if I would help him move a boat. Move a boat? Move it where? I had told him about my experiences with the fishermen before the war and he thought that I was handy to help him tow a fishing boat to St. Petersburg. His father had sold it to another fisherman at the north shore of Tampa Bay and it required a helmsman and someone to assist in the tow. That sounded like a lot of fun and I agreed to help tow the boat to its new owner in a bayou up there. Our destination was more than 60 miles north and without any problem, it would be a long day. That was wishful thinking.

I arrived at Danny's dock at 5:00 a.m. on a clear cool Saturday morning with a bag of food and a light jacket. He had already warmed up the engine so we pushed off and fastened a line to the second boat and worked our way down to Sarasota Bay in the pink dawn light. I steered the boat that we were towing, making sure that it cleared the narrow confines of the waterway and then got on board with Danny to work our way up the bay to the north. He was an experienced boatman since he had fished with his father from an early age and he showed it as he worked his way through the pilings under the causeway that connected Siesta key and Longboat Key to the mainland. Then the throttle was opened and we began to cruise at a good speed, at least 12 mph. The trailing boat was behaving itself and didn't show any sign of deviating from our course but the water was calm at the time so we charged ahead with our journey.

As we passed the town we could see a few lights of vehicles

moving about, milk trucks, garbage trucks, newspaper delivery boys, and the early risers who had to open their businesses. I looked up Main Street and recalled with humor the incident when I was helping my football teammate, Cy, deliver milk one morning. We were leaving steel baskets full of milk bottles at the rear of restaurants when Cy screamed," Oh shit!", and I heard him scrambling up on garbage can lids amid hissing and thumping somewhere on the other side of the fence that separated us.

"What is it?" I yelled.

"There's a damn alligator back here!"

I looked over the fence into the little courtyard behind the restaurant and sure enough, there was enough light to see an eight-footer guarding the back of the restaurant. An eight foot-alligator is quick as lightning, has a head full of teeth, and is ugly when cornered, so Cy was lucky to have spotted it in time to climb up on the fence. We let the police deal with it and gloated over the fact that this was one incident for which we wouldn't be blamed. But it did give us some ideas.

It wasn't impossible for a 'gator to take an excursion to better eating places, the bay was only two blocks away and there were plenty of creeks and bayous for them to live in but it was a bold and hungry animal to come up Main Street as far as it did. It made the Herald Tribune if I remember correctly and it was the only time that an alligator was a customer at that fine establishment.

Danny got the boat up to a steady plane and we cruised up the bay past Sarasota-Bradenton Airport, a new name now since it was turned over to the county for civilian operation after the war. Just one year before it was Sarasota Airbase and at this time of the morning we would have heard the growl of P-51's warming up to begin their day of training. Now there was probably a light plane warming up for a student learning to fly on the G.I. Bill.

On we went at an easy clip and our estimated time of arrival in Old Tampa Bay looked possible. We passed Anna Maria key at 0730 and headed into Tampa Bay on a northeasterly heading until we picked up the shoreline of St. Pete in the distance on our left some two hours later. We shed our sweatshirts as the morning sun got higher and warmer. We made our way onto the vast glassy surface of the bay. Off to the right in the blue haze we could see a couple of cargo vessels making their way to Tampa and I recalled a poem about "the painted ship on a painted ocean". That's all that I could remember at the time. We were getting into the shallows so we decided that I should go back to the towed boat and stand by to steer in case we had to dodge a sand bar or something.

That "something" happened no sooner than I had settled at the helm and Danny got under way again. His boat suddenly looked like it was going to fly the rest of the way to our destination as it rose out of the water in a shower of spray. Danny was thrown violently to one side as his boat rolled on its beam ends.

"What the hell was that?" I yelled.

My question was answered when the wing tips and the body of a huge Manta Ray broke the surface in its frantic effort to escape, flapping and thrashing to leave us. We watched in silence as it left a swirling wake in its run to deeper water.

"Man! That has never happened to me before." Danny yelled back

"Me neither. It must have been asleep or eating something. Any leaks?"

"No, we're okay, just banged up some."

We gathered our wits, got the boats going again and started out across the bay in the sultry heat of the afternoon. By one o'clock we neared the place where Danny had to locate the bayou to deliver the boat. It wasn't like finding a street address because of all the little creeks and inlets that confronted us but after an hour of searching, we finally found the correct bayou and delivered the boat. Since time was becoming a problem we declined the offer of lunch and headed out of the bayou for the trip home. We had a little bit of food left so we figured that we would be okay.

Little did we know.

By two o'clock the weather began to change. There was a little breeze at first that generated a nice chop. The boat seemed to enjoy it but an hour later, we ran into a stiff wind and some serious quartering waves. Danny reduced power to minimize the impact with the waves that were beginning to break over the starboard bow as we were getting drenched and cold. Our progress was substantially less than we had planned and by the time we were in the middle of Tampa Bay the sky had darkened and the wind was howling. The stinging rain added more to our misery and the long range view of the horizon was shortened to just concentrating on the next wave that not only threatened our progress but our survival as well. One after the other crashed over the bow and exploded over us with water that began to collect in the bilge. The diving rolls that the boat was taking demanded considerable physical exertion to stay attached to something. We were getting concerned about the amount of water that we were taking on because these boats weren't designed for rampaging seas. They were open from stem to stern and the only bilge pump was a hand-operated device with a plunger that was used to remove modest amounts of water from loading fish. It was nowhere near what we needed but I tried to use it even as we were being thrashed about.

The storm appeared to be reaching a crescendo and Danny yelled that he was going to head directly into the waves and head for deeper water where the waves were less steep and spread out. Good thinking because we could see the bottom sometimes when we were diving down into a trough. It worked but we had no more than reached our goal when the engine quit.

"Take the helm!" Danny yelled. I scrambled forward and took the little wheel that was mounted on the bulkhead aft of the forward decking.

"Keep it dead on into the waves," he yelled as he rushed back to the engine box that had been knocked askew.

"The plugs are wet and shorted-out. See if you can find some rags in the forward locker."

I found some dry rags and managed to get them back to him without their getting wet. He crouched over the engine to try to shield it from the spray with his body while he frantically worked on the spark plugs. This went on for what seemed like an hour but he eventually got the job done and replaced the engine box over the engine.

He pushed the starter button and the response was   silence.

"Either a dead battery or a dead starter or both. See if you can find a pipe wrench up there."

A pipe wrench! Okay, you know what you're doing, I thought as I handed him the wrench. What the heck is he going to do? Whack the engine back to life. Danny immediately tore off the cover over the propeller shaft aft of the reversing gearbox and started to crank the shaft with the pipe wrench. I thought for a second that if he was cranking with the jaws of the wrench in the wrong direction, it wouldn't release when and if the engine started. It would then be turned into a heavy whirling club that would try to beat its way out through the bottom of the boat with obvious results.

He cranked frantically as fast as he could trying to get the engine to catch. I kept the boat heading into the waves as best I could but I was frantically looking over my shoulder at the rocky shoreline that was getting nearer by the minute. Neither of us said anything as we worked and worried our way through our mounting disaster that could give us, at the least, a long cold swim. At the worst it could end things for us right here.

Our fears were at their zenith when, after a shot of starter fluid, the engine POPPED! Danny accelerated his cranking and set the choke a bit richer and finally we heard the sweetest sound in the world! After a hearty barf of flame out of the exhaust stack, the engine caught and produced a healthy bellow, but best thing of all, the wrench slipped free of the shaft as the engine came up to speed.

Danny slowed the rpm some so that it could warm up and, then put in gear and we slowly made our way out into deep water again. I stayed at the helm while Danny tied the engine box down and tried to catch his breath. He didn't rest very long.

"What the hell!" he yelled as he looked back at the box. I turned to see a spray of water shooting up from behind the engine box and immediately froze with fear that a hole had opened up in the bottom of the boat. Here we were in the middle of Tampa Bay and the boat had split open.

Danny rushed back to the site of the spray with the rags to try to plug the leak. All I could see was his rear end as he crouched down to do whatever he could to stem the flow but he soon popped up with a grin on his face.

'What the hell are you grinning about?" I asked.

"No leak! It's the starter gear teeth on the flywheel shooting water up from the bilge. I forgot to put the floorboards down after starting the engine. Keep going."

As we made our way out into the channel, we started giggling and ended up laughing our way almost into silliness. It was the kind of laugh that tension produces -- the kind of laugh that is a tenth of an inch from crying but we laughed until our bellies hurt. Danny then attacked the bilge water with the pump but gained little. The flywheel may have done more than he did.

As we reached the middle of the bay I gradually turned south again to head for the mouth of Sarasota Bay with the hope that it would be more sheltered from the waves that had such a long fetch in Tampa Bay. Our hopes came true as the squall abated somewhat as evening approached. Our course down the bay positioned once again to take the waves on the starboard side and we slowly proceeded south in a drunken sailor's gait. Rolling-to-port climbing the wave, then rolling-to- starboard on the slide down into the trough with a thump with more spray breaking over the bow. We were in control now and modulated our speed and maneuvered the boat to work the swells instead of bashing into them.

As we cruised along, shivering in our wet clothes, I thought about the change from the glassy windless journey north, baking in the sun and running free. Now, we were wet, cold, and shivering uncontrollably as it got dark. We brought some sweatshirts with us but they were wet and cold as we were so we alternated huddling near the engine exhaust pipe to absorb a little heat, and that is exactly what is was, VERY LITTLE HEAT, but enough to keep us going. The boat was running perfectly and the waves were subsiding along with the light as we entered the Sarasota Bay. Rough water still slowed our progress and we ran at half speed while both of us fought to navigate through the sparse channel markers while we watched the lights on shore. We still had 40 miles to go and we were miserably cold, tired, and hungry. We were beat up, too. Both of us had bleeding shins and arms, bruised legs and cut up hands from the rough treatment of the storm. BUT, we had beaten the threat that could have ended everything for us.

It was totally dark now. All that we could see were the lights in the distance and the foam of the waves breaking near us.

"Okay, I can make out the lights near Little Manatee and we ought to see some glow from Bradenton soon." Danny said after a long cold silence. He was more familiar with this part of the bay than I was and totally competent in nighttime navigation. I put my trust in him and tried to recognize things as he did but I was outgunned this time, a lost Boy Scout. Our speed down the narrow waterway between Anna Maria Key and the mainland increased as the effects of the squall diminished to the point of almost calm sometime around 9:00 PM, but we were still very tired and cold. Hunger took the back seat to our misery and all we could do now was to visit the exhaust pipe often as we could.

"See that glow up ahead? Sarasota" Danny stuttered.

"Good! It's after 10:00 o'clock and I'm freezing to death!"

We cruised in silence after that and we pushed the boat as fast as we thought it could go in the remaining chop and pretty soon we were negotiating the passages under the causeways crossing Sarasota Bay and headed for Philippi Bayou, the entrance of which was known only to my companion at the helm.

Sure enough, he somehow found the entrance and we crept into the waterway and finally pulled up to the dock at his home. We found that it was difficult to move about as we should have in docking and tying down the boat. We made mistakes that caused other mistakes but we finally got everything accomplished like responsible sailors and staggered up the dock to Danny's home.

When we shuffled into the kitchen, Danny's mother already had blankets waiting to throw over us and his father was standing before us with a very serious look on his face.

"The boat's okay, dad. Got beat up a bit but it's okay. I think the starter went out when the engine got drowned by a wave and we had a little trouble getting it going again. The money is on the table in the pouch." Danny quickly reported to his father as he sat shivering under the blanket. I said nothing while Danny's parents listened to their son with obvious relief as he told them about our struggles in the storm.

"Yeah, we heard about that squall an' we figured you was gonna' be in it but it was worse than we figured."

"I never saw one come up so fast. It was dead calm when we went up and then all hell broke loose around noon."

MAGGIE AND HER TOUCH

"You boys get out of those wet clothes and get in the tub. I started fillin' it when I heard the boat go into reverse an' I figured that you was gonna' be cold an' wet. You go first, son, we only got one tub an' you are the guest so you get it first." She ordered me with a firm but friendly voice. I obeyed. After a short and life-giving soak I turned the tub over to Danny and found some dry and warm clothes on the chair outside of the bathroom. Something else was waiting for me that made me forget how cold I was and it greeted me as I made my way into the kitchen … food. I could smell something delicious ahead of me and I wasted no time finding the source.

"You set down, I have some ham, eggs, an' grits for you." Mrs. McCann said.

"You get that blanket around you while I get you some coffee."

"I have something better," Mr. McCann said as he shoved a tin cup in front of me and put one on the other side of the table. They were half full of brandy and I didn't dare refuse this man's firm but kind offering. Danny did the same thing when emerged from his bath. Then we honored Mrs. McCann by rapidly consuming her late night snack that kept coming as long as we ate it.

It was well after midnight when we arrived but Maggie and Big Danny sat with us and listened to our story while we refueled ourselves with food and warmth. It wasn't long before we were sagging in our chairs and sometime around 1:30 AM, Danny's mother escorted us to our cozy beds and we quickly disappeared from the world.

The next morning I woke to the smell of cooking again that urged me out of bed to see what Danny's mom was cooking for us. Jumping out of bed was something that little kids do. I realized that I was stiff and sore from the beating that we took in the boat and I had some ugly abrasions and bruises. But that didn't slow me down from getting into the kitchen. Danny's mother was at the stove pouring a cup of coffee for us and I sat for a minute at the kitchen table trying to wake up. She sat with me with her coffee while the pancakes were cooking and it gave me the opportunity to see what a beautiful woman she was. The night before was so occupied with getting our brains and bodies back to normal operating temperature that things didn't fully register as they should have.

MAGGIE

Maggie McCann could have been on the cover of Vogue Magazine when she was 19 or 20, I'm sure. She was a slender woman who was just shy of being thin and probably would have been if she hadn't had a life of activity and hard work. But that in its self, had dressed her in a patina associated with a healthy but stressful life. Her hands were those of all others who toiled in the fishing trade: tan on top and the white palms like sandpaper. Calloused from simple and hard manual labor, not housework but man's work. Her arms were tan and muscular with scars here and there but still feminine and graceful. Unlike most women of the time, she didn't wear the inevitable cotton dress. She wore faded jeans that did nothing to hide her lovely figure. Her feet were bare and, like her hands, tan on top with bleached white soles.

She moved with sinuous purpose: direct and smooth, with nothing wasted. She was taught in the way she did things, leaving no chance for a sloppy mistake. Her white broadcloth shirt appeared to be a hand-me-down from her son or her husband because it was slightly large and a little bit threadbare. It was bright and clean, however, and accentuated her blazing auburn hair that was loose about her shoulders this morning. The night before, it had been pulled back and tied with a cloth but now it fell in waves of deep red streaked with grey. "Crow's Feet" radiated from the corners of her green eyes and there were some wrinkles in her brow that told of some worries but she wore it all very well. Her nose was a classic straight, sharp, and properly proportioned feature that so many movie stars wished that they had. She was in her mid-forty's and lived a harsh life but she remained a remarkably pretty woman.

She seemed out of place to me but at the same time, she was the perfect wife and mother to the men in her life. She wore the signs of hard work that came with it and she shared her part of it without fanfare. We sat at the small kitchen table and sipped coffee while the sausage cooked and I realized that Danny was absent.

"I should kick Danny out of bed to have breakfast with us," I said.

"Oh, Danny was up an hour ago, he and his dad went down to the boat and took the starter off and then went to town for another one and a few supplies."

"Well, I feel guilty that I didn't wake up to help them."

"Now how is three of you gonna' fit in the bilge of that boat to git' one starter out!"

"Well, I feel that I should help instead of sleeping all morning."

"You helped plenty yesterday. Big Danny and I are grateful that you were with Danny 'cause he wouldn't be here now. That boat needed two people to git' outa' that squall. He told us about it this mornin' an' we're jes' glad he had help."

"I just did what he told me to do, nothing great about that."

"Maybe not to you but it is to us." She glanced at me with a look of stress in her face.

"Danny is pretty important to us now since we lost Jake in the war.

"Jake?"

"He was our oldest boy."

"I didn't know that he had a brother, I'm sorry about that."

"Yes, he has a sister, too but she lives in Jacksonville with her new husband. She run off at seventeen and got married last year."

Maggie looked down at the table with a smile and thought for a moment.

"Jes' like her momma done."

"You got married at seventeen!" I asked.

"Lordy, yes. Me an' Big Danny run off and got hitched when he was nineteen and I was seventeen an' we didn't know how to come in outa' the rain but we took off an' managed to survive doin' all kinds of work. But we did it. Then Jake come along in 1925 and Jess come along in 1930 an' the only one with us now is Little Danny. His sister an' her husband are doin' good up there in Jacksonville with him working as a' auto mechanic. He's makin' almost 80 cents an hour."

Maggie acted as if she had to purge herself of everything as she exposed the facts about her family, somewhat painfully at times.

"So, Little Danny an' me have to work the boat now with Big Danny." She looked out at the bayou and the boat that was now safely docked and I could see the concern in her face and eyes. I knew why her hands and arms were so scarred and at the same time so sinuous and strong. Pulling in the nets after a strike was physically demanding and at times dangerous when saltwater catfish and rays were caught with the fish. For that matter, working the nets could be hazardous without the addition of nasty sea creatures. It was easy to see why Maggie was in such athletic condition; she was doing man's work as well as caring for the home and her men. It was obvious that she was doing a good job of it but the demands were making their mark on what was once a beautiful young lady. She was still an attractive woman but her youth and beauty were being robbed from her at a rapid rate.

"Lordy, I shouldn't be going on like this! I don't know what come over me. I guess it's nice to have somebody to talk to about somethin' besides fishin'."

She chuckled and looked out to the yard again.

"Big Danny is buildin' another boat to replace the one you boys was in yesterday. That's why we sold the other one so's we could git' a better one goin' for us. I tried to talk Big Danny inta' keepin' that one we sold but he's bound to build another one fer some reason. I'm guessin' that he has some new ideas about it so…"

"He does about everything, doesn't he, the boats, the house. What else does he do?"

"Oh yes, he can do anything 'cept making money right now. I shouldn't have said that in that way, Lord knows he's tryin' but…"

Before I could answer, the sound of a car pulling into the yard broke her confessional. I quickly downed the rest of my breakfast and followed her through the back door to greet Big Danny and Little Danny on their return from the auto shop. Big Danny had the new starter in his hand and purposefully made his way to the boat.

"Maggie, I could use a cup of coffee if there is any left," Big Danny said without looking back. Maggie returned to the house to make a fresh pot while I stayed with Danny and his father who quickly replaced the starter and tested it successfully.

"Looks like we can fish in the mornin' but there's a split in one of the planks that we'll have to watch. The boat got a good beating but it'll do for a spell 'till we get the new one in the water." Big Danny looked at his boat and turned to me and said," You can go fishing with us."

Young as I was, I understood this taciturn man's mannerism as a "thank you" and an invitation to go with them any time I chose to do so. He was no different than the other fishermen with whom I had gone out when I was younger. For them, putting a long string of words together was a waste of time and energy.

"Thanks Mr. McCann, I'll try to make it back soon and thanks for your hospitality." He nodded a response as I went to the house to thank Maggie. Little Danny waved as drove away from their small home and past the new boat sitting on the temporary "launching way" so that it could be slid into the bayou when it was finished. The frames were all in place on the keel, supported by braces and boards that were nailed to large pegs that were driven deep into the sand. A taught wire stretched from the stem at the bow to the center of the transom at the stern. Plumb bobs, a level, and a yardstick completed the array of alignment tools. Block plane, hand saw, brace and bit, and a 24-ounce hammer completed the equipment. Every fisherman with whom I was associated built their own boats this way and I never saw one that wasn't a handsome piece of work.

I thought of the Blounts and how much I enjoyed going out with them in their 26 footers before the war but some of the "hands" that worked on the boats had personal histories that weren't disclosed or discussed. The work was hard, injurious, and sometimes very dangerous. You never knew what was in the catch sometimes, stingrays, barracuda, and sharks, occasionally. For a moment, I went back to the last time I worked freeing the lead line inside the net when we had a big catch. I came up for air and heard someone yelling SHARK! I must have made the water boil with the speed that I made getting over the cork line to the free side and sure enough in the boiling thrash of fish I could see a fin. It turned out to be a Bull Shark, one of the most dangerous sharks that you could encounter.

Getting it separated from the catch wasn't much fun because it was still dangerous even out of the water and tried to bite anyone who came close. After a quick photo, it was dispatched by captain Blount.

I never went fishing with Danny and I never visited Maggie and Big Danny again. It wasn't that I didn't want to, I did very much, but I had a feeling that I could have been swept into a whirlpool from which I couldn't escape. The adventure and working in the open air was inviting but dead-ended and not quite inviting as the sweet song of the Lady Siren In The Sky who was calling me.

I had to go flying.

Bull Shark in the Catch

Chapter 12.

Hollywood at the airport.
A swim with a mermaid.
A chat with a movie stunt pilot.

A KID IN A CANDY STORE

In 1946, the airport was filling with all sorts of airplanes that were being purchased from military surplus as well as a lot of new stuff: Aeronca Champs, Cessna 120's, 140's, then Cessna 170's, Stinson 108's, Fairchild 24's with the Ranger engine or Warner, the new Luscombe 8F and fancy new Cubs with brakes and tail wheels. Exciting as they were, my interest went to the war surplus trainers, the Stearman PT-13, Fairchild PT-19 and PT-23, but they would have to wait until I returned from a year in college.

The next summer was even better with more airplanes showing up, some old and some new. I was hired as a flight line jockey and general maintenance worker so I was at the airport 10 hours a day servicing airplanes and flying after work and sometimes before work. The rich had arrived during the winter and the hangar was full of big stuff, DC-3's, Lodestars, some more PT-19's, Ercoupes, many Pipers and some old Stinsons.

In mid-summer a well to do hot-talking real estate broker bought a new Bellanca Cruisair, a "cardboard Connie", a slick and beautiful little fabric covered four-seater that was faster than anything on the airport. I worked with the mechanic to increase the cruise speed by removing propeller weights on the Aeromatic prop and we got a cruise speed at sea level of 155 indicated. Several months later the owner stalled it while approaching the field and totaled it. How do you do that!

There were two PT-19's owned by the manufacturer of business machines that he hangared with his DC-3. His son liked to try to fly them and by the end of the summer, both had been ground looped -- on takeoff. They were ugly anyway, painted black and dark red, maybe like his business machines.

I was too young and myopic to see the rapid influx of the rich and well endowed who planted their airplanes at Sarasota. I was just enthralled that I could fly a lot of airplanes if and when I wanted to, money permitting, and sometimes I was able to benefit from the generosity of the owners who allowed me to fly their machines if I put gas into them. I quickly got checked out in the PT-13, PT-17, PT-19, PT-22, PT-23 and a Brunner-Winkle Bird that had been pulled out of the rafters somewhere and brought to the field. It was a pretty old thing, painted cream with red trim and powered by a 125 Kinner. It was doughty looking, though. The finish was dull and the trailing edges didn't run straight, but I got the chance to fly it and I took it.

The first thing I noticed was the top-heaviness of the big thick top wing and the tendency to waddle and wander when it was taxied. I learned that that was typical of the older planes and one had to stay on the rudder and stay wake. In the air it was not something to love. It flew like a hunting dog trots, a little bit sideways and you had to keep the stick a bit into the left corner. I thought it was best to make a circuit and land because it felt a little rubbery in the air.

A few days later, another guy ground-looped it and chewed up the right wing tip and the "wood" that poured out of the torn fabric had the consistency of a soda cracker. It disappeared into somebody's shop or garage and we never saw it again. The Bird wasn't the only antique that popped up.

A Rearwin Sportster arrived from someone's garage and we got to fly that. I thought it was interesting but heavy on the controls and just plain heavy with its 90HP LaBlond engine. So, up to that time I had flown a 55HP 1937 Cub, a 40HP Taylorcraft, an Aeronca 7AC, Fairchild 24, PT-19, PT-13, PT-17, PT-23, a Rearwin, a Globe Swift, Cessna 120, Cessna 140, a Bird, a Stinson 108, a Piper PA-11, PA-15 and had some stick time in a BT-13 and a Cessna Bobcat.

It was a time that will never be repeated. The post war euphoria and the release of the war load opened a period of freedom and sometimes we escaped the scrutiny of the CAA. That really wasn't in its all-encompassing operation yet. The heavy hand of officialdom had not yet completely throttled the free spirits that abounded at this civilian airfield. Aviation sort of sang its own tune for a year or two. Many times we simply did things without fear of dire consequences as the old stuff briefly tried to assume its old place again but was soon replaced by all the newer airplanes.

Many of the fields lacked radio communications so we relied on lights and pattern etiquette with very few incidents. There were few restrictions or special notes or instructions on the sectionals in our area then and we flew from place to place with a comparative freedom. Many times I would take one of the new Cubs up to an area east of the field and dogfight with the big turkey buzzards. The only thing that could out turn one of those big black birds was another big black bird that didn't spin out of a tight turn.

Buzzing the cows in the dry lakes was fun in the dry season and so was running down a beach at wave top height -- except when the surf was up. I got a quick lesson that the rollers coming in on a rough day produced some rollers in the air over the beach. I was having a fun day in a PT-19 when I was low enough to smell the salt spray and it was like something grabbed the right wing and almost pulled it down into the surf. The short rough ride over what seemed like a cobblestone road, some wrestling and a climb away from the rollers, as they say, got my attention.

Pilots coming through on cross-country's, brought some interesting machines in for fuel. We welcomed a beautiful little Luscombe Phantom one day and some older Stinsons and a smattering of Waco's at times, the designations of which escaped me then as they do now. We were impressed by several new airplanes that were flown in by company demonstrator pilots. The first Beechcraft Bonanza was one of the first and what an exciting airplane that was with its all aluminum construction, modern design, tri-cycle landing gear and the exotic Vee tail. It was fast, too, and could fly as high as its price: seven thousand five hundred dollars!

Shortly thereafter, another racy looking aircraft arrived that had a most bizarre appearance. It too had a tri-cycle landing gear but it was constructed of a combination of steel tube, wood, and fabric and had an odd seating arrangement with the pilot front and center and only two passengers in the back. It was very fast but, obviously, the Johnson Rocket didn't seem to make sense to anyone.

One interesting transient was a man who taxied to the tie downs and had his Cessna 170 secured before I could get there. He went to the baggage compartment and removed a small sketch board and a small bag. Having an interest in art, I asked him about the board and he told me that he was a cartoonist that did a strip called "Smilin' Jack". He said that his name was Zack Mosely and when I looked at the number on his airplane I got a glimpse at his ego, NC 11111. He was a nice guy, though, and I got a nice tip when I refueled his airplane.

After the summer of 1947 I went back to school and while I was there I met an ex-Eagle Squadron pilot who owned a PT-13 and I flew with him several times in the winter, but it wasn't much fun when the clothes that I had were no match for the icy blow torches of air that found their way through any seam in my apparel. Things got better, however, when he purchased a beautiful little Culver Cadet and we flew it many times. "Just like a little 'Spit", he said when referring to its handling.

Well, I had to agree; after all, I had thousands of hours in a Spitfire -- in my dreams. It was a wonderful little airplane to fly, however, quick and smooth and we had many nice flights in it. One of the less than nice flights occurred on one Saturday afternoon late when we were preparing to land at Raleigh-Durham and the landing gear lock mechanism failed to lock. We circled the airport with darkness approaching frantically trying to get the gear to lock and when Stan decided that we were going to have to belly it in, we finally got the lock plate to line up and made a safe landing in almost darkness.

I flew some Cubs and Champs out of the little airport there in Durham and buzzed the Duke campus once, but I realized what a neophyte and a nothing- pilot I was when two of my fraternity brothers came visiting one afternoon in an F6F and F4F and tore the place up. Duke is laid out as a classic English university in the form of a cross. East-west Avenue of the quadrangle terminates at the beautiful church patterned after the Canterbury Cathedral. The north-south leg has lower buildings that house some of the classes and dorms.

These navy pilots came in from the north and had their airplanes down in the north-south leg below the trees and made a pull up at the south end with feet to spare. No one knew they were coming and I just happened to look in the right direction and picked them up as they started their pass. Great stuff!

1948 - EXCITING THINGS AND PEOPLE

The airport manager was kind enough to give me another summer job at Sarasota-Bradenton and I put my third year of school behind me. The almost frantic influx of people into the town and flyers and airplanes at the airport startled me when I returned. The flight line was almost full, several new flight schools had started operation and there were many struggling businesses that had rented the ex-military buildings.

My job had expanded also from airplane stuff to help with the maintenance of the grounds and buildings so that meant mowing the tall grass that rapidly grew in any area not traveled. There was a marshy area in the southwestern area in the intersection of the main runways and I had the job of mowing it with a tractor towing an eight-foot sickle bar cutter. If the bar hit something that it couldn't cut, like a stump or rock, a breakaway cam would allow it to snap back.

THE BAG OF BONES

Mowing the tall cattails and saw grass was slow in that area and I hit something that popped the bar back and I had to dismount from the tractor to examine the obstacle. One had to be cautious in the grass because of large rattlesnakes that thrived on the rats and rabbits that lived there and they didn't like to be disturbed.

I found the obstruction to be a tangled mass of half buried aluminum wreckage. It was so extensive that I couldn't mow around it so I had to get some help to dig it out. It was deeply imbedded in the sand and most of it was fairly large with long pieces and after looking the debris we determined that it was part of a P-51. It was more debris to add to the pile that we had collected from wrecks on the field. In the bottom of the hole, peeking out of the sand, was some silvery gray cloth with heavy cords wrapped around it.

We dug it out and after opening the large silken bundle, we were dismayed to see that the contents were some of the broken bones of what was left of the pilot, wrapped in his parachute and buried there.

As we reburied the remains I recalled seeing the crash of a P-51 that spun in four years before and hit in this area of the field.

HOLLYWOOD!

In mid-summer, we were told that a movie was going to be filmed here on the field and that we were going to support the aircraft being used in it, AIRCRAFT BEING USED IN IT? Wow! Now that sounded interesting! I couldn't wait to see who and what was going to be on the airport and what airplanes were going to be used in the film.

We didn't have to wait long. A crew from Los Angles descended on the place as if they owned it. They set up tents and fences and gear that was to used in the movie called "On an Island with you" starring Peter Lawford, Jimmy Durante and Esther Williams. Okay, yeah. That sounds like an epoch -- Peter Lawford and Jimmy Durante? Esther Williams and who?

They were set up on the eastern side of the field and the party got started early in the morning even before I started my 0700-1500 shift. Fake palm trees were set up at the end of the runway and other south sea trappings were spotted around. Then the important people arrived one afternoon, Paul Mantz and his crewman showed up in a Grumman Avenger. Typical of the day, it was a war surplus plane with crudely applied civilian markings slapped on it, with a mop I think, and the navy markings slopped over with the same mop.

He taxied to the ramp and opened the torpedo bay doors as soon as the engine stopped and the gasoline fumes were frighteningly strong. He and his mechanic were unimpressed with the situation as they got out of the plane, but I was getting ready to run. I asked him if I should get the fire truck and Mantz said, "Naw, it's just a heater fuel line leak." He showed me where the tube had been cut and the end pinched with pliers after the navy removed the heater. Well, so much for their aviation safety protocol, but that was the first thing we fixed on that airplane.

The airplane was repainted all dark navy blue with proper insignia applied and it was ready for action. A companion plane was hired for the film and soon a Grumman Widgeon arrived from Lakeland for its makeover. So we had two airplanes to service. No big thing? It's a big thing when the airport was not equipped with a fuel truck that had mass fluid delivery systems. We had to have the Avenger taxi in to the pumps for gas and we replenished oil not by the quart but by the case -- by hand, one quart at a time. This airplane liked its oil.

The pilot who flew the Widgeon in was just out of the hospital from crashing a Widgeon while attempting a landing on a glassy lake. He told us how it landed nose first and started porpoising and eventually tucked under and broke the nose off. His broken jaw was wired shut but he could still speak and was willing to fly another Widgeon.

Sometimes during the lunch breaks in the maintenance hangar, we cooled off and chatted with him and Paul Mantz about things of which we had no knowledge. Mantz shared many of his Hollywood stories that kept us enthralled for hours. One of his most interesting tales was the making of "Blaze of Noon," written by Ernest K. Gann. The opening sequence of the film took place as a couple of barnstorming biplanes are spinning down to open a carnival somewhere in the Midwest. Mantz had hired three young duster pilots to fly the Travel Air's for this sequence and they developed a competition between them to see who could do the most spins in the specified altitude. The winner's last turn was just that, his last turn. He took the Travel Air into the ground.

He talked about his working with Amelia Earhart and had nothing good to say about her skills or attitude as a pilot. It was quite a surprise for us to hear his comments, but he spoke without derision; he was simply being factual. We listened to many stories about Hollywood stars and their exploits while he was working on flying movies, but we only saw him during the day and had no idea where he was staying or what he did in the evening. Not so with the big star of the movie, Esther Williams. She was on stage at all times and you knew when she was on the set because her voice carried quite well and we could hear her where we were.

She enjoyed the "quaint" nightlife in the little town and almost every night one could see her in one of the nightspots. My buddy and I decided to follow her one night. After two or three stops, she made an appearance at the "41 Tavern" on highway 41 leading out of town where they had turtle races every night. Anyone who sponsored and raced a turtle had to name it, so she named her turtle Broken Zipper with the lengthy explanation of how she broke the zipper on her skirt before leaving the hotel for the evening sortie.

I remember that she wore a white peasant blouse, a multi-colored broom skirt and sandals that made for a nice contrast to her tanned body. This lady was an absolute dynamo and after four hours of tracking her while she drank crème de-menthe frappes at all the stops, we had to quit. We had jobs that required us to awaken at 0600. The next morning when I arrived a bit bleary eyed, I heard that Miss Williams was already on the set at breakfast.

On weekends I often swam at the fresh water pool at Lido Beach Casino as it was refreshing and had a bar at one end of the patio where one could have a beer and relax. Esther Williams appeared one Sunday afternoon and immediately emptied the pool of everyone but me. I'm a swimmer and competed in high school and college, but I was no match for this lady.

She was powerfully built and could still swim like she did in her competitive days. I was able to see how attractive she was when she was close up and she had beautiful teeth, nice skin and a lovely face. But she was almost as wide in the waist as she was in the shoulders, and they were powerful. We chatted a bit and swam around for a brief period but I thought that it best that I left the pool for her to entertain the crowd that had gathered on the balcony of the pavilion. She was a beautiful mermaid.

Near the end of filming, I met Peter Lawford briefly one evening when he picked up his date, a girl who attended high school with my sister. He was a polite gentleman and behaved himself while he was in town during the filming, leaving no gossip or bad feelings.

The filming went on for weeks with the Avenger and Widgeon running up and down the runway at times and flying around aimlessly. Some days were quiet while the crew was up at Anna Maria Key shooting other sequences and life went on. It did anyway after the initial excitement of having Hollywood in our front yard.

I still enjoyed swimming and diving at Lido Beach, but chasing somebody around town just once was enough for me. I teamed up with a fellow worker at the field who owned a pretty 40 HP Talyorcraft that was clean and totally basic. It had a bright red glossy finish with cream-colored numbers and something never seen now: a wind driven generator between the landing gear struts. Not that it had any equipment for it to power but it did power the navigation lights and that was important because we flew it at night many times.

I know that doesn't sound exciting and it wasn't, but flying over the Gulf and beaches with the light of the full moon reflecting off the water was simply magical. In the clear night one can see quite well when the moon is up. It is calm and cool then and the little airplane purred along at 55 MPH and was very happy to let us ride along with it.

Without verbally agreeing to it, we flew in silence while we enjoyed our gift. Seldom did we see other aircraft lights and when we did, they were far off and above us. We did witness beautiful displays of lightning darting inside and out of the towering moonlit clouds roaming around out in the Gulf. Some were ghostly leftovers from the heat and turbulence of the afternoon and like petulant monsters, they retreated into the night, sulking while they plotted their return the next day. Malicious looking as they were, bathed in ghostly moonlight; they marched off to the horizon, flashing their lightning to let us know that they were still alive.

These bullies assert their nasty strength during the day when the heat, humidity and thermal physics allow them to build enormous thunderheads that climb into the sky in a few hours, starting from a few wisps of condensing moisture in the morning to pretty little cotton puffs that join forces to form cumulus. They then gang up on us when they become towering monsters by late afternoon that rise to 30,000 feet and then proceed to beat the hell out of anything below it.

This happened one afternoon when the movie people came rushing into our hangar and asked us to get one of their airplanes ready to film a sequence near one of the huge thunderheads that had formed just east of us. The Lakeland pilot was donned with a blonde wig and jumped into a Navion that we had cranked up and quickly took off after the Widgeon camera plane and headed for the build-up. They filmed a sequence of the Navion flying in front of the thunderhead for another movie that was in the works starring Lana

Turner and Spencer Tracy entitled, "Cass Timberlane." She was supposed to be doing the flying in the film and from what I saw of the movie, it was a beautiful sequence and one could think that Turner was flying the Navion. Again, the wonders of Hollywood.

"NORMAL" OPERATIONS

The movie thing seemed to disappear as fast as it had appeared and we went on with our normal operations at Sarasota-Bradenton until a radioman had completed his job of installing a new navigation device in a Beechcraft Bonanza. We had heard about this new wonder and found it difficult to believe that it could do the things they said it could. We sure as hell believed what happened when the radio installer hit the master switch in the Bonanza to see if his installation worked.

The airplane was positioned at the front of the huge hangar that was filled with airplanes of every variety. Cubs, Champs and Stearmans were jammed into one area, all stacked up on their noses. Behind them were the Lockheed Lodestars, BT-13's, T-6's and DC-3's; most of the big ones had fuel in the tanks.

The radioman had just finished installing an OMNI system in the Bonanza and when he turned on the master switch to power up the new nav system, ALL of the airways flares fired and sent three flaming thermite flares back into the hangar. It is difficult to reassemble all that happened when we saw the fire in the hangar, but somehow everybody in the vicinity took some action. Somebody ran to the buckets of sand that were placed at intervals along the base of the hangar walls, some tried to move airplanes away from the hangar, and I ended up on the fire engine that was driven into the hangar to spray water on the fabric covered planes that were in danger.

The mayhem that ensued defies description, but somehow we got the flares contained under layers of sand and prevented the more fragile airplanes from igniting the larger ones that were filled with hundreds of gallons of fuel.

After we inspected the airplane that caused the problem, it

was determined that drilling shavings had fallen down on the contacts of the flare switches and when the master switch was energized, so were the flares. That was the most frightful episode of my duties there at the airport -- or for anywhere else up to that time. Those thermite flares burned deep holes in the concrete floor of the hangar.

As if it were to be the finale' of the summer, we witnessed a most bizarre incident the Monday after Labor Day. I remember fueling an Ercoupe with two locals in it on Friday, who said they were going to fly to West Palm Beach to celebrate the long weekend. Late on Monday afternoon, an Ercoupe overflew the field in an erratic manner and made a wide circle in the distance and made an approach to the main runway that would carry it into a restaurant on Highway 41.

At the last minute it pulled up and tried to make a diving stab at the runway, but again pulled up at the last minute to clear the palm trees at the end of the field. I alerted the airport manager that we had an airplane with a problem.

In a minute all the gang was in front of the office to watch what was evolving. Comments were they were having control problems, but the manager nailed it immediately and said, "The problem is with the pilot, not the airplane. It seems to be doing everything okay but not when it's supposed to." Another attempted landing and it was all over the sky, but on the third attempt he got it down in a hard impact and we started to run out to it. Before we were half way there, IT TOOK OFF AGAIN.

We were presented with another frightening ballet while the airplane wallowed around the field. "GET THE DAMN FIRE ENGINE!" the manager yelled. Run it out to the edge of the runway and if this idiot lands again, run into the airplane!" The airplane came around and started another descent that again just missed the trees and finally jackrabbited to a hard impact near the middle of the runway.

With the fire engine jammed into it, the airplane was finally stopped, but we had to climb up to it to kill the magnetos. The pilot and passenger sat there in a drunken stupor in a cockpit fouled with vomit, urine and an empty gin bottle. They were so drunk that they couldn't get out of the airplane, or what was left of it. It was evident that it had been flown through a hailstorm because the nose bowl and wing leading edges were peened and dented from fairly large hailstones. From the oil streaks and the sound of the engine, it had been run at 100% for too long.

When the airport manager asked the pilot why he took off again the pilot said, "I just wanted to show Cuzey that I could do it again." They and the airplane would never fly again.

Chapter 13.

Alligators, snakes, spiders, and a fish camp in the Everglades.

Our camp in the Evergades, 1948 | Robert Parks

FAIRWELL TO THE GOOD DAYS

My last summer in Florida was spent in real Florida, the Everglades. I was hired by the Gulf Oil Research and Development Co. to help operate a mobile ground based radar station, with which their DC-3 navigated while it was towing an aerial magnetometer to survey the state for oil domes.

We worked three different locations in the state, two of them in the deep swamps and one in Belle Glade. The first location was the most interesting and the most difficult. Even though it was deep in the Everglades, the pay of 280 dollars per month was too good to pass up and the job sounded interesting to me.

I was hired as a ground crewman of a two-man mobile radar station. The head crewman was a radar/radio technician who operated the equipment. I had to help set everything up and monitor the operation of the generator and other equipment. The entire station was carried in a 1947 Dodge Power Wagon, a vehicle based on the WW2 one-ton weapons carrier. It took the two of us most of the day to inventory and to load everything. That included all our food, clothes, and housing.

The purpose of the mobile station was to locate on a pre-determined point as a navigation aid to the DC-3 survey plane that flew precise lines over the state while it trailed an aerial magnetometer to read the subterranean structure of the earth. Searching for, you guessed it, oil. There were five radar stations located on geodetic survey markers placed 50 years before. As the aerial survey moved to different locations, the mobile ground stations moved to different markers somewhere else in the state.

My fearless leader was a man who looked the antithesis of a self-reliant woodsman. He was a bespectacled rail of a man who looked more like a physics teacher. Paced in his movements, he plodded through the process of checking all the equipment and then

we spent the rest of the afternoon checking the maps to figure out where the survey marker would be located. John decided that he could find the marker so we locked everything up and went home for our last night under a roof.

Susie, Our truck | Robert Parks

We departed early the next morning to search for a six-inch diameter bronze plaque embedded in a marble shaft that was sunk into the sand in a swamp somewhere south of Highway 41 approximately 20 miles east of Naples, Florida. A piece of cake! The area in question was in what was called "Alligator Alley", just to make it interesting.

We drove south on the Tamiami Trail, Highway 41 that went from Tampa to Miami, hence the tricky name. It wound its way to Ft. Meyers and Naples and then east across the Everglades to Miami. Twenty miles after we left Naples, John decided that, "This is where we turn off." One could barely see the remnants of an ancient trail winding through the scrub off to the right. Off the road we went and John wisely put the Power Wagon in four-wheel drive so that we could churn our way through the palmettos and swamp grass.

The trail kept disappearing but it would re-appear again as we probed deeper into the woods. Soon we got to a relatively clear area where the underbrush had thinned and we could see for more than a few yards. I thought that it was odd that the trees were widely spaced and underbrush was so thin that you could see the bright green of the cabbage palms and bare sand. The terrain was flat and I thought that it would be a perfect place to set up camp.

John started snooping around in the brush and somehow quickly found the marker. He never looked at the map but he somehow knew where to look. He was a quiet studious Swede from Minnesota and in his laconic tone he said, "Okay. We set up here."

I won't go into all the facets of setting up camp except to mention that it took us all afternoon to unload the truck and set up the antenna mast. By nightfall we had the tent finished, the generator running, and all the cables connected to the transmitter. We were ready to go at 0500 the next morning. That meant that we had to arise at 0400 to get the equipment warmed up and sending a strong signal.

Perhaps there should be an explanation of our purpose in the field. The Gulf Oil Co. was making an aerial survey of the entire country to find geological evidence of dome-like features under the surface that would indicate the presence of oil. To accomplish this feat efficiently, the used an airplane to trail a magnetometer behind it to read the magnetic forces emitted by the subterranean masses. Every state was surveyed by means of a mosaic of blocks 100 X 100 miles square. The blocks were delineated by "tie lines" flown by the airplane. Within those blocks they flew parallel lines one mile apart that ran east and west.

The magnetometer took readings at set intervals and recorded them in the in the airborne equipment. The parallel lines then had a series of numbers on them when the "mapper" made a drawing of the grid. Identical numbers were connected to form a contour or relief map and soon one had a picture of the subterranean shapes.

To keep the lines straight and exactly one mile apart, the airplane had a radar set that read the signals from two ground stations that produced a set of numbers on the instrument in the airplane. The challenge of the airborne operator was to keep the numbers at equal values, thus keeping the airplane on a straight course. This is a simple explanation of a complex system and I hope that it somehow clarifies the reason for our being in the middle of nowhere.

A look in any direction will give the viewer the same scene, thigh high palmetto palms, tall pine trees, and all of it blending into a grey-green haze as far as you could see. The pines are indigenous to the southeast. Tall straight bare trunks carried a cap of green fuzzy foliage of long needles. Unlike hardwood forests, the trees are widely spaced and one can see for quite a distance through them but even then, we had to chop several of them down to set up the transmitting mast and tent.

Our camp was set up in a circular arrangement, the radar mast in the center and in a clockwise rotation, the tent, the truck, the generator, and the latrine. Cooking was done in front of the tent on a Coleman stove placed on some empty boxes. Breakfast was almost always eggs bacon, and fruit. It was consumed quickly while the equipment was warming up. We operated until 1430 when the airplane returned to the airport to unload data and to service the airplane. We then cooked our lunch of soup, bread, and canned fruit. Most everything was out of cans and boxes. The evening meal was somewhat the same except that we had spam or some other kind of canned delight like beans.

Bedtime came at 2030 or 2100 because we had to be up by 0400 and on line by 0500. Cots were set up in a large two-man tent, a box between them at the head end on which to place the lantern.

Footlockers at the foot of the cots contained our clothes. A 30-30 rifle and a 22.caliber pistol were inside the tent with us. Our other weapon was a can of mosquito spray.

Every night we could hear the wildlife that roamed the brush. Catamount, painter, and panther were the names that the locals gave to one animal: the Florida Cougar. We heard them every night off in the distance and occasionally a bull gator drumming in concert with the giant bullfrogs. The hooting of owls often was mixed with something screeching and we never did figure that one out.

Every day we followed the same routine. This suited John just fine because he was teaching himself Spanish and he sat in the truck with his books and listened to radio traffic. I read some too but I also did some sketches of our camp that I still have and when I got bored I went exploring. I discovered a canal close by that was teeming with alligator gars, small fish, frogs, water moccasins, and I imagine, alligators. I didn't see any but I knew they were there in a "land of plenty … or a canal of plenty." Snowy Egrets, Great Blue Herons, Wood Ibis, lesser Herons, and Mudhens were chattering and wheeling about. Cottonmouth moccasins sunned themselves on the logs with the turtles and that is why I carried the rifle. The snakes weren't always on the other side of the canal the banks of the canal were raised slightly above ground level and one could walk along a fairly clear path and observe the activities in the water. The landscape was relatively sparse in this area, not barren but it did not support the thick growth of cypress and under growth as did other areas of the big swamp.

We were located on the western edge of the Everglades and very near the Ten Thousand Islands area. It was still a wild place, though, and lacked only the vast body of water that covered most of the southern half of Florida. The alligators that we could hear were obviously in the canal and ponds that dotted the area. Scrub oaks bordered the canal in isolated but tightly formed groves Small birds squabbled and fluttered about in them much like a New York tenement, but much more beautiful.

Away from the canal the floor of the forest was sandy and dry with thin grasses and plants growing between the palmettos. That meant that there were swamp hares and that meant that there were rattle snakes, so we had to walk with caution, even in camp. There were many other things that we had to watch for that could bite or sting and most of them could be life threatening. Every poisonous snake in North America lives in Florida: Copperhead, Coral, Moccasin, and Rattlesnake. In addition to those nasty neighbors were Black Widow spiders, scorpions, tarantulas, and scores of huge horse flies.

We had a screened tent flap to protect us from flies and mosquitoes but during our outdoor activities during the day we had to put up with everything that flew or crawled in the 85-95 degree heat. The pick-up bed of the truck was equipped with a five-foot tall box that held all of the equipment. Each metal side was hinged at the top and lifted up to form an awning. The radar equipment and radios were installed on the right side and across the front. A bench was formed by a row of lockers on the left, so that is where we sat when we were on line. One morning when John was chatting with the pilot about a course correction, I began to hear a DC-3 and sure enough, there it was to the north of us and heading east at about 900 feet. About an hour and a half later we heard it again. It was about one half mile to the south heading west so that put us in between two lines. It was nice to actually see the results of the black magic going on in the buzzing and clicking boxes in front of us. We were near the west end of one of the "boxed grids" over which they were running the magnetometer test.

Every day was the same. Hot, humid and boring. Get up before sunrise, get the equipment running, eat breakfast and watch John study Spanish. Oh, we chatted once in a while but the conversations were mostly about things esoteric. John was easy to get along with and had a good sense of humor but he was a bookworm and thrived on the quiet isolation of the Everglades. So, I left him on his studious maximus while I explored deeper into the course of the canal.

One Sunday morning I persuaded John to go snooping with me. We headed east until we came upon a trail that looked like a road little used. We decided to see if it went to the water so we traveled south for about a mile when we heard the rumble of an engine, a muffled sound that soon was close enough to determine that it was coming our way. It was very close but we couldn't see it because of the thickened brush and the tight bends in the road. Then what finally appeared was something straight out of Hollywood.

A 1928 Packard, or what was left of it, came slowly around the turn toward us. All that was left of the once elegant car was the front of it -- the fenders, the hood, nickel plated radiator shell, windshield, and a moth-eaten front seat. It still had the solid disc wheels but they were badly rusted. The frame rails extended aft to a fully exposed fuel tank behind the rear axle. Immediately aft of the front seat a couple of wooden boxes were nailed to some boards that served as the floor. Two young girls, one a teenager, precariously perched on them while they clutched the back of the seat in front of them.

Occupying the front seat appeared to be their parents with a little boy sitting between them. The "car" was driven by a stocky man who bore evidence of hard work. His face was tanned by long exposure to the sun and his lips had the characteristic smooth bleached look that fishermen and farmers often get from too much sun. His dark bushy eyebrows hovered over intense eyes that fixed on us with an unnerving intensity but they remained bright even in the shade of his battered straw hat that he wore low on the front of his head. His black jeans were clean but well worn as was his white rough cotton shirt.

The lady of the family had that telltale look of total subservience and overwork but she sat straight and looked at us with eyes that said, "I would like to talk with you". She was worn thin but she still had the beautiful features that had been inherited by her daughters. Her dark cotton dress appeared to be handmade, neat and clean. Her long blonde hair was pulled back into a bun on top of which was a small straw hat, placed squarely on top of her head.

None of the women wore make up but it didn't detract anything from their handsome appearance. The girls sat in silence but one could detect their desire to speak, particularly in the older girl. Her long blonde hair was much like her mother. The younger of the two had dark hair like her father, and the little boy looked like he was going to be like his father. They appeared to be on their way to church. After all, it was Sunday morning and all were dressed in their Sunday best.

John broke the silence as the car stopped and introduced us, telling the man that we were doing some work for the Gulf Oil Company and we decided to take a little walk on this fine Sunday morning.

"The name is Williams, George Williams. This here is my wife Jenny, my daughters Sarah and Rachael, and my boy, Jacob. You ain't drillin' wells are you?"

"Oh, No sir!" John countered." We're just a radar station that helps the airplane to navigate while it's surveying the area."

"Surveying fer what?"

"Well, they are looking for certain land formations that might hold oil'. John wisely and quickly threw in a qualifier, "But it doesn't look like they will find any." It was apparent that George William's hackles were raised and John was on the defensive.

"Won't cotton to no drillin' here!"

"I wouldn't worry about that, Mr. Williams. The company is surveying the entire country and they haven't found much to indicate a reason to drill." A little lie to further calm the waters.

"We're on our way to church. Don't want to be late." Mr. Williams put the car in gear and slowly drove away.

"Nice meetin' ya'". Jacob was the only one brave enough or innocent enough to say something to us as they drove away. As I watched them drive away I wondered about their safety on the highway without any doors or even a body on which to hang the doors. The rear wheels were completely exposed, the gas tank was hanging out in the open between the frame rails, and those two pretty young girls were sitting on a couple of wooden boxes in front of it while they hung on to the back of the front seat. John interrupted my thoughts, "Sure hope that church is close by and what in the world do they do when it rains?"

His question must have triggered something "upstairs" because tropical rainstorms on Monday and Tuesday kept us from working. The airplane was grounded so we had a chance to do some maintenance on the generator and ourselves. When the rain was pouring down we were able to take wonderful long showers with lots of soap and an endless supply of water. And it cooled down and gave us some much-needed relief from the heat and insects.

Wednesday Thursday, Friday and Saturday were full workdays to make up for lost time. As we were shutting down Saturday, Mr. Williams came strolling into camp to make a proper" hello", in his words.

After looking around for a few minutes, he looked at the ground and said," Not a good place to camp."

John explained that we had to set up here because of the location of the survey marker. There was no reply from our visitor, then John proceeded to explain how our station operated by showing him all of the equipment. Then he swept his arms around and said, "AND, there's not a drill in sight." Mr. Williams was pleased with what he saw and he warmed up to us a little bit.

"The Mrs. and I thought you folks might like some home cooking and we would like you to have supper with us after church tomorrow." He looked up from the ground at John who accepted the invitation.

"Jes follow that road you was on and you will see the house on the left. Two o'clock sharp."

MISTER WILLIAMS FISH CAMP

We were late. It was 1410 when we could see the house on the left as he described it. It was situated in a clearing as bare as a pool table and sat on a series of concrete blocks and bricks like any back woods house should be. We quickened our pace to make up for our tardiness. We had walked from camp thinking that the camp was maybe a mile in distance but it was much farther and we worked up a sweat to get there.

Mr. Williams accepted our apology as he beckoned us to the front porch where he pulled out some old chairs for us. Mrs. Williams came out with glasses of lemonade. "Supper will be ready shortly but you two look like you need a drink so it's best if you set a spell." As she handed us the drinks she gave a furtive glance at her husband as if to seek approval and disappeared into the house.

The house was what I had imagined it would be, a single story simple structure that rambled over the ground in several directions. The entire structure was supported by brick and block piers approximately three feet tall. Chickens and a few lazy dogs occupied the space underneath where it was cool. Smart animals! One of the dogs, a skinny flop-eared hound greeted us with a "Halloo-a-roo-roo" while he wagged his tail. With that duty accomplished, he sauntered under the house and went back to sleep. There wasn't a speck of paint on the house, bare grey wood like any other Florida Cracker's home. The porch ran the full length of the house and deep enough to fend off the rain. The corrugated metal roof was red with rust.

The main part of the house consisted of a large living area on the left and the kitchen on the right. I could tell what the layout was without going inside because I could see through the window openings from the porch. The windows were not glazed because there was nothing in which windowpanes could be set; it was just an opening in the wall with screen cloth tacked on the outside. Hinged above each opening were wooden shutters that could be quickly dropped. Sometimes the wind could drive the rain horizontally in this area.

Sitting on the porch was a treat for us as we enjoyed the breeze coming from the Gulf that we could see in the distance through the mangroves and the palms. We sipped our lemonade and petted one of the hounds while we chatted with Mr. Williams about the beautiful view and his fine home.

"Jenny an' me built this ourselves. Only had one room an' the kitchen space but when the younguns' came we added on them other rooms an' we jes git along fine."

"You should be proud, too! You have a fine family and a lovely place." John was in fine voice and he was making a good impression on George. I had not seen John put so many in a string since we started working together.

The aroma from the kitchen was beginning to overpower my ability to think about anything but food. Mrs. Williams and the girls were bustling about in the kitchen and the soft clatter of cookware signaled the event for which we had anticipated long before our arrival.

"Supper's ready." It was Rachael who came halfway through the door to call us for supper. She was still wearing her church dress, a white affair with short puffy sleeves and a tight waistband that appeared to be homemade. The cloth looked like cotton muslin and the stitching was precise throughout.

"That's a pretty dress, Rachael," I said as we entered the room.

"Momma made it for me." I guessed that one correctly.

We stood behind the chairs, to which Mr. Williams had directed us, while he said a blessing. Then we sat down to a table that was barely large enough to accommodate everyone. It was obvious that Mr. Williams made the table for it was an example of heavy-duty simple craftsmanship, sturdy, clean and handsome. A platter of fried chicken sat at the end of the table in front of Mr. Williams. From his end of the table to that of Mrs. Williams spread an array of good ol' Southern cooking: a bowl of collard greens, a plate of yams, a bowl of big hominy, a plate of biscuits, covered with a cloth, molasses, and a huge pitcher of lemonade. The food was enthusiastically passed around and put on a mixture of plain white plates, and blue speckled porcelain ware. There was no tablecloth but there were white muslin napkins freshly ironed for everyone. The host and guests had glasses from which to drink but the rest of the diners had a mixture of cups.

Jacob was a likeable little guy who was comfortable with company even though we knew that they didn't have many people dropping by. They weren't exactly on the mainline and one could sense that Mr. Williams was the typical patriarch by the guarded manner that his family responded to questions. They self-consciously checked with him with quick glances to see if he approved. All except Jacob, he seemed to instinctively know how far he could go without getting into trouble.

"I'm sure glad this is Sunday 'cause we git' somethin' to eat besides fish." Jacob launched an attack on a drumstick and offered no more profound statements except to ask for more chicken. His blonde hair had been bleached white by the sun like mine so that made us sort of partners. He made one mistake, however, that earned the immediate attention of his father. Like any hungry seven year old might do, he wiped his hands on his overalls.

"Jacob! You have a napkin, boy, now use it!" His father delivered his reprimand in a firm even voice and it carried enough weight to get a serious response. "Yessir!"

I felt the urge to break the tension that this family felt to tread the narrow path that their father had obviously laid out for them, and not just for this meal with guests. He ruled.

"Mrs. Williams there is only one person that I know who can cook chicken this good." Before I could say anything she spoke up and said, "I bet your going to say, your mother."

"You're absolutely right, mam. It's light and crisp like hers and has that same good flavor from the spices she puts in it. I won't ask what it is but it is delicious. The biscuits melt in your mouth, too." I went on to rave about the dinner because it was outstanding fare and this lady could use some praise. I caught her looking down at her plate with a faint touch of a soft smile.

John chatted with the girls, asking about their school subjects and all the things that they were "just dying to talk about." Typical studious John, but it did break the ice and the girls appeared safe enough to talk with him and they seldom flicked those side-glances at their father. The pace quickened and everyone relaxed and enjoyed the meal. The father chatted with John about the weather in Minnesota and how anybody could measure things underground.

I didn't feel that I should start a conversation with the girls because I was certain that their father was keeping a tight rein on them, at least on Rachael. She was the oldest, very pretty, and anyone could see that she was ready to bolt. The isolated life in the fish camp was behind her now and she could see that there was an exciting and interesting world out there. I caught her looking at me several times and so did her father so I steered clear of engaging her in too much conversation.

After a dessert of rhubarb pie, the "men folk" had coffee on the porch while the ladies cleared the table. Our retirement was orchestrated by Mr. Williams and he firmly diverted any of our efforts to help with the dishes. As we sipped our strong black coffee he turned his attention to me and asked where I was from. When I told him that I was from Sarasota he leaned forward with an almost imperceptible move in my direction.

"So! You are a Florida boy!"

I told him about my background and his demeanor changed from cool inquisitiveness to a genuine interest, not enthusiastic interest but something in my direction, anyway. I no longer felt like an alien who threatened him and his family but someone closer to his level with whom he could talk.

"I haven't seen your fishing boat. I thought that you would have it moored near the house."

"Don't want 'em tied up here 'cause it's too open. I have 'em tied up in a nice little bayou up the line a tad."

"How many do you have?" It takes a crew to operate one boat and he made no mention of anyone but himself.

"I have two. One's kinda' old and I still use it some but I built me a new one last year that's doin' good."

"Could we take a look at them, Mr. Williams?"

He perked up and said, "I suppose we could if you don't mind walkin' a bit."

We walked into the scrub on a narrow path with him in the

lead. After about 200 yards I could see a thinning in the trees and finally an opening where the bayou emptied into the Gulf. It was protected as he said. Tall pines stood on either side of the bayou and a very large island of mangrove sat directly across from the mouth. At this point it was wide enough to run his boats upstream for quite a distance if he had to protect them during a hurricane. Hurricanes seldom hit this area but some of the storms can be dangerous.

The boats were tied up to either side of the narrow dock that jutted out into the black water of the bayou. A large net rack had been constructed to the right of the dock where he could dry and repair his nets. To the left was a shed where he could repair his engines. A haul-out winch occupied the center of the little building and a cable ran from it down to a carriage on the ways to pull the boats out of the water. The arrangement was very neat, clean and well built. Unlike most of the fishing set ups that dotted the coast, this one had a mark of pride on it.

The boats were prime examples of the craft used by the coastal fishermen in western Florida. They were usually 26 to 28 feet in length with a beam of eight to ten feet, shallow draft, hard chine, open hull with a very handsome look about them. They were like a vee-bottom version of a Maine Lobster Boat. Invariably an old auto engine was placed a little forward of amidships and housed in a box that could be quickly removed. At the stern a large decking was built to carry the carefully folded net. The rest of the hull was open except for a small deck at the bow to facilitate docking operations and to provide a small cuddy in which the crew could store clothing, tools, and sometimes a bottle of whiskey (the first aid kit).

The engines were usually obtained from large cars such as the Cadillac, Chrysler, Packard or Buick. They weren't equipped with anything marine except the water pick-up in the hull and a reversing gear. The exhaust went up through a pipe that stuck straight into the air and at full speed, about 30 MPH, the sound could be deafening. I recall as a youngster seeing them running by our house at night with the exhaust stack glowing bright red. They were fast and maneuverable to negotiate the twists and turns when they went after a school of mullet.

Mullet is a bottom feeding fish and does not strike at a hook so they must be caught in a net. They travel along the shore in shallow water from 50 to 200 yards out. They grow up to three feet in length, and no matter how large they are, they are delicious. The smaller examples were usually fried after being filleted and rolled in flour and cornmeal. But the best way to prepare them is to smoke the fillets over a smoldering fire of Hickory and Osage Orange. It was a very popular delicacy in western Florida but it has become scarce from over-fishing.

I looked at Mr. William's new boat and I could see that it was built with skill and good materials. It was similar to the other boats in the business but somewhat better.

"I see that you have a little more re-curve in the bottom near the stern than some of what I've seen in the other boats."

He wheeled around quickly at my comment, "You know about these boats?"

"Yes sir, I used to go out with them all the time when I was a kid and I have looked at them many times under water."

"Where was that?" He was excited to find someone who could talk about the boats.

"Off Siesta Key. When they made a strike in front of our house we would help to haul in the nets sometimes. Sometimes I would go out with them for the next run and they would drop me off on the way back to the market."

"Oh, you were with the Blounts up there at Siesta Fish Market."

He was totally relaxed now but he asked me more about my experiences with the Blounts as if he were trying to verify what I had told him.

Some digression is needed at this point to explain how these fishermen plied their trade. Most of us picture commercial fishermen going to sea in large boats equipped with cabins two deck high and with masts and booms arrayed on the after deck. Having already described the Florida mullet boat, there is no need to expand it except to emphasize their simplicity.

Three to four men completed the usual crew. Boots and slickers were not a part of it because they spent their time riding in an open boat barefooted or they were in the water hauling in the nets and throwing fish into the boat. They were rough men living a rough life and unless they were boat owners like Blount and Williams, they were dirt poor with a future of hard work and little else. Their clothing consisted of sun-bleached jeans, a sun bleached shirt that was sometimes rolled up and stowed forward. Hats were of all descriptions but the captain invariably wore a battered sweat stained fedora. As mentioned before, their feet were bare and tough as sandpaper. Scars showed white on their legs and feet from encounters with sharp objects on the boat or fish that they wrestled. I remember one fellow with whom I fished had an ugly festering wound above his ankle. I asked him what had happened and his answer was short and simple, "Stingaree." Evidence of one of the dangers of walking on the bottom and stepping on a stingray, some of which could be three feet across.

Talk was sparse and one learned quickly not to delve into a man's past or present. One of the crewmembers who fit this description was a big blonde Swede with sun-bleached hair down to his shoulders and a weight lifter's body. You stayed out of his way and out of his life. He had just been released from prison for stabbing a man in a fight. Some of the crewmen were too old to be doing this kind of work but a man has to eat. The younger men usually ended up hauling the nets and left the fish sorting to the older guys. None of the work was easy.

When I was 14 I took my first all day trip with one of the Blount's boats. Looking back on it I wonder how my mother felt about allowing me to go riding away on a boat with a bunch of rather tough men who made a tough living. I suppose that she got to know the Blounts well enough from her patronage of the fish market to purchase fresh or smoked mullet from them. All of us got to know the crews from helping them on the beach when strikes were made nearby. So, I suppose that she trusted them with her little boy.

They told what time they would be rounding the point where we lived near Big Pass. I swam out to meet them when I heard the roar of the engine. They swung in toward me, slowed down a little bit; the Swede put his arm over the side, hooked my arm and swung me into the boat as if I were another fish. Everyone staked out their spot in the boat and one did not violate it. Swede silently pointed to where I was to stay and I assumed my spot. Ahead of me the open hull amidships awaited the fish yet to be caught. On the left, the Swede leaned against the coaming, on the right a non-descript young man dressed in ragged black pants and a well-worn chambray shirt and acknowledged my presence by raising his hand as he stared ahead.

Forward, the captain was at the con standing at the small galvanized metal ship's wheel gazing ahead. Next to him, stood "The Greek", an old man of possibly 65 years of age. His bullet shaped bald head was shiny and brown as was his bare torso. He, too, wore faded black pants and was barefoot. His gaze was ahead and toward the shore, searching for fish. No one spoke as we sped along the shore, 250 yards off the beach in the bright blue-green of the Gulf of Mexico. We could see the bottom even though the water was 20 to 30 feet deep.

It wasn't long before the Greek touched Mr. Blount and pointed toward the shore ahead. Blount turned the boat in that direction and held his course until we were into the shallows. Then he made a sharp turn to the right and yelled, "Willie, you and the boy take the net!" Since Willie was on the starboard side and I was on the port side, we grabbed our respected sides at the end of the net and bailed out over the stern with it as the boat sped away out into the Gulf. We anchored the shore end of the net that was spilling out of the stern of the boat that was making a long sweep to the left that would take it back to the beach 100 yards south of us. They had circled a school of mullet and closed any escape route by running the boat ashore. Our end had been pulled up on shore to close the other end.

It was now our arduous task to pull the net into an ever-tightening purse toward the boat where the fish would be tossed into the hold. The water became a seething mass of flopping thrashing as the space in which they were trapped became smaller. It was not a simple task of just pulling in the net because the heavier lead line often became fouled as it dug into the sand. That required someone to go into the water and follow the lead line into deeper water to free it. I did this many times and it could get very exciting when a shark was discovered inside the net. Coming up for a breath of air, many times I felt like I was being shot at as hundreds of Skipjacks and Yellow Tails flashed by as they were jumping over the cork line to escape only to be snatched up by the Bottle Nose Dolphins (porpoise) that were waiting for them on the outside.

For the best part of an hour we struggled with closing the net and getting the fish into the boat while we watched for stingrays, salt water catfish that were equipped with long, sharp gill spikes that could inflict serious deep cuts. We had a good strike this time and the boat was filled to the gun'ls with fish. With six inches of freeboard left, we made a slow careful trip back to the market. There, we spent several hours unloading and cleaning the boat.

I was exhausted when my mom came to pick me up that evening and we went home with some nice fish. I went back many times after that and I was welcomed any time I asked to go out with the fishing boats.

All trips were not as successful as the one described. Many days were spent cruising far down the coast with little to show for it and those days were tougher in some respects than the busy ones. Inactivity and short attention spans were not the best mix for those who made up the crews. Hunger could be a problem, also, because in the 40's there were few stores on the many miles of deserted coastline. My first experience with eating "boat style" came one day when we were running down the coast on an unexpectedly long run. One of the crew chose a large mullet and dressed it by cutting off the head and gutting it. He then spread it out flat, sprinkled some salt, pepper, and spices on it and placed it meat-side down on a flat steel plate that was welded on the exhaust manifold of the engine and cooked it in its own fat. I learn fast when I'm hungry so I followed suit and soon I was eating a lunch of delicious mullet out of a plate formed by the skin and scales. After lunch, the Greek dove down into the Gulf and came up with fresh scallops that we had for dessert, raw.

So, this is essentially what I told to Mr. Williams when he asked me how much fishing I had done. My first outing was in 1939 when I was 13. I continued my association with the Blounts on and off until I went into the Air Force in 1944. Every time out was a new adventure. Each trip was different and had its own new version of excitement. The joy of cruising out on the Gulf in the warm sun, charging up one side of a big roller, and diving down the other side was pure fun. It was always a thrill to "take the net" at full speed and tumble out over the stern into the foaming wake. Then there was always a feeling of accomplishment when we pulled in a good strike.

Wonderful memories.

John interrupted our "water talk" and said that we should take our leave. We had a long walk back so we bid our hosts a thankful goodbye.

As we walked back I could see the large fenced garden behind the house, the outhouse was some distance behind that.

Before we left, Mrs. Williams removed her apron, dried her hands, and went to a lovely old pie safe and removed a plate covered with a white cloth. Under it was another rhubarb pie still warm from the wood-burning oven.

"We would like you gentlemen to take this with you. I reckon it will be better than those stale cookies you have been eatin'. The rhubarb is right out of the garden."

After many thanks, we hurried down the road hoping that we could beat the darkness. John remembered to bring a flashlight for these woods were no place to be at night without some kind of protection, like a cal. 50 machinegun. Indeed it was dark when we got back to our camp and we hurriedly cleaned up and got ready for 0400 next morning.

The next week was routine and rather boring until several thunderstorms came to visit us. It was mid-July, the time of year when usually rained every day. The rain came down in a deafening barrage from black clouds that served as a perfect backdrop for violent and brilliant bursts of lightning. We were in a vulnerable location, not so much from the tall pines that surrounded us but from the radar mast and high voltage electricity that we were generating. John wisely elected to stop transmitting during the storms and I disconnected the heavy cables from the equipment for a little more insurance. The strikes were close and numerous on several occasions so we retired to the tent in case the truck got hit. The drop in temperature to 75 degrees was a welcomed relief.

The time passed slowly with the daily rainstorms and we hadn't heard from the Williams'. We discussed our not being able to return their hospitality and humorously figured that we could take them a can of beans but any thoughts of re-visiting the family were dashed by a rainstorm straight out of the bible.

One of the afternoon thunderstorms stuck around longer than an afternoon. What we thought was a local system turned out to be a very large and wide spread storm that seemed to be dedicated to pumping the water out the Gulf and dumping it on us. We secured our station early in the afternoon as the rain began to get heavy. It slackened some before dark but not enough to make things any easier for us when we attempted to cook our evening meal under the fly that we erected over the kitchen area. Everything was wet. We retired for the night and listened to the deluge until we fell asleep.

Four thirty A.M. was colder and damper than usual. The rain was still coming down in the darkness and it was doubtful that we could get the station up and running. All doubts disappeared when I swung around out of my sleeping bag and put my bare feet into 12 inches of ice-cold water.

"JOHN! WE'RE FLOODED!"

John jumped up and put his feet in the water and never at a loss for strong words said, "My Word."

We turned on the lantern and discovered that indeed we were camped in a fast rising lake and we had small fish swimming inside our tent. I grabbed most of my clothes and stacked them on the cot. The rifle and flashlight went on top of that and we tried to retrieve the equipment and supplies that were floating around in the tent. Then the two of us went through the ludicrous attempt to find and don dry clothes. My socks were wet, my boots were wet, and before long my pants were wet. Then, when we rushed outside, we got everything else wet in the downpour.

The generator was our first concern but we found it in good shape because we had wisely set it up on some heavy boxes and it was out of danger for the time being. Everything else that wasn't in cans or was on a high place was ruined or had floated away. The Power Wagon was okay but the high voltage cables connections at the mast were under water. We were out of the radar business but we still had a radio that John turned on immediately and tuned in to the office in Sarasota. There wasn't much else for us to do but to wait for daylight and to watch the rain come down. As I sat in the truck I recalled Mr. Williams' when he visited our camp. "Not a very good place to camp."

He knew that we were in a drained swamp and my thoughts went to the canal. That meant that there would be some "little water critters", as John called them. "Little water critters" could alligator gars, alligators, cottonmouth moccasins, and some minnows that we could see wherever we waded.

"John. We should keep the rifle handy because we might have some visitors now that the canal is over-flowing into the swamp. He answered, "Yes, I thought about that. We're going to have to watch where we walk...or wade, I should say." He was correct because the water was now deep enough to hide a small critter, like an 8-foot alligator.

After we had accomplished all that we could do we had a cold breakfast of cold beans and Vienna sausage. We even had some coffee afterwards like any high-class outdoor restaurant. John made contact with the office and they ordered us to vacate our position soon as possible. That was sound advice because we were in trouble. The swamp was filling, we had no food or dry clothing, and if the water got much deeper the truck would be immovable and we would be forced to wade out to the road leaving thousands of dollars of equipment in the swamp.

We started immediately. The process of taking down the radar mast was the most difficult of all because the mast itself would be under water after it was swung back down to the ground. The "bedspring", the antenna, would be a simple operation that involved several bolts but the mast was a molded wooden tube that was assembled by slip joints. Sure enough, the joints had swollen from the moisture and it took most of the afternoon to disassemble it and get onto the rack on top of the truck. I might add here that that the loading sequence had to be followed to the letter because every item had been carefully planned to fit into a specific place on a specific rack or cradle.

By nightfall we only had 60% of the work completed. We were exhausted, wet, cold, hungry, and very concerned that we would not make it in time. It was still raining. Have you ever heard of the old saying, "Here I am up to my ass in alligators and they want me to drain the swamp?" That was us.

The next day we completed the job and we started our retreat in deeper water. Soon the truck started to sink in some of the soft spots. It was heavy and progress in four-wheel drive and creeper gear was slow and delicate. Even that wasn't good enough in several spots and I had to get out and hook the winch cable to trees winch our way from tree to tree. I didn't care what was in the water after a while. I was numb with cold and fatigue. We made it to the road just before dark by heading directly to Mr. Williams' road instead of the highway because we remembered that it was on higher ground and closer to us. When we reached it, we were barely out of the water, just barely. The roadbed was perhaps a foot above water level and the distance increased as we approached the highway that was a welcomed sight.

We turned left and headed for Naples to find the nearest motel where we could get a warm shower and some dry clothes. Dry clothes, we didn't have any. Everything in the truck was wet. When we emptied the tent our clothes were the first items to appear. Everything we owned went into the truck first and the tent, which we couldn't properly fold in the water, went in on top of everything else. I think that you can get the picture.

We arrived in Naples before closing time for the stores and happily purchased some dry clothes and underwear before we could get cleaned up back at the motel. We went to an old Penny's store and I can still see the oiled wooden floors and wooden display cases AND the fearful stares of the women who waited on us. We didn't think about what we looked like when we were in the swamp. Our clothes were torn and now streaked with black mucksoil and sand and, of course, wet and smelly. I hadn't cut my hair in months and it was bleached white and nearly to my shoulders, something that wasn't accepted in the 40's. My beard would have made a calico cat jealous with its orange, black, and blonde stubble. I was dark tan from the sun so the ladies had reason to be nervous, I suppose.

We left for Sarasota the following morning in the rain and it diminished after our arrival. It took us the best part of a week to dry, repair, and to replace some of the equipment. Then it was off to another assignment in Belle Glade. It wasn't half as interesting as Naples.

BELLE GLADE

Our station was near the edge of town so we usually had dinner in a little café on the main street. When we entered town one evening, we were astonished at the infestation of Giant Water Bugs. The town was crawling with them and some were even inside the café. Just before we finished our meal, we heard an airplane roar over at very low altitude. I recognized the sound of the engine as a 220 HP Continental and we asked the proprietor what the heck was going on after the second pass.

"Oh, that's the sprayer plane puttin' somethin' down to git after these damn bugs. Ol' Man Hughes is probably flyin' it."

We quickly paid our bill and drove out to where he said the

"airport" was located. We weren't sure that we had gone to the correct place, because darkness had fallen and all we could see was a canal over which the bridge crossed in front of us.

To the right we could see a single light bulb on the front of a building, and we could barely see a grass strip below and to the right of the bridge over the canal. Then to our left we could hear an engine in the darkness and soon, the sight of an exhaust flame came into view. To our amazement we followed the flame coming right over the bridge. The lights illuminated a Waco biplane as it descended into the dark hole alongside the canal and made a perfect landing.

We found the road that allowed us to drive down to the "Airport" where we saw a wiry white haired man who had to have been in his seventies getting out of his airplane. We chatted with him for a while and I asked him how he could see to land in this black hole. He pointed at the light bulb on the hangar and said, "I've got plenty of light." I quickly re-evaluated my personal assessment of being a "hot pilot."

My job in the Everglades was adventurous and interesting, but once was enough. After my vacation time was up, I returned to "people" again. Shortly after my return, I learned that I had to quit school, so I went back to work at the airport again. Shortly thereafter, I met a pretty and exciting girl and we got married -- too soon. I thought that I had a job in at an art studio in Philadelphia and we left Sarasota. The job disappeared in the recession that occurred in 1950, so I saw an ad in the Philadelphia Inquirer that Boeing was hiring mechanics. Fast-talking and a fake smile got me the job and off we went to Seattle in our Jeepster on a 3300-mile trip.

Robert Parks

"John, when did you say the plane was going to drop our supplies?"

Robert Parks

PART FOUR
Chapter 14.

Out of Florida and to Seattle.
In a recession but got a job with Boeing.

A cross-country trip in 1950 was unlike a trip in the 2000's. There were no freeways and much of the traveling was done on narrow two lane roads. And the motels were small, very plain and usually stinky.

BOEING

We arrived in Seattle on September 30th and I reported for work on October 5, 1950. The personnel man noticed on my application that I had been in the air force and had worked on the line. So I was assigned to work on the flight line as a field modification mechanic. Working outside added ten cents an hour to my wages and that brought it up to an even $1.00 an hour. After taxes and deductions I took home around 30 dollars a week. Even then, those were starvation wages and my new wife and I were in dire straits in spite of living in war surplus housing for 40 bucks a month and eating a lot of pancakes and peanut butter. She couldn't work because she was expecting our first child, so it was a typical hand–to-mouth existence.

Then I was put on an overtime crew and I was working steady overtime for the next seven months. The winter of 1950-51 was a typical Seattle event: raining from the start of October to ice and snow in December and January. Coming from Florida sunshine and

80 degree days, to standing in ice water 12 hours a day was a difficult transition. I suffered a continuous round of sore throats and colds, but soon I adjusted and actually relished working on the flight line. In the spring of 1951 we were rich enough to move to better accommodations with central heat. Just in time for our son to make his arrival.

FROM MEAGER BEGINNIGS

The Boeing Company had won a contract to modify 15 B-50 bombers into K-3 bombsight trainers and 15 B-50's into electronic counter measure and surveillance airplanes. I was assigned to the KMP program and there is where I really began my journey through The Boeing Company.

Boeing earned a worldwide reputation in WW2 by producing a magnificent bomber, the B-17, and established a reputation for manufacturing prowess when they were producing 22 airplanes per day. Five years later in 1950 the company population was down to 33,000 and it was struggling to stay afloat. So the B-50 modification program was a big shot in the arm with 30 airplanes to modify. The "Cold War" was hot then and these programs had an unlimited budget and no limit to overtime work. December in the Pacific Northwest can be cold and rainy or cold and snowy. 1950 brought a cold winter with freezing temperatures and lots of snow. That was the environment in which we worked on the flight line on the east side of Boeing Field. The B-50's were randomly parked on the ramp near the "B-17 Hangar" where, 15 years earlier, the original Model 299 was prepared for its first flight.

Our workday started at 0400 in darkness and I soon learned to climb on the crowned surface of a metal airplane that quickly froze the rain that constantly fell on it. Then many jobs were inside the airplane where I traded the cold for working with someone who hadn't bathed for a couple of days. I started work at 0400 and staggered home at 1600 and we soon became Zombies, numb to the time of day or the day of the week. One day I got angry at seeing the same guy punching out 4:00 AM in the morning when I arrived, after "just" seeing him punch in at 1600 the previous day.

As work progressed, so did the fatigue and so did the number of accidents. While working on the top of the number four nacelle, a boy slipped and fell to the pavement and received some serious injuries. We got a lecture on being careful but I don't recall that any safety equipment installed. Speaking of safety equipment, one dark dreary morning we were in the nose section of an airplane wiring a panel when it was rocked by an explosion and sprayed with shrapnel. After scrambling out of the airplane, we could see a crowd gathering around the adjacent B-50 to see what had happened. It lacked the nose dome and almost all the glass in the flight deck.

There was glass everywhere from the blast and frantic confusion among the crowd. We soon learned that the airplane was being pressure tested and it failed, blowing off the nose dome that actually hit the Boeing Field control tower. The next pressure test that took the structure to 12 PSI was conducted again there on the ramp, but with a heavy cargo net draped over the nose and sighting blisters. Luckily, there were no more 0430 wake up calls. My memories of those days were darkness, ice water on the ramp and relentless work. Then before we completed the KMP work in the spring of 1951 that sprung forth in glorious warmth and sunshine, I was transferred to the BMP program INSIDE OF PLANT II and there I spent my time out of the beautiful weather.

BMP stood for British Modification Program named after the British aerial refueling system that would extend the range of these planes. This was a monstrous modification that required the complete gutting of the fuselage from nose to tail so that 11 radar operators could be accommodated. The airplanes were run through a production line type of process, going in the door to enter a "U" shaped line where they were gutted by the deletion crew and gradually rebuilt as they moved through the succession of stations to roll out as a completed BMP B-50D. Sounds simple, doesn't it?

The forward pressure bulkhead at station 218 was cut out and a new one was installed 12 feet aft at the end of the forward bomb bay. The aft bomb bay was fitted with a 2500-gallon droppable fuel tank. The aft fuselage was configured to hold five radar operators and their equipment in the same arrangement as the forward fuselage that held six operators. With the operators positioned on the left side of the fuselage, the right side was filled with radio and radar equipment, tons of it from the copilot's position aft to the bulkhead. The electronics were operated by vacuum tubes then and they required huge amounts of cooling air. There was a huge NACA type scoop on the right side to feed air to an intercooler imbedded in the racks of equipment. The tail compartment was arranged the same and the fuselage from nose to tail was a dense array of radar and radios kept alive by miles of fat wire bundles.

Near the end of spring, 1951, I was promoted to the Pick Up Crew where we worked off last minute inspection items before the airplane was moved to flight line for re-flight tests. One morning an inspector discovered that the racks in the forward section had not been riveted and were still being held together by Cleco's, temporary hole clamps that held the structures together prior to riveting. That meant that we had to disconnect and remove 20-30 boxes to empty the racks. So we set up a chain-line inside the airplane to hand the equipment to a guy at the pilot's window who dropped them to an accomplice on the ramp. It was working beautifully until the catcher below was called away by a supervisor. I'll never forget the sound of that expensive box of electronics hitting the concrete.

As I write this, I cannot remember a fatal incident occurring on the flight line at Boeing Field after the commercial jet programs started. But in the 50's, there were several that illuminate the hectic pace that we were on. The summer of 1951 was one of those unforgettable Seattle weather anomalies with bright sun, clear skies and an almost total lack of rain all summer. The best part of it was my working outside for once when the weather was good.

One of my jobs was to install a drift meter mast on the upper fuselage and I had a good view of the runway while I was up on the aerostand. I was drilling some holes when somebody yelled, "What's he doing!" I looked up to see a B-50 slowly climbing away from the field but instead of a left heading for Elliot Bay, he was drifting to the right and getting very close to Beacon Hill.

He had four dark and healthy trails of exhaust but the airplane was losing speed and altitude and suddenly rolled onto its back and plunged into Beacon Hill near or on the Rainier Brewery, destroying a large wooden apartment complex, the Lester Apartments. It was so close to the brewery that a wing tip left a scar where it scraped the side of the administration building. The ball of fire and mushroom of smoke was a nasty thing to see and it was difficult to concentrate on anything the rest of the day.

The cause was attributed to the Curtiss electric propellers on engines three and four going into full feather on takeoff.

Shortly after that incident while working on another B-50, we were startled by a sharp bang nearby and saw flames and smoke rise from and airplane several parking slots away. When we got to the site, we witnessed a B-50 with the left wing opened and broken, flames pouring out of it. A brave mechanic with a fire extinguisher was attempting to quell the fire but the firemen quickly knocked it down.

We didn't know it at the time, but an inspector had been killed in the explosion. We later learned that he had his ear up to the wing lower surface to listen to the operation of a faulty boost pump when the wing exploded. Over-used pickling fluid saturated by high-octane fuel ignited when the incorrectly wired boost pump sparked.

In the fall of 1951, I was accepted for a job in the Experimental Lab where I worked on the Boeing 502 Gas Turbine Engine. During that time I learned of the loss of fifteen airmen in "an airplane off the Russian coast." The Russians had shot down one of our surveillance airplanes and we knew that it was one of our BMP B-50's. Several more were shot down without any response from our government.

THE BUF

Boeing supplied airplanes not only for the hot war of WW2, but also the Cold War that went on longer than the "big one." Their next contribution was being assembled in mock-up form in the building next to the lab. I was tired of being a mechanic so I sought and gained a transfer to the Production Illustration Group where I drew three dimensional drawings of the structure, wiring and tubing installations of the   B-52. It was 1952 and I was working on the largest airplane that I had ever seen and I thought, "Certainly this airplane can never become airborne."

I retired in 1992 and as I write this in 2014, I cannot believe that that airplane is still in service and will be after I'm gone. That is simply mind-boggling that as a kid I worked on the original B-52 and never thought that it was going to be the epitome of excellence and longevity.

I saw the first take off in April 1952 and listened to Tex Johnston talking to the T-33 Chase plane after he was airborne and circled to the west over Puget Sound. He then came back over Boeing Field and headed for Moses Lake when he told the chase plane to tell his wife that he was looking forward to some Jack Rabbit stew for dinner.

As the B-52 passed over the field we could not believe the beauty of it. The swept wings and machine-like grace of it was awesome and the takeoff was a startling revelation of its size. It appeared to making a fast taxi test but the outer wings began to lift and to our amazement the rest of the airplane followed. It simply levitated at what appeared to be a speed far below what it should have been.

We had now lived in Seattle for two years and it was a little bit better than it was when we arrived; but still way behind the cities on the east coast when it came to amenities like good restaurants, transportation and street lights. I had trouble with the traffic signals. They were either red or green, no yellow caution light in between so one ran red lights most of the time. There were restaurants in the city but they were limited to Triple-X at the low end and Canlis at the high end, where a fresh lobster tail dinner cost a whopping $4.00 and filet mignon was $6.00. The art of cooking the abundant seafood was woefully lacking.

However, the place was naturally beautiful in any direction. Elliot Bay was full of salmon in the fall and one could easily catch a 20 pounder during one of the many fishing derbies. Seattle was still a rough and tumble town in spots, but very livable with population of 390,000, surrounded by waters to the west and thick forests to the east that were bordered by the Cascade Mountains. To the south it had a beautiful peak, Mt. Rainier.

When I went to work in the month of October 1950, I never saw that mountain. It was raining, remember? One cold winter morning on my way to work, the clear sky allowed me to make out a prominence south of town that appeared very close. When I settled down to work I asked what that hill was south of the city.

"That HILL is Mt. Rainier!"

"Damn furriners!" Came from the bowels of the airplane.

I should mention that it was frigid that morning and there was a heavy layer of snow on the ground. We never see that now.

Chapter 15.

Swept wing beauties and the dawn of the Jet Transport Age, the 707.

Credit: Boeing Co.

THE VIEW FROM THE FACTORY FLOOR

In the summer of 1953, I was transferred to Renton facility to work on the modification of the   KC-97, the G model. Not much to describe about this job, the airplane was long in the tooth and the modification was an effort to stretch the performance of an aging propeller driven tanker. The dual role mission of carrying troops and refueling other planes was simplified in favor of increased fuel capacity and a single mission of refueling.

As work progressed on the KC-97G mock up airplane, we noticed that a canvas curtain was erected next to it in the northwest corner of the final assembly building. No one knew what was going on but something new was afoot. Since we could see over the curtain our suspicions were correct, a new airplane was being built. When we could see the planform of the tooling as it was being set up on the floor, we could tell that it was a swept wing vehicle!

As the year went on, we saw the form of the new bird emerge out of the jigs and it looked like a low wing B-47. We also began to receive requests from the Production Planning Group to prepare illustrations of items on the new airplane that confused them. The wing center section and the main landing gear placement and retraction sequence in particular.

The word PARADIGM was unheard of in 1953 but the meaning was understood. The planners requested an illustration of the landing gear simply because they couldn't understand why it retracted into the fuselage instead of the engine nacelles like they always did. There were many discussions about how the wheels couldn't protrude beyond the loft of the fuselage, etc. so we "dumb arteests" had to make three dimensional drawings of it so the "brains" could tell everyone else how to build it.

The secret airplane became a fact and when the jigs were removed, we could see what it looked like. It was nothing like the bulbous KC-97. We could see a sleek four-engine swept wing transport. From then on the work on the KC-97 was boring, but it was broken by the rollout of the new plane on a bright sunny day in June. When it came into the sunlight, we couldn't believe the color scheme: bright yellow topside, bronze lower half with white trim, and polished aluminum in between. The refreshing departure from the over-used red, white, and blue livery was a welcomed change. The airplane with its strut-mounted engines departed from all the older designs as well and we all felt that something good this way comes.

In mid-summer, power on tests and engine runs were accomplished and taxi tests began a few weeks later. The taxi tests were a crucial element in the proof of the new landing gear design that cantilevered the gear off the rear spar by means of a trapezoidal torque box. Drag loads from heavy braking and side loads from sharp turns had to be adequately reacted by the wing and body structure. This, then, was the series of tests that Tex Johnston had to put the airplane through to literally see if something would fail. I knew what he would be doing so I stayed after work to watch him repeatedly run the airplane up and down the runway at full power and slam on the brakes.

In between these runs, he put the airplane though a series of violent "S" turns at full power, the tires smoking and then full application of the brakes. After the third or fourth run, he was taxiing the airplane to the north end of the field and unbelievably it sagged down on its left side, putting engines one and two on the taxiway. Well, maybe the taxiway caved in. Oh No! There are landing gear parts sticking up through the trailing edge! The torque box failed. Maybe not, all we could see were landing gear parts so that meant that the supports failed.

The airplane was moved into the final assembly building for inspection and repair. We were shocked when we sneaked a peek several days later to see the airplane completely dismantled. It was on jacks and looked like a plucked chicken after having everything removed except the wing. All the inspection panels were opened and the floors were littered with pieces. The entire empennage, stabilizer center section, struts and landing gear were on stands and cradles while the crew removed parts from them. The engines had been quickly "re-owned" by Pratt & Whitney and never seen again. It was time for a visit to my contact in engineering.

Beside his drafting board sat a yellow metal "tub skid" filled with the parts of the failed landing gear trunnion bearing with the strain gage wiring still attached. He answered my questions while he pointed out the various pieces of evidence that led to the failure and I got a valuable lesson in metallurgy, heat treat and landing gear design. As in most failures of complex structures, the landing gear collapse was due to a symphony of events. First the trunnion bearing showed signs of embrittlement and indeed, the fractures showed a crystalline nature and the breaks were jagged. My friend explained the rest of the arrangement to me as he displayed the broken metal.

The metal in the trunnion support was not the alloy that was specified and in failing the Rockwell hardness test, evidence showed that it was too hard. They traced the parts that were made from the same batch and found that the horizontal tail terminal fittings, the vertical tail terminals, the strut attachments and many other fittings were suspect and would have eventually failed. Some of the tests had somehow been bypassed. The other contributing factor was a change in the geometry of the drag strut and trunnion to eliminate the bending loads in the trunnion that twisted the support bearing. A long interconnected chain of assassins was exposed and repaired before the first flight.

A NEW ERA

The first flight occurred July 15, 1954 without any problems and a steady stream of flights followed. Probably the most memorable, was the flight that included the barrel rolls over the Gold Cup boat race course on Lake Washington.

Being a good Seattleite and an avid race boat fan, I was at the shore when the Dash 80 came from the south for a flyover. I trained my eight-millimeter movie camera on the airplane as it approached and followed it as it came in until I saw it start a climb with the left wing coming up. I stood there in disbelief as I watched the historic roll -- my camera at my side. I yelled that he just rolled the airplane. A fellow next to me said, "Oh no. You can't roll an airplane that big."

As I was trying to convince him that the airplane indeed did a barrel roll, Tex Johnston came back from the north and did another one.

"What was that?" I asked.

There was no reply.

Our supervisor's wife worked for one of the VP's on mahogany row and she said that Tex was literally on the carpet listening intently to Mr. Allen for several days in succession. But his maneuver impressed the airline executives on the Boeing yacht, almost gave coronaries to some of the Boeing exec's, but gave Wellwood Beal, VP of Engineering and unofficial salesman, a shot of adrenalin. Out came the order book.

For those who are not familiar with aerial maneuvers, it is important to know the difference between a slow roll and a barrel roll. A slow roll is done while the nose of the airplane is fixed on a point on the horizon while it is rotating about that point. This requires a considerable amount of forward stick while the airplane is inverted, imposing a negative G on the airplane. A barrel roll or aileron roll is just what the name implies. The airplane inscribes a path as if it were flying around the inside of a barrel with back pressure applied throughout the maneuver maintaining positive G on the airplane as if it were flying right side up. The flight engineer on the -80 said that if he had closed his eyes during the roll, he would not have known that he was inverted at one point. Tex did it right.

If he had not done it correctly and gone negative at any point, the constant speed accessory drives would have lost oil feed and in the wing, the tank vent stringers would have filled with fuel and possibly siphoned the tanks dry. The wing structure would have probably survived it.

High-speed shallow dive tests exposed a serious rudder flutter that could have done the airplane in. The T/C (thickness/chord) ratio near the tip was too low and abrupt. The turbulent flow caused strong enough flutter that it failed the yaw damper. The rudder chord was extended 24 inches at the tip and this modification can easily be discerned in early and later photos.

367-80 First Take off | Robert Parks

- 80 Barrel Roll | Credit: Boeing Co.

Chapter 16.

Climbing the ladder at the Kite Factory.
The 720 and 707.

AN AWAKENING

It wasn't long before the Air Force was interested in the airplane as a Tanker/Transport. DUH! It's no wonder because the company had installed a pod and boom on the -80 and demonstrated its compatibility with the B-52 and other jets.

I have long since forgotten the time span between -80 and the tanker, but we were soon drawing parts for the Model 717 tanker ordered by the Air Force. It must be explained here that Model 707 was actually the model number of the prototype that was called the 367-80, a spurious designation to hopefully confuse the competition into thinking that it was a modified Model 367 propeller driven transport instead of the jet. In spite of the present day marketing ploy of the sales people to call the MD90 a Model 717, the real Model 717 was the KC-135 Tanker.

THE KC-135

The workload accelerated rapidly as the new airplane took shape. A wooden and metal mock-up airplane was constructed to a tolerance of something less than $1/10^{th}$ of an inch. It was used to establish spatial relationships of internal equipment and configuring the wire bundles and tubing runs.

While this was going on, we were busy drawing three-dimensional illustrations of the aircraft structural backgrounds for our drawings that showed the mechanics how to install the wiring and tubing on the production airplane. We then went to the mock-up and "sketched" the wire bundle and tubing installations onto the structural backgrounds and then transformed the sketches into finished drawings that were printed and made available to the installers. They then installed the bundles that were duplicated from the mock-up patterns. Though it was a labor-intensive process, it worked beautifully and I got to know the airplane in depth.

The speeds and gross weight doubled so the structure changed accordingly. No longer were there .050 and .080 wrought sheet wing skins and hydro-pressed sheet metal ribs. The wing skins were replaced by roll formed plates that were anywhere from .25 to .75 inches in thickness.

The wing thickness of previous wings was twice that of the new wings that were subjected to extreme flexing and harsh load reversals in their new flight regime. This required the use of high shear steel fasteners in the heavier materials so a new genre of processes and techniques had to be put in place. One fastener was actually named the High Shear Rivet, but it was really a steel pin with a swaged on collar. Then there was the Hi-Lock, also steel. Both required a close tolerance reamed hole that meant retraining the mechanics.

The 7078 and 7075, alloy wing skins were machined to a three way taper with machined "pad-ups." At this time Lockheed was acid-etching the pad-ups and touting their modern techniques, but Boeing engineers were not convinced that there was adequate control in the etching process so they stuck to machining. Instead of the short plates on the -80, the long continuous wing skins were rolled into contour. The inter-spar ribs were built up with webs, heavy chords and stiffeners to support the thick "Z" section stringers, some of which on the upper surface were changed to "U" shaped section to serve as fuel tank vents.

Reaming close tolerance holes requires a precise technique and wax lubrication of the reamer was essential. Those who were used to simple and quickly drilled holes had trouble sometimes in changing their technique. They would find themselves with a seized reamer or they had put a side load on the reamer and chipped out a piece of skin in the comparatively brittle metal. Fortunately good design practices prevailed and the edge margin of the holes would accept the next larger fastener.

The wing was built in five sections with the center section mounted in the fuselage and the two outer sections on each side. Wing panels consisted of a spar box formed by a front spar and rear spar connected by the inter-spar ribs. This assembly was closed by the upper and lower skins to form the box that would then be the fuel tanks. The leading and trailing edges were then attached and the wing was transformed into the streamline shape that lifted the airplane.

The technology to build a one-piece outboard wing was not yet available and the old Renton final assembly was too narrow to accommodate the wingspan of the new jet, so the outer wing was made in two pieces. A steel fitting joined the two panels. It was the source of a serious problem that showed up during the shaker test. The test exposed a disparity between the oscillation frequency of the fitting and the rest of the wing. Everything was out of phase.

I never found out how they solved that one but they did. The engineers did solve one design hurdle with a unique feature that was fun to mention to the uninitiated, which I did on a 707 flight when I told him that the wing was attached by four bolts. Well, that wasn't the truth but it wasn't far from it.

There are many fasteners in the upper and lower joints where the wing is mated to the center section that transmit the wing compression and tension loads. But the wing terminals and bottle pins take the wing/fuselage loads during flight, landing and turning on the ground. The load paths are too complex for a neophyte to adequately explain, but they all were concentrated at the terminals and bottle pins and fed into massive forgings in the fuselage frames and center section.

The pins were made of steel, nine inches in diameter, a foot and a half in length, and shaped like the old glass milk bottles -- remember those? The milkman would put them on the front stoop in the winter and the milk would freeze, pushing the cream up out of the bottle, wearing the cardboard stopper for a cap. You don't remember that? Never mind. Anyway, that must be why they were called "Bottle Pins." After multiple checks and adjustments in the position of the wing assembly, it was time to install the bottle pins.

A large steel bucket was brought out from the freezer where

the pins had been cold-soaked in liquid nitrogen for 48 hours to shrink them as far as they could shrink, and that was only a few thousands of an inch. It was enough, however, to allow the mechanic, donned in a thick pair of insulated gloves, to grab the pin from the container, insert it into the hole and quickly slam it home. Once there, it quickly expanded and was seized in place forever. Any delay in the process would invite disaster.

My fellow passenger exclaimed that if he had known that the wing was attached by four bolts, he wouldn't have flown in the airplane. Of course, he got an explanation and a sketch to allay his concern.

For the first time in a transport, the fuel was carried in the wing structure instead of rubber bladder tanks; so the Boeing Processes Unit devised a new and very successful sealing process. This generated a new skill in the work force, the Wing Sealers. They squirmed their way into the interior of the wing with their sealant and guns and performed a valuable but hardly thought about job. In all the years that have passed, I have never heard of a Boeing wing ever leaking any fuel -- even after some extreme in-flight incidents.

Overtime was once again a normal work regimen and a seven-day work week was in place. We weren't the only people hitting the over time, the engineers were burning the lights late, too. This was the typical wartime approach: flood the problems with manpower and overtime. It worked and we got the job done on time and a beautiful airplane rolled out to go on to a 50 year-long career characterized by strength and reliability.

The population of the company was about 35,000 at the time and the workload almost exceeded the staff available. The engineers and draftsmen on the model 717 program occupied both floors of the small 417 building near the entrance to the Renton plant. The engineering staff not only configured the airplane but they worked on the prime lofting drawings, the MLO's.

Master Layouts were full size definitions of the outside shape of the airplane. Think of it. How does the shape of a huge airplane come in to being? It is formulated in sketches that determine what must be done to contain and lift the payload, and then define the vehicle in slippery shapes with low drag/high lift wings and engines powerful enough to push it through the air for great distances with minimum fuel burn. It's easy, right? Well, one preliminary designer described it as an exercise in "spoon and bottling one thing to please another and then doing the same over and over to please everybody and ending up by pleasing nobody". It was a monstrous compromise.

It was difficult to separate the engineers from the draftsmen, because they all worked together on their hands and knees drawing the full size parts with silver solder pencils on 4 X 8 sheets of aluminum painted with matte white lacquer. The layouts were done on aluminum because it had the same thermal expansion as the aluminum parts that were being drawn. The work was labor intensive but that was the only way it could be done then. The points were laid out with excruciating accuracy, usually locating everything with a magnifying glass.

The MLO's were recorded by huge cameras the size of a small room that made exact duplicates of them on photosensitive sheets of aluminum called REPT's, Reference Photo Template. These were used to cut the first flat patterns of the parts from which router cutting templates and a variety of other tools were made. Each fuselage station from nose to tail was cut out and carefully filed down to the loft line and then set up on a base like slices of bread. Then the spaces in between were filled with plaster and smoothed to make a full size three-dimensional model of the compound curved parts of the airplane, like the nose and tail sections.

From this Master Model, a series of tools were derived. Skin trim lines were translated into trim jigs, drill jigs for compound skins and most important, "splashes" or molds were made for the Kirksite dies that were used in the stretch forming of the compound curved skins. These were then trimmed with the trimming tools that were derived from the same master model. It was a good system, but it was successful only if those working it were exacting in their work and adhered to the tight tolerances required. The labor-intensive time-consuming work in those days was tolerable because the pay was low. I don't know what an engineer earned then but I, in a technical grade, was earning $1.64 an hour.

Our group completed the three dimensional illustrations of the entire structure of the KC-135 for the planners to use in their planning to break the airplane into production units. Soon thereafter, the full sized mock-up was completed and the wiring and tubing routing was established. Using our structural background drawings, we then sketched the wiring and tubing runs from the mock up and produced finished drawings from them that the production people used to install the wire bundles and tubing made from the mock-up patterns.

A humorous incident occurred during this phase that illuminates the quirks that surface in the interactions of the hundreds of people involved in a project of this size. A black mock-up electrician named Sam was in charge of mocking up the anti-ice heater wiring for the stabilizer leading edge. It was signed off by inspection and the harnesses were made-up in the wire shop. We prepared the installation drawings to match. When the first production airplane hit the line, we got a call that our drawings were wrong; the heater wiring could not be installed as shown.

We checked the problem and sure enough, the installation was impossible. The last clamping points were deep inside the leading edge and no one could reach them -- except Sam. He was six-foot seven and his arms were much longer than the normal mechanic and only Sam could reach the clamp points. So, the installation had to be redone and Sam wasn't the one to do it. He smiled and said, "Guess I won't have that long term job insurance after all."

THE 707

"The 707 is just a civilian version of the KC-135." How many times have we heard that? Okay, from the outside they do look alike until one takes a closer look. The KC-135 set the style with what could best be described as a beautiful piece of sculpture. Its form, proportions and symmetry adhered to the axiom of industrial designers, "Form Follows Function." A graceful shape that was designed for aerodynamic efficiency and 600MPH was applied to both airplanes, but the tanker's structure was heavier because of its mission and as the 707 program developed there was an almost invisible difference in the fuselage.

Boeing had a prototype that was proving its concept every day BUT Douglas had more orders for their DC-8 that hadn't flown yet! Why? The answer lay in two things: first, Douglas's reputation, second, the DC-8 had a wider fuselage cross-section that allowed butt room. The 707 fuselage cross section was the same as the KC-135, 144" diameter. The Douglas DC-8 had room for one more passenger seated abreast than the 707. This was a serious defect and Juan Trippe had placed an order for 20 DC-8's and none for Boeing.

Boeing president, Bill Allen, told the vice president of engineering, Wellwood Beal, that we had to widen the fuselage of the 707 to be competitive with the DC-8. Drawings had already been released and parts cut for the circumferential frames of the 707. To increase the diameter of the cross section would mean an increase in drag and wasted money on parts that were already made. That was the argument presented by the VP of engineering and he balked at the change. Predictably Mr. Allen prevailed and soon we were drawing the new frames with an increase of six inches diameter.

The change raised the crown line of the upper fuselage and moved the tangent point of the forward fuselage curve further aft, thus destroying the symmetry of the KC-135 profile. It also added a crease line at the level of the passenger deck and caused an interruption of the smooth transition into the Section 48, producing a bulge forward of the pressure bulkhead. All of this is unnoticed by the casual observer, but I see it every time I look at a 707.

Soon the orders were coming in with not only sales to Pan Am, but to American and TWA. It was dizzying to hear that an order for 25 airplanes had been announced! Wow! The total orders had almost reached the 100 mark! The government gave us permission to build the 707 on the same line as the KC-135, an important decision and good news for the company. Work accelerated. Again we were on a seven-day workweek and I practically lived at the Renton plant.

On Sundays, the plant management duties were assigned to the Tooling Department Manager whose office was in our area. One Sunday morning, after receiving a phone call, he bolted out of the office and rushed to the production line. He returned an hour later shaking his head and told us that a foreman instructed a "mechanic" to remove a faulty rivet in the lower forward skin of the first 707 nose section. When the foreman returned to follow up on his orders, he almost had a coronary when he saw a jagged one-inch diameter hole in the skin and supporting structure.

When he confronted the worker and asked him what he did,

the man told him that he did it the same way he would have done it on his tractor on the ranch: drill holes all around the rivet and knock it out with a ball-peen hammer. It turned out that the "mechanic" was a tool room janitor who was picking up tools to return them to the tool room. The foreman never ascertained that the worker was actually a mechanic, because he was standing there with a drill in his hand and the janitor, being an obedient worker, did what he was told. The repair was extensive and expensive. The foreman got a week off without pay.

The rest of the year, 1957, was a whirlwind of work to get the 707 ready for first flight and a never-ending stream of problems kept popping up seemingly on their own schedule. Careful inspection techniques and some good luck exposed some that would have caused more than heartburn.

One occurred when the airplane was in the last position before rollout when an inspector checked the steel splice plate on the forward lower surface of the wing and center section joint. He found a long crack in the apex of the fitting. The curvatures in this area are complex and to get an external part to exactly match the contours is impossible without shimming the gaps. No shims were evident and the plate had been pulled up to the surfaces by the installation bolts that were tightened almost beyond their tensile limits. Eventually the steel fitting was replaced with an aluminum part and shim training was emphasized.

The 707 hydraulic systems operated on a pressure of 3,500 pounds per square inch like the KC-135, but it used the new fire resistant Skydrol fluid. This new high pressure system caused a few problems in the beginning, but when one of the hydraulic reservoirs burst during pressure testing, blasting hydraulic fluid through the inside of the left wing fillet area, we discovered that Skydrol was a good paint remover. It stripped the zinc chromate primer and all the identification tapes off the tubing. Hence the invention of SRF ... Skydrol Resistant Finish, that bright glossy white paint that you see in the lower confines of the airplane.

IT FLIES!

In the fall of 1957, the first 707 was rolled out and went to the flight line where it went through functional tests and engine run-ups. During the engine tests the EGT, Exhaust Gas Temperature harness, was being incinerated by the exhaust gases that it was supposed to measure -- an engineering problem caused by engineering.

The nacelles were designed to minimize frontal area and the cowl panels were tightly wrapped around the engines, causing huge headaches for the systems people who had to route round tubing through areas that were half the diameter of the tubes. So, many tubes were flattened to pass between the engine case and the cowl frames. There was virtually no space for airflow in some areas so things got hot -- like the EGT harness. We were told that the Douglas DC-8 had big fat round cowlings with plenty of clearance.

In spite of all the problems associated with the new airplane, it was fired up one dismal December 20, 1957 and taxied to the north end of the field, waited for a clear interval in the thick misty showers, spooled up, sending sheets of rainwater out into Lake Washington, and took off to the south over the city of Renton. I believe this was the only time that a jet airliner took off over the city much less the first flight of one, but it happened.

As soon as it gained enough altitude, it banked right and disappeared into the mist. Seven minutes later it landed at Boeing Field in Seattle. It was the shortest first flight on record, but it was made before the end of the year, thus escaping a contract penalty imposed by Trippe and PAA if it failed to do so. It missed the planned first flight date of December 17th, the day of the Wright brother's first flight, but it was on its way.

A strenuous flight test program followed and it fed back many things that required changes so many PRR's (Production Revision Record) came in to the program. One of the most expensive and misguided was the installation of retractable wind deflector panels at the leading edge of the main wheel wells to quiet the rumble of airflow when the landing great doors opened. The jets provided great speed, but with it came new and louder sounds and there was concern that the passengers would be frightened when they heard the noises during the deployment of the main landing gear. Vast sums were spent on a complicated and ineffective system of rods, cranks, actuators and panels to attenuate the sound. It didn't work and the system was abandoned. Passengers hear the sound nowadays and hardly notice it.

Sound was a serious problem in the early days. Engine exhaust noise from the J-57 was not only damaging to the ears, but it could destroy metal. The early engines were designed to move air at high velocity and produced ear-splitting shrieks at full power, especially when using water injection. Two hundred and fifty gallons of distilled water was carried in the wheel well keel beam and all of it was used at takeoff. The injection of water had the effect of closing the clearances between the compressor blade tips and the case thus raising the pressure ratio. It also allowed a healthy increase in fuel flow to the combustion chambers without the danger of flame creep and pre-ignition. So it boosted the power output of the engines.

There was no noise worse than a KC-135 taking off at 100% with water injection, except maybe a B-52 that had twice the number of engines. The effects of the supersonic sound from the KC-135 engines can be seen in the addition of belly-bands on the aft body skins that were being destroyed by the noise. Now you certainly couldn't have that on a civilian airliner so the "daisy petal" exhaust pipe was designed to attenuate the sound by quickly mixing cooler air with the exhaust gases when they were slowing down and going through shock speeds. That muffler worked well as did the clamshell thrust reversers ahead of them. It appears that the same sound attenuation design is being used on the 787 by the chevron edges of the nacelle near the tail pipe.

TROUBLE AT THE KITE FACTORY

Near the end of the 1950's, the pace was beginning to bog down in spite of massive overtime and a huge work force. We were told that the company was having financial problems and in spite of finally pulling ahead of Douglas, we weren't making money, just spending it. Bill Allen, the president of the company, abruptly announced the removal of the VP and manager of the transport division. The company comptroller, J.O. Yeasting, was in charge. And indeed he was!

The successes of the war production days still pervaded the thinking and actions of those who drove the company through those frantic times. The old "cost plus 10 and kill it with overtime and manpower" paradigm was still in force after ten years. Yeasting changed that in a matter of days, literally. His first move was to fire ONE HALF the production line workforce, scaring the daylights out of everyone. The grade of notepaper pads was lowered to the absolute bottom, mimeographed memos (remember that process?) were not thrown away, but cut up and glued together to be used again as note pads. Overtime was cut to an absolute minimum and many support employees were reassigned to real work positions. Even the grade of toilet paper was lowered to the minimum and, thank the Lord, we didn't have to use that over and over.

I don't believe that I ever experienced such a rapid, wide-ranging and deep attack on a problem. No one escaped the effects of Yeasting's actions. The lowest level employees were scrutinized and those who had not been consistent performers were let go.

Some lower level supervisors were demoted and soon everyone was looking over their shoulders. We never got the feeling that this was a vindictive inquisition. It was a cathartic cleansing from stem to stern that eliminated all the unnecessary expenses, poor performers, ineffective employees, excessive overtime and deadwood. However, the concern over the release of 6000 production line workers turned to amazement when the production rate increased. No longer were people waiting for others to finish their jobs so they could move into the area to do theirs.

The demeanor of the work force began to change. There was direction instead of busy work and everyone settled into a more structured routine where the links between operations were shortened and clearly defined. Directives from Yeasting's office filtered down through all levels of management and they not only acted on them, but also added their own initiatives. Their heads were on the block, too.

Intra-organizational cooperation appeared to be part of the change and old fiefdoms began to disappear. Engineering that formerly enjoyed an elevated and autonomous position in the company began to work within the schedules to which the rest of the factory was bound. In earlier stages of the programs, they took whatever time they deemed necessary to achieve near perfection in their design work and figuratively threw the drawings over the wall for manufacturing to scramble as best they could to produce the work on schedule. They worked to their own schedule. Missed dates for the release drawings became a reason for a "hot" meeting with engineering, planning, tooling and manufacturing to iron out missed schedule milestones.

When engineering said they had met their drawing release dates on a certain installation, a planner stood up and said, "Do you mean this drawing?" He then displayed a blueprint that was released as stated, but the drawing field was blank except for some grid lines. Soon this sort of thing was eliminated and engineering was integrated into the rest of the work force.

Yeasting had orchestrated a "Perils of Pauline" rescue of the company at a time when the previous director was a successful veteran of WW2 production battles but was unable to adjust to a more lean and austere civilian type of business where there was no "cost plus 10" profit structure. Yeasting was the comptroller and he saw the books every day and knew what had to be done and he knew how to do it. I'm convinced that his rapid and surgically deep action saved The Boeing Company from a financial disaster.

"Donald Duck" Kiddie Pool | Boeing Co.

BACK TO THE SHOP FLOOR

One thing that mollified the seriousness of the times was a product of the company suggestion system. An employee noticed the similarity of the engine nacelle intakes diameter and the six-dollar plastic wading pool in which his children played. The dimension of the pool diameter wasn't close, it was exact. He suggested replacing the expensive intake plugs with a plastic wading pool and received a handsome reward. Touring visitors were amused to see Walt Disney's Goofy and friends stuck into the front of a 1.5 million dollar engine.

Nineteen sixty was my tenth year with the company and I had seen it change from a rather rough and austere organization that relied on its engineering prowess, to one that began to recognize the benefits of communicating with the public AND its employees. When I started in 1950, the company was still in a WW2 mode of operation: factory management by intimidation, isolation of "lower level" employees from information regarding company operations and plans, isolation of the company from the public and an overall company attitude of introversion. Everything corporate was close to the vest and no need to share anything with outsiders.

Now, the huge success of the 707 had thrust the company into worldwide fame for something other than the B-17. The struggle to regain some postwar footing had turned into a headlong scramble to keep up with its own progress. Certainly the B-52 and KC-135 could not be discounted for boosting the company, for these were huge successes on the military side and would continue to be so for the next 60 years, but we didn't know that then. Seattle in the 50's was an unsophisticated conservative sleepy sort of town for its size. The people, mostly of Scandinavian descent, were rather clannish and newcomers got a jaundiced eye. There was nothing really outstanding about the city, but the scenery and fishing were magnificent.

Following close behind the 707-120 series came the Intercontinental 707-320 and then behind that the 720 and the 720-B. Orders were pouring in from all over the world and the assembly lines in the old saw-tooth building were jammed nose to tail with 707's, KC-135's and 720's. Boeing had quickly and wisely filled most of the route requirements with airplanes that fit: medium range, long range and shorter range. The company had become the international icon for air travel. In Europe, the "707" became the ubiquitous word for any jet transport. A jet was a 707, just as any facial tissue is a "Kleenex." Work methods and attitudes changed. They had to in order to address the more sophisticated construction of the airplanes, but the changes became routine quickly and smoothly.

We were getting things running pretty well and then the company announced a new SHORT RANGE airplane and a huge factory expansion in which to build it. The 727 had arrived.

At this time, my work kept me in engineering more and more and I visited Preliminary Design many times. I met a man in my search for design data who was a German ex-patriot. He was an impressive man who, for some reason, took a liking to me and we struck a quick friendship. We talked for hours about airplane design and what Boeing was doing. He stated that the 707 was a "stupidity" for having so much dihedral and sweep back combined and for being so low to the ground. His name was Henry Quenzler and he told me that he had been an engineer and test pilot for the Dornier Company before and during the war and had been a test pilot on many of the pre-war flying boats.

To illustrate the difference in flight test in 1938 and the flight test of today was his story about a possible hull defect in one of Dornier's flying boats. The hulls were leaking after rough water landings so Henry took one up to find the problem. He found the ocean liner Bremen in the Atlantic outbound for the U.S.A. and landed the flying boat 90 degrees to the wake of the ship, directly into the wave. The impact was so tremendous that a solid spray of water erupted between him and the co-pilot. Henry said that he thought that his "bottom had come up to his back teeth" (a cleaned up version of his actual words). They had found the problem.

Then near the end of the war, he was one of the designers and test pilots on the DO-335, one of the most bizarre and potentially the most deadly bomber-killing fighters of WW2. He related how angry and frustrated he was when he couldn't complete a flight test without some "damn P-51 shooting holes in my airplane". He wasn't a Nazi. He was a total aeronautical engineer and pilot who didn't give a hoot about the Nazi's, but did his job as a German. He taught me many things about aircraft design and later in the 707 program, his predictions came true.

The 707 was inflicted by a phenomenon called "Dutch Roll" caused by over stabilization from coupling seven degrees of dihedral with 35 degrees of sweep-back. Then when the company tried to stretch the airplane it was impossible because the landing gear was too short and a lengthened tail could strike the ground on takeoff.

I learned much later that Henry was involved in a secret squadron, KG-9 I think, and he flew huge Junkers transports over Russia to Japan and back during the war. He never mentioned that part of his life to me. He was all about aeronautical engineering and flying. I lost track of Henry when we both were involved in those hectic days and I regret it. He was a fascinating and brilliant man.

MEET THE AOG

In the mean time since there was no competition that equaled the 707, almost every overseas airline purchased the Boeings and as the number of operators increased, so did the accidents.

The first incident occurred at Idlewild Airport in New York when a TWA pilot overshot the runway and bellied-in the airplane in an unsuccessful attempt to make a go-around. Remember, this was a transitional period where long time "recip" pilots were changing to jets and many deeply ingrained propeller procedures had to be un-learned. In this particular incident, the pilot used a DC-7 go-around sequence:

1. Apply power,
2. Initiate climb while you retract the gear.
3. Reduce flap setting and gain altitude.

In a jet, the procedure is a bit different:

1. Apply power,
2. Wait for the engine to spool up to 100%,
3. Allow the airspeed to increase to climb speed,
4. Initiate a positive rate of climb,
5. Retract the landing gear and reduce flap settings.

A propeller-driven airplane benefits from instant thrust when power is applied. The propeller sends an immediate stream of air over the wing providing instant lift. A jet can climb only when a build-up of thrust from the engines accelerates the airplane to the point where the wings start to lift. The landing gear must be left in the down position until a positive rate of climb is established. The TWA airplane settled on to the runway while the landing gear was retracting and slid 5000 feet, grinding off most of the belly and losing all of the struts and engines. Fire heavily damaged the lower skins of both wings. The pictures of the wreckage showed us what we all thought was a write-off. Not according to AOG.

AOG means Airplane On Ground and Boeing had devised a crew and support system to respond to damaged airplanes anywhere in the world to get them airborne again as fast as possible. The earning power of these airplanes was worth the expense. What the AOG teams accomplished was astonishing. "AOG" was a signal that, when received, put in motion a team of experts in all disciplines of airplane design: production and operation. The most qualified people in every discipline went into action on a minute's notice.

A survey team was dispatched to the accident site to assess damage while a team of mechanics packed their bags, gathered the tools and portable equipment and flew to the accident site to begin work in a matter of hours. Field service engineers and planners armed with illustrated catalogues of major and minor assemblies ascertained what parts were needed for the repair.

Soon crates of preassembled major tools arrived by air and in a day or two the work started. Once the damaged parts were identified, they were ordered from the factory and flown to the site. This included things like entire fuselage panels, engines, struts, landing gear assemblies, seats, plumbing, wiring harnesses, carpets and exterior paint. If the part wasn't in spares or readily available, it was pulled off the assembly line.

The AOG crew performed miracles without the benefit of all the fancy equipment in the plant -- like a roof sometimes. They jacked the airplane up and most times supported it with wooden cribbing and makeshift jigs. They aligned the airplane with piano wire and transits, locked it in place and cut out all the damaged parts. Then the frantic but careful rebuild began.

The TWA airplane was back in the air in an amazing 33 days. Time to breathe easy.

Nope. Soon thereafter an Air France 707-320 undershot the runway at Guadalupe Island and ripped off the main landing gear and suffered the same damage as the TWA airplane. The AOG crew repaired it on the spot but before they finished it, a South African Airways 707-320 performed the same stunt in Nairobi and the crew had two airplanes to repair at the same time. As usual, they were all back in the air in about 35 days.

An incident that no AOG crew could fix occurred during a training flight over Washington State. We got word that a 707-227, a Braniff airplane, had gone down in the Skagit River near Arlington. Confusion and disbelief preceded the reports because larger JT-4 engines to improve high altitude take off performance powered that particular model. We soon found out that it happened during a customer training flight when he was learning how to control the airplane in an engine-out situation during takeoff. A swept-wing airplane is more dangerous than a straight wing plane when they are allowed to skid. The advancing wing generates more lift than the retreating wing and that's what happens when power is lost on one side. The yaw must be stopped with aggressive application and power adjustments to regain symmetry of forces.

The Braniff pilot failed to feed enough rudder quick enough to stop the yaw and the airplane went into a violent skid and did a snap roll, throwing off two of the engines. The Boeing test pilot took the controls as the airplane entered another snap roll after which he stabilized the airplane, but it had lost a third engine. There was only one engine to keep the airplane under marginal control but it was nothing more than a 200,000 pound powered glider and it was on its way down.

Full power was applied to remaining engine, the pilot ordered everyone into the rear section of the airplane and he made a crash landing in the rock-strewn riverbed, destroying the airplane and losing his life. The other crewmembers survived but with serious injuries.

There were other problems that surfaced that no designer could ever predict. An airline customer reported that the floors in their airplanes were getting spongy. Now this was a puzzle. The floors panels had been designed and tested to take the loads of many passengers standing in a small area. Vertical grain balsawood cores were sandwiched and bonded to .032 aluminum and they could take quite a load. However, when they were examined it was evident that their stiffness had been destroyed by extensive denting from something sharp.

The culprit, or culprits, were hundreds of well-dressed women wearing high-heeled shoes with stiletto heels. The metal sheathing had been pocked by heels no wider than 3/8th of an inch. Engineering calculated the load on the floor under the heel was in the range of almost 1500 pounds per square inch. It was back to the drawing board to cope with women's fashion, not to correct a design flaw.

Operational ambushes became a regular event after the 707 entered service and they weren't always man made. A Pan Am 707 came in for a C check and when they opened up the fuel tanks they were greeted by a sight that could have come from a science fiction thriller movie. The interior was covered by black slime. After the initial shock wore off, they successfully cleaned it up and to their dismay they found that there was some surface etching in the aluminum structure.

After a frantic investigation, the culprit turned out to be secretions produced by an airborne microbe living in the moisture condensed in the air space of the tanks as they fed on jet fuel. The airplane had been operating in the Caribbean so all of the jets received an anti-microbe coating in the fuel tanks.

Then it was man's turn again to upset the best laid plans. A 707 operator ordered an interior trim panel to replace one that had been damaged. The replacement panel was returned because the color did not match the airplane. Another was sent and it too was returned because it didn't match. The color codes on record matched those of the customer's airplane and a representative was sent to see what the problem was. The problem was in the airplane, not with the color of the replacement panel. The 707 had been in service long enough to be discolored by cigarette smoke. Remember how everyone "lit up" in the 60's?

The tars left behind by cigarette smoke also gummed up the works in some of the delicate electronics and the fuselage skin aft of the cabin air outflow valve was streaked with brown goop.

The airplane's operational advances had left its human creators lagging behind in many areas, mainly, high-speed performance. It brings to mind an aviator's axiom: "Never let the airplane reach the destination 15 minutes before you do." No longer could aircrew set the airplane up in cruise and let it drone away on autopilot. Certainly the new jets had autopilots but unlike the prop jobs, when something went wrong, it went wrong quickly.

This was the case of a PAA 707 near Gander Newfoundland with near fatal and unsolvable results. The 707 was at a cruising altitude of 33,000 feet heading for London. The captain left the flight deck to go aft to chat with the VP of Pan American Atlantic Operations. While he was visiting, he noticed an increase in wind noise. Looking out of the window he saw stars when he should have seen the ocean. He made his way back to the flight deck, struggling with increasing G load. When he reached his position, he saw that the co-pilot was incapacitated and the airplane was in a steep diving spiral at an alarming speed. The Mach warning light was illuminated.

After a struggle to pull the airplane out of the dive, he succeeded at an altitude of 6000 feet and managed to make a safe landing. A thorough examination showed that the wings had reached the yield point and had a permanent bend in them: I recall two degrees of additional dihedral. The horizontal tail was replaced because of deformation and many sheet metal access panels were missing. The upper wing-to-body fairings were crushed and buckled from the extreme bending of the wing. Unbelievably, there were no fuel leaks.

A reconstruction of the incident uncovered some rather simple conclusions. The airplane was not monitored as it was burning off fuel and getting lighter. As the airplane reduced its weight, the cruise Mach increased, the center of pressure moved aft and the airplane proceeded into a spiral dive.

What about the autopilot? It had tripped off line and couldn't respond to the problem. What about the Mach warning light? It was working but no one was watching. It was soon replaced by a bell. What about the humans? They weren't replaced, but there was some retraining was initiated. And the airplane? It had exceeded Mach 1 and the yield point of the wing without a failure of the primary structure. After repairs, it was returned to service. More proof that Boeing wings are supreme.

If that airplane had been recovered from its dive, the cause of its disappearance might never have been determined. Fate did not find its quarry this time.

Of all the problems that surfaced in the initial debut of the 707, some were quite mundane, like decorative paint. Sometimes it wouldn't stay on the airplane even though the best grade was applied and a plane came back with the paint literally blown off the nose. Okay, what do we have to do now! Something else has popped up. Taking a look at what happens to the paint when it goes from, let's say, a standard 60 degree day at sea level to 35,000 feet and -60 degrees in probably 20 minutes. The aluminum base is shrinking, the paint is also shrinking, but at a different rate and it is being blasted and battered by 575 mile-an-hour wind.

One cannot blame it for giving up and losing its grip and that was too much to ask of regular paint no matter how good it was. So the Boeing Processes group devised a primer that had an etching component added that bonded to the aluminum and a finish coat that bonded with the primer.

ENTER THE 720

By the late 50's, Boeing was on a roll with a full stable of 707's that fit most routes, but there was one more to be filled: the short-to-medium range "lighter" routes. The Boeing engineers put the 707-120 on a diet and they shortened it and reduced its weight down to a bit over 100,000 pounds. The 707-120's empty weight was about 25,000 pounds more.

The 720, the model number assigned to this new airplane, was pitched to the domestic airlines but this time, Boeing had some competition from another company, General Dynamics Convair. They were offering their 880 and it looked promising. Lockheed was busy sorting out their problems with the Electra, Douglas was concentrating on the DC-8, and so Boeing and Convair were in a tight race to sell their lightweights.

United Airlines was considering both airplanes and was leaning toward the smaller and very fast 880. To meet the weight and range requirements, Boeing was waiting for Pratt & Whitney to guarantee that they would have a lighter JT-3 for the 720. William Patterson, CEO of United, had opted to go with Convair and was in San Diego ready to sign an order for the 880 when he received a phone call from Bill Allen to inform him that Pratt & Whitney had guaranteed the lighter weight engine for the 720.

If the call had been 15 minutes later, the contract for the Convair 880 would have been signed but Bill Patterson performed a "180" and flew to Seattle to sign an order for 25 720's. Boeing continued to win big and Convair eventually folded and dropped out of the commercial airplane business.

The demise of Convair was an interesting example of "the right hand not knowing what the left hand was doing." They had a brilliant engineering staff, but serious problems in the developmental and manufacturing areas were successfully hidden from the executive level of management who were told only what their subordinates wanted them to hear. By the time they heard the truth, it was too late to fix the problems and their commercial airplane program collapsed. Fortune Magazine published an extensive analysis of this incident entitled "How To Lose Control of A Large Corporation." It illuminated the differences in the way Bill Allen handled a similar problem at Boeing.

Like its predecessors, the 720 was an immediate success and it was purchased by many airlines here and abroad. More changes to improve the airplane came in rapid succession from the engineering department. It seemed that we had a new airplane every other month and if we didn't, it was a major modification to something. One of the most interesting was the fan engine, the JT-3D where a large-ducted fan was added to the front of the compressor section.

Instead of attempting to cram more air into the engine to increase jet thrust, it was discovered that the great torque of the basic engine could turn a larger fan that passed air down the outside of the engine, thus increasing the mass flow. The thrust of the basic engine was increased by 4000 pounds with a minimum increase in weight.

The changes at this time did not involve materials as much as it did techniques. Admittedly the new engine had a lot of titanium in it but nothing really new in the airplane, just steel and aluminum. When the drawings were released for the fan engine cowl, it caused an outcry from manufacturing because of the tolerance requirements of the cowling aft of the fan. Surface ripples and depressions from manufacturing operations were to be held at one ten thousandth of an inch. Sonic and supersonic airflow out of the fan would not tolerate a rough surface.

Manufacturing said that they couldn't achieve the tolerances called for. Engineering said that they HAD to. Manufacturing did it and the installation was a roaring success. As an added benefit, the cuff of fan air covering the exhaust acted as an effective silencer.

All of the 707 series were modified to take this engine and they benefited from the increased power as well as lower specific fuel consumption but the airplane that used the fan to its fullest was the 720, now labeled the 720B. Concurrently, the aero guys came up with a modification to the inboard wing that eliminated a serious drag problem and boosted the cruise Mach. A Fiberglas and aluminum glove was added to the leading edge between the inboard struts and the fuselage.

It reversed the curvature of the wing upper surface at the wing root and diverted the flow from the upper surface to the lower surface eliminating a standing drag wave caused by the collision of wing airflow and body airflow above the wing. The increased chord at the wing root also increased the sweep angle at the wing's thickest point so the combination of the fan engine and wing glove made a hotrod out of the 720B.

An interesting incident occurred with the 720B operated by Western Airlines. They were chronically splitting the bleed ducts that supplied air to the turbo compressors that provided cabin pressure at high altitude. The duct was made of 1/8th inch stainless steel and should have withstood normal operational pressures and heat at the 14th compressor stage bleed.

Western Airlines was the only operator splitting these ducts so an engineer went to Seattle-Tacoma airport to talk to a Western Airlines representative to find out why. When he asked what power settings they were using, the answer was, "Anything to beat United, yeah, we're running just under the bell" (the critical Mach warning bell). Indeed, that airplane could exceed critical Mach if it wasn't monitored as the fuel burned off.

As an example, I was on a production test flight of a Northwest Airlines 720B in 1963 when we climbed to 35,000 feet in less than 10 minutes after takeoff. The airplane weighed 163,000 pounds so it was light. The climb was steep enough so that all one could see was clear blue sky until we leveled off.

The 720B was the final expression of the 707 series. The -80 design was slightly enlarged to fit the requirements of the KC-135 and the 707-120. Then it was stretched and the wing area was increased for the -320 series. Then the KC-135 was morphed into many different electronic surveillance marvels. All through these modifications and disguises, the original 367-80 configuration prevailed not only in Boeing airplanes but also in most other successful jet airliners.

The DeHaviland Comet, with its engines buried in the wing root and external wing mounted fuel tanks, initiated a comment from Wellwood Beal that held true, "They put the engines in the wing where they should have put the fuel and put the fuel in tanks hanging off the wing where the engines should be."

Chapter 17.

Up-grade to Employee Development Training Instructor.

STEP UPWARD

In the middle of the 720 program when I was a lead in the illustration group, I was offered a job as an engineering instructor in the Employee Training Group. The company was approaching a rapid build-up to produce the new airplanes that seemed to be popping out of the walls once a week. We were hiring new engineers not only from colleges in the U.S, but from almost every country in the world. They had to be trained in the Boeing engineering systems and I had to develop a program to train them.

The fact that I lacked an engineering degree weighed heavily on me, but at that point I knew more than the new students did about the subjects in this instance so I had to play it accordingly. We studied the Boeing drawing system that was and is the most convoluted arrangement that anyone could devise. But once you have mastered it, you could rule the world. Then there was the use of the hardware standards manuals and the Boeing Design standards manuals that segued into the design of flat patterns for detail parts and the proper standards required to install them. Then there were several sessions on manufacturing processes from lofting to the assembly of the thousands of parts that made an airplane.

The most interesting part of this training program was meeting men who had been in Europe when the Nazis were in power and those who came from Germany after the war. The Polish students were so violently anti-Russian that I had to avoid any discussion about what they endured during the war and after it. Some of the German students were still arrogant and could not admit that they lost the war.

One engineer was a Polish ex-patriot who escaped his country on skis while Russian troops were in pursuit and firing at him. He minced no words in his hatred for Russia and Germany. Unbelievably, twenty years later I worked with him AND his son in the 767 program. Some of the English guys had a rather glib and dispensing attitude about America as being rather basic and uncouth. I noticed later that many of them had moved to the rather fancy neighborhoods in Bellevue and had put on a lot of weight in a few years. 1960-1963 was an interesting period when we drained a lot of brainpower from Europe and the company certainly benefited from it.

The 727 program used many of these engineers and the program joined the 707, KC-135 and 720 that were in full production. Boeing was operating like a blast furnace with one new commercial program after another.

Just when you thought it was safe to go to work and work on something you knew, out popped another airplane. Boeing saw that the shorter-range feeder routes needed an airplane so away we went again. It was only four years since the 707 hit the airways and in that time we built the -120 series, the -320 series, the 720/720B series and we were pumping out KC-135's along with the civilian airplanes. In a few months, the empty fields east of the old Renton plant were filled with sub assembly and new engineering buildings including a new administration building.

"YOU GUYS WILL NEVER GET ALL THAT TO WORK AT THE SAME TIME!"

The new 727 airplane was a huge jump in mission requirements, design and technology. The mission profile was that of an aerial Jackrabbit serving a string of short fields that were a short distance apart. All the jets so far were designed to take off from improved facilities, climb to very high altitudes and cruise for thousands of miles in calm smooth air.

The new airplane had to be designed to take off from short unimproved fields, quickly climb to a cruising altitude where the engines were efficient and in a short time, descend to another unimproved airport, pick up passengers, deplane passengers with its own equipment and then take off again and rapidly climb to altitude to repeat the same routine in a short time. This required some thinking "out of the box" to design an airplane that would have to be "out of the box."

At the time I was a training instructor and had been given the assignment to design several training courses to apprise employees in all departments in what was to come. Therefore, I spent most of my time in engineering as the airplane went through many design iterations and saw it emerge as a three-engine tee-tailed bird with all kinds of innovations in the structures and systems.

The engines were mounted on the fuselage instead of on the wing and the wing took full advantage of advanced manufacturing technology. It was one piece from the fuselage out to the tips, no splices and very much like a good light line fishing rod. The absence of engines left the wing as a clean highly efficient fatigue tolerant answer to the difficult mission.

The wing was comparatively short to aid in a fast cruise, but to enable the 727 to get into and out of shorter fields, it was provided with powerful high lift triple-slotted flaps and leading edge slats. These devices effectively changed the shape of the wing from a high-speed, low drag section to a highly curved, high-lift shape. This allowed a steeper slower descent and a steeper climb out of short fields. When it was deployed for landing, this system required 80% thrust to push it through the air so that it would work. And it did work! I witnessed Lew Wallick, Chief of Flight Test demonstrate the airplane to a potential customer. One day he made a maximum performance approach into Renton and had the airplane stopped 1800 feet down field from the fence. Being an ex-navy fighter pilot, he came very close to setting it up to land on an aircraft carrier -- I was told.

The wing was a masterpiece of design and engineering and the manufacturing people worked out a system to shot-peen the one-piece skins into the complex curves to match the lofting. The fuselage skins were joined not only with rivets, but were bonded with a new adhesive to extend their fatigue life. A lot of ribs in the tail were precision one-piece forgings instead of being fabricated with rivets and many small pieces. The 727 was highly successful in every respect and we sold more of them than any previous airliner: 1800 of them.

The wing and the high-lift devices were the secret and at first, the machinery in the trailing edge was almost frightening to look at. One day when I was taking a group of airline pilots on tour of the mock-up, one of them shook his head and said, "You will never get all of that to work at the same time!" Well, it did and it turned out to be one of the most reliable systems on the airplane.

The public interest in the new products and especially the 727 brought the company to realize that it had to respond to its rapidly rising status in the world and not only was it modernizing its production skills, but it had to open up its response to the public. Internally it initiated Employee Relations, Industrial Relations and then Community Relations to supplement Public Relations. I spent 90 percent of my time either conducting tours of public dignitaries, schoolteachers and civic organizations. I traveled to many states to give talks and lectures about the 727 and I trained over 2000 people in-plant in how the 727 was built and how it operated.

Then I did a similar job when I was transferred to the 747 where so much of the 727 wing concept was used, but in a much bigger scale.

I was working a heavy load of overtime and my wife decided that there were more entertaining things to do and our marriage ended. I eventually ended up with our four boys and a goofy housekeeper who I soon dismissed. So, it was just us guys and a lot of confusion and fear. I determined that I would be available for them 24 hours a day every day of the week and that meant sometimes leaving work during the day but it worked. We spent every evening and every weekend together and many times we would go to the old Issaquah airstrip to watch the gliders and airplanes.

Chapter 18.

Princess Judy and flying adventures in air shows.
Enter the 747.

HANDS ON AGAIN

One Saturday afternoon, an Aeronca Champ landed and I started a conversation with the pilot, a bachelor and a Boeing engineer. Nothing fancy here, the Champ was just a plain silver airplane and the pilot was just as unimposing. We struck up a friendship and soon he had me flying again after 15 years on the ground. So, the kids and I were soon enjoying the aerial delights of that little Champ and instead of driving to the nearby airfields we flew.

I slowly regained some of my touch, but not all of it and the responsibility of four little boys attenuated my desire to do anything risky. It was wonderful to be able to fly again. I went through all the drills and regained coordination almost to where I wanted it but the lengthy layoff had a permanent dilution of the sharpness that I once had. My boys and I had already been making regular visits to an airport south of us, Thun Field, a private strip that was full of antiques and homebuilts and was almost off the radar of the FAA. It was also off the beaten path of urban development and we had the most wonderful sunny weekends there in the summer of 1966 flying everything you have never heard of and some that were well known. The freedom that we enjoyed was something that will never be seen again in private aviation.

There was only one large closed hangar on the field, all the rest were T-hangars of various health conditions and some even had doors on them. Valuable and extremely rare antiques were rolled out into the sunshine for their owners to work on or to fly. Have you ever seen a Student Prince? A Corben Baby Ace powered by a 40HP Salmson radial? There was a Monocoupe 90, a Curtiss Robin with an OX-5, a Monocoupe 165, UPF-7, PT-13,PT-17, several Flybaby's, 1913 Curtiss pusher, Cubs, Fokker Triplane, 10 homebuilts, "his and hers" Ryan STA and PT-22, T-6, Pietenpol Aircamper with a Ford Model B engine, an early helicopter, several Pitts's, and I almost forgot, a P-38.

One never knew what he would see in the air or what they might do when they were up there. There were shows every weekend. The P-38 belonged to a WW2 Ace, Capt. Larry Blumer, who shot down 5 Fock-Wulf 190's in less than 10 minutes in a dog fight over a German airfield. His tales of WW2 action were like something out of a book.

He went through five P-38's all of which were named "Scrap Iron". After the first one he began to add numbers after the name and his WW2 token airplane was finished in the décor of his final P-38, "Scrap Iron 5."

His favorite war story was typical Blumer and one might not believe it but he had pictures to substantiate the story. He instructed the crew chief to remove the radios from the mounts on the wing that passed through the canopy directly behind the pilot. He was going out on a "test flight". As he told it, "To my great surprise at the end of the runway a pretty little French girl was there in the tall grass with a picnic basket. She managed to scramble up on to the wing with my help and just fit in that space where the radios were! So we flew to another wheat field and had a nice picnic lunch and a special dessert." It was a very important test flight.

The range of expertise and ability in flying and building was extensive. And one of the homebuilders decided to enter his Pitts in the Biplane Race at Reno and performed a variety of modifications to lighten the airplane and to clean it up. The Scott tail wheel was replaced by a little furniture dolly wheel for one.

When he was preparing to qualify for the Biplane Race, he was informed that he had to wear "A hard hat" in order to meet the racing rules. That afternoon he appeared wearing a child's toy plastic soldier's helmet. Facing the safety committee's objections, he held them to the wording in the rule book that simply stipulated a "hard hat". He had them, but it lasted only one race because when he started his take off the prop wash and wind lifted the hat straight into the air until the elastic strap broke. Bruce was a lot of fun.

One of the funniest incidents happened when one of the less educated homebuilders decided to fly one of his creations one Saturday. It was a rather flimsy contraption powered by two chainsaw engines mounted on 2x4 struts protruding from either side of the cockpit in the nose. The creator could reach the starter ropes from his place in the cockpit and yank the engines into life.

After he herded his mount to the end of the strip, he applied the full force of his screaming power plants and ACTUALLY took off -- but not for long. His elephantine body, that weighed more than half of his airplane, was too much for it to sustain flight and we watched as it staggered over the trees at the end of the strip and settled into the brush in a cloud of dust.

Before anyone could fully respond, another antiquer jumped into his 1950's era helicopter that my son called "a blown-down TV tower" and flew over to the crash site and lowered a sling for the downed pilot to affect his rescue. The comic opera reached its climax when the ponderous "victim" climbed into the sling -- AND PULLED THE HELICOPTER TO THE GROUND. Even Buster Keaton would have laughed at this routine.

My kids had a wonderful world on our weekends at Thun Field. They got to watch an array of airplanes that were flying historic artifacts in some cases and many times they got to fly in them. When they tired of that, they walked over to the drag strip east of the field to watch the cars. I learned 30 years later that when they were tired of the race cars they were teaching themselves to drive our Volkswagen bus while I was up flying. And today, every one of them is a "motorhead". I got to fly quite a few airplanes and got some of the feel back, but I was nowhere near what some of the gang were doing there. One was an ex-air force pilot who was a Monocoupe aficionado and an accomplished aerobatic performer. He rebuilt a 1941 Monocoupe and powered it with a 165 HP Warner and put on weekly shows with it while he practiced for air shows.

In the L-3 South of Roseburg, OR | Robert Parks

I flew with him several times while he practiced and I experienced his routine called, "Four and a half G for Four and Half Minutes." That is a real work out! When the flying gang at Thun Field was picked for a local TV show, the producer wanted their cameraman to film the routine from the cockpit. He refused, so I got the task of operating the big 16mm camera with the Mickey Mouse ears. It probably weighed about 15 pounds or more. Pulling out at 4½ G and going negative at 4½ G is not conducive to good filming.

While I was being driven into the seat on a pull up with 65 pounds of camera on my shoulder, I got great shots of my shoes and rudder pedals. Then on the negative maneuvers I was struggling to keep the camera from flying out through the skylight. The TV people said they couldn't use any of the footage. I thought that it would have been funny.

The next year we were again a part of a TV show called "Exploration Northwest" that featured the interesting activities of local people. They wanted to do a feature on our second flight to Merced, California to attend the annual antique fly-in. Pete Bowers would be in his Fly Baby biplane, my friend would fly Pete's Pietenpol Aircamper and I would fly an Aeronca L-3 that we had restored. A description of that will follow. Total horsepower for all three airplanes -- 200 HP.

Flying over the flat lands of the mid-west in this type of equipment is no problem. Flying the spine of the Cascades and Sierras was a problem. The route would take us from Thun Field south of Seattle to points south along I-5, over flat valleys until we got to Eugene, Oregon. Then the mountains started. We didn't stay over the road all the time and we cruised along the sides and crests of the mountains where we could see deer and other animals just below. Pete's airplane had a 16-gallon tank and had more range than the rest of us who had 10 gallons and a 120 to 150 mile range. So, we had to refuel every hour and a half.

The TV crew followed us on the road in an air-conditioned motor home and they were always waiting for us at our scheduled fuel stops where we inevitably drew a crowd after we landed. The Pietenpol looked like a Mickey Mouse airplane with its simple slab wing and the Model A engine sticking up in the front. Pete's airplane looked like an old biplane from the 30's, the L-3 was finished in accurate WW2 camouflage and markings since it was an old liaison plane from WW2. The trio was unlike the usual Cessna's and Pipers that frequented the airports.

As we flew south, the sunny clear weather held and we had smooth legs between fueling stops. Since the L-3 had two seats, I got to carry several of the TV crew on different legs so that they could take movies. In the middle of the boring stretch between Salem, Oregon and Eugene, the Aircamper pulled alongside of us and the TV photographer started filming just as the Aircamper did a snap roll and entered a spin. I followed him down spiraling outside of him and we got some outstanding and dizzying footage. The studio didn't use it for some reason.

Working our way down through the mountains south of Eugene, we easily flew through the passes that gave us some real heartburn the year before when the ceiling pushed us down over the road in Wolf Creek Canyon. With the peaks in the clouds, all we had in front of us was the dim light of an inverted delta that was getting smaller by the minute. The road in that section of the pass is steep with tight curves so we went into a trailing formation and wound our way up to the summit, flying just over the cars.

Some were passing me since I was only five to ten miles per hour over stall speed at times. We made it over the hump and reached our stop at Ashland, Oregon where we stayed for the night.

We were greeted by a very pretty girl instructor who was totally undone by the Pietenpol. After looking into the cockpit she had some questions.

"Where's the magnetic compass?" she asked.

"Doesn't have one", the pilot answered.

"Where's your radio?"

"At home on the night stand where it belongs!"

"Is THAT BOARD the seat?" she asked as she looked down into the wooden structure.

"Yup, first class."

"I have never seen and airplane engine that looked like that."

"Not an airplane engine it's a car engine."

She looked at us with a pained expression, threw up her hands and went into the office.

The next morning we filled the five-gallon gas cans that we had to carry because there was no FBO (Fixed Base Operator) at our next stop, Dunsmuir, California. We would need it too after a hard climbing spiral after takeoff at Ashland so that we could clear Siskiyou Summit at 5500 feet and close by. This is where the overweight and underpowered L-3 showed its displeasure at high altitude flight. It was a liaison plane designed for close cooperation with army ground operations and it was sturdy and heavy.

We scooted through the cut in the rocks at the summit. The clouds were still hanging around and we started the long run across the high plateau to Dunsmuir. Here we hit strong headwinds and turbulence caused by the lumpy terrain below. We were getting kicked around like we were in a washing machine, up, down, sideways and wings vertical a few times. Ground speed wasn't measured but I knew that I was way behind the other two airplanes.

Approaching the town of Shasta, I got trapped in the rotor behind a good-sized hill and realized that it was out-climbing me. The L-3 simply quit trying to go up and after staring at the upturned faces of two girls on horses, I decided to head for the flat to the west where I did catch some smoother air coming up out of the canyon. The calculated ground speed for the last ten miles = 40 MPH.

The north landing approach to the strip at Dunsmuir somewhat parallels the glide slope, at least for the L-3 and I succumbed to the visual trickery of it and seriously undershot my approach. Almost too late, I applied full power and could almost feel the ragged stumps as they went by. It would have been literally a pain in the ass if I clipped one of them. The L-3 threw up a cloud of dust as it hit in the runout 20 yards from the end of the strip. I was getting some quick lessons in flying in the mountains. It looks like I missed that lesson when I was training in Florida where the highest point is 300 feet.

Sure enough, as we were refueling the airplanes, a parade of cars roared into the strip hangar area to see the airplanes and we became aware that there were antiquers wherever we landed. From Dunsmuir to Red Bluff was downhill finally and we arrived there in late afternoon, passing over the baseball field as we entered the pattern.

By the time we had landed and taxied up to the ramp, there must have been 30 people already at the airport. There was a strong crosswind to the main runway that wasn't too much of a problem, but when the Pietenpol came in to the ramp it had a tailwind and a good head of speed. The line boy, eager to show his good service, ran out to the Pietenpol like he always did with normal airplanes, but the pilot had to yell twice, "NO BRAKES!" The kid darted out of the way as the airplane was put into not one but many ground loops, going round and round.

One of the guys in the crowd said, "Maybe I should go home and get my shotgun and shoot the damn thing!"

We finally got everything under control and began refueling. The poor line boy had no idea what to do with the Aircamper and asked if that thing in the front behind the engine was a bug screen. The pilot admitted that it did serve as that when it wasn't a radiator and then asked the line boy if there was a coffee maker in the office.

"Would you like a cup?"

"Nope, just one of the pots with some water in it."

The line boy stood in amazement as the pilot climbed on the wheel and added some water to the radiator with a Silex pot.

We over-nighted there and resumed our journey down the San Joaquin Valley in good weather until we got south of Manteca where the visibility went to zero in a hurry. We had flown into heavy smoke that made things IFR, blind. Still over Highway 99, I started to make a rapid descent when a Grumman Albatross emerged from the murk coming right at me. I made the descent much more rapidly, like in a dive, until I was a few hundred feet over the road and made my way to Merced which was in the clear by then. Unbeknownst to us, the farmers were burning their fields.

It was my first time to the Merced Antique Fly-In and I felt like a kid in a candy store with every conceivable type of old airplane in attendance. We gave rides in our airplanes and rode in others and I managed to do some right seat time in Bill Harrah's Ford Tri Motor. For me it was about the same as flying our living room but it was fun. Some of the visiting "Spam Can" pilots asked interesting questions about our flight down from Seattle. One fellow asked how long it took and upon hearing 14.5 hours spread over two and a half days, he said, "Hell, I can drive it faster than that!"

"I think you should go do it," was one of the pilot's answers.

One little old lady asked the Aircamper pilot what he would do if the engine stopped since he didn't have a radio.

"I'd land."

"But you wouldn't be over an airport. Nobody would know."

"Lady, the whole world is an airport. And I would know."

After flying in some of the aerial parades and looking at some wonderful restorations for 2½ days, we headed home and, of course, the God of the wind switched them so that we had a head wind going north just as we fought a headwind going south. Then as we got close to the higher passes, He added rain and clouds. We were held up for a day at Yreka-Montague until the weather changed from rain and fog to just rain clouds. We headed for Siskiyou Summit in "iffy" conditions and when we got there, the pass was in and out of the clouds. I was last to get there, as usual, and I watched Pete disappear into the roiling mists and saw the Pietenpol climb over the pass to the right side. The L-3 wasn't too sure it wanted to try it and with a bit of coaching we approached the pass to take advantage of an opening, but being the slowest airplane in the bunch, by the time we got there, the clouds dropped and started to close it up again. I spotted the tail lights of a truck as it crested the summit and followed it across until I figured that I should turn left a bit and drop down to follow the road as it descended on the north side of the mountain.

I timed it just right and broke into visible conditions as we paralleled the road down into the valley. When we refueled at Ashland I commented that I was glad that there were no wires crossing the notch through which I flew and the FBO said, "Whaddaya mean? There's wires going over to that cabin." I remember catching the flash of a metal roof to my left as we went through the gap. Hmm. The sectional charts didn't indicate any wires crossing the gap. Did I go over or under them?

The rest of the trip home was uneventful and all we had to dodge were a few rain showers and headwinds, but now in our 1970 trip, we enjoyed clear skies and the favor of the Wind God who blessed us with tail winds all the way.

When we stopped at Roseburg, Oregon the producer of the show wanted to ride in the front cockpit of the Pietenpol and do some of the filming. Ordinarily that wouldn't be a problem but Tim, the producer, weighed well over 200 pounds and he wasn't a typical person, he had been the center on the Rose Bowl Champion University of Washington football team and he hadn't shrunk any in his succeeding years.

The Pietenpol was a small plane with a parasol wing mounted directly over the front cockpit so the struts and wires presented a challenging entry for even a small person. So, after threading Tim through the obstacle of lift struts and wires, three of us supported his upper body while he struggled to pack his legs into the tiny and cramped forward cockpit. Then, with his knees almost jammed up to his chin, he was in place with a grin on his face.

Of course, we were concerned about exceeding the gross weight of the Pietenpol, as if one had ever been established, but the pilot said that if he could get the tail up, it would fly. To our amazement, it flew quite well and it didn't seem to bother about the heavyweight up front that decreased the rate of climb a little bit.

When we arrived at our next fuel stop, Ashland, Oregon, the Aircamper displayed an increased rate of descent, like a brick. I had landed first and knew that the Pietenpol was behind me so I waited off on the shoulder at the halfway point on the strip. The Pietenpol three-pointed at the very beginning of the strip and went by me like a runaway freight train, the pilot yelling, "Whoa! Dammit!" I saw a cloud of dust rise in the runout at the end of the strip and figured the worst had happened. After a minute or two, the Pietenpol came taxiing up the strip none the worse for wear.

Then the fun started when we had to extract Tim from the little torture chamber in which he was trapped. It must have taken us twenty minutes to pull him out and another twenty minutes for him to get his cramped and numb legs working again.

Our little sideshow gave the airport people some free entertainment. Tim managed to get some interesting footage of the left side of the Model B engine and its ice covered carburetor that could deliver a cold chunk in the face to an unwary pilot who happened to look around the left side of the radiator after pulling on carb heat.

The next morning we left Ashland and cleared Siskiyou summit with empty seats in the Pietenpol and L-3. The TV crew decided to meet us at Dunsmuir where we would refuel. Unlike the previous year, the airport now had an operator and we didn't have to carry our own fuel. The guy operating the strip was just that, an "operator". He presented himself as a very bad reincarnation of Gen. George Patton, the pompous air and gravelly voice coupled with an announcement that he had been an Air Force Colonel, or something, completed the picture. He orchestrated the parking arrangement of our old airplanes and got on the radio to order a transmission line check pilot to land and see "all these old airplanes."

After we refueled, the TV crew said that they wanted to film us in formation flying by Mt. Shasta that loomed clear and beautiful that day. "Ace" announced that he would fly the cameraman to film the formation in his Citabria. Great! That would work just fine and then after the shot we would continue on our way. Dunsmuir/Mott was at 5000 feet and we had to climb to approximately 6000 feet to get set up for the picture. That took wide-open throttle for a good 15 to 20 minutes to climb up and to get formed in a three plane Vic. When we had gotten into position, I caught sight of the Citabria roaring by on my right at flank speed for ONE PASS! And too far out! Okay. I guess that's way they were going to do it, but I thought that Ace would close up with us and stay a while to get some good footage.

After he peeled away and went back to the airport, we continued down the valley to Redding/Enterprise. Ten minutes later I stole a look at the sight gage, a glass tube with a cork float in it that showed fuel level in the tank over my head, and realized that I should have gone back to "Ace's Place" to refuel. The gage was well below the half tank level and I had about 60 miles to go. At normal cruise settings the I-3 burned 4.5 gallons per hour at 70mph. I estimated that I had about 4.0 gallons left.

I pulled back to 1100 RPM and started to look for lift, after all, it was downhill from Dunsmuir and I didn't have to hurry. The temperature was 88 degrees when we took off from Dunsmuir and wasn't the best formula for lift, so I slid over to the weather side of the canyon walls and sure enough I could feel a little bump at times in my rear end and we began to ride some ridge lift. To my amazement, I could spot the Pietenpol ahead of me doing the same thing. Aha! He was low on fuel, too! We zigzagged down the canyon riding the hot wind that was splashing up the sides of the hills.

As I neared Lake Shasta I couldn't get a bounce out of the fuel gage float and I started to look at gaps between cars on the road below as possible landing spots. Crossing the bridge over the lake, I got lower and a bit nervous because I knew that the engine was close to not making that nice noise up front. The Pietenpol headed to the right because there was a golf course over there but I could see Enterprise strip ahead and I kept it in sight as I lowered the nose and hoped that there wasn't traffic in the pattern because it was going to be a one-time straight-in approach.

I couldn't believe that I had made it when I crossed the runway threshold! Level off and flare for a nice three-point landing. Whoa! No noise up front! The engine just quit! I had been running on the two-gallon header tank for the last 10 minutes or so and when I pulled the nose level it quit feeding. Never mind! We made it.

The L-3 took 11 gallons, the Pietenpol took 9.6 so that meant that his tank had .4 gallons left and the L-3 had used everything in the 10-gallon main tank and half of the 2-gallon header tank. It cost a whopping $6.50 to fill the tanks in the L-3.

The heat after landing was unbelievable! As we were parking the airplane we saw the Pietenpol coming in on a right hand descending approach. It got straightened up, but it didn't flare as it neared the ground and the Pietenpol flew into the runway shattering the prop! A hard bounce preceded an excursion off the runway where the airplane sat with no movement from pilot. When we got there he was semi–conscious. The radiator was hissing steam and we quickly figured out that the pilot had been overcome by the ambient heat that was hovering around 110 degrees and flying behind a radiator that indicated 210 degrees. He was fortunate to have made it.

He quickly recovered with copious quantities of water and cool towels and then we turned our attention to replacing the broken propeller. Thanks to the generosity of the Enterprise guys, we were allowed to remove any wooden propeller from any airplane on the field to see if it would work on the Pietenpol. The rest of the day was spent trying out at least six different props and none of them were the correct pitch/diameter combination. Some had the correct diameter but the pitch was too flat and it would be like trying to cruise a car in first gear.

Others were just the opposite, with too much pitch so the little Ford engine could not get high enough revolutions. That would be like starting a car off in fourth gear. As we sat there exasperated, one of the airport guys said, "There's a tavern in town with a prop mounted on the wall behind the bar, I'm gonna' go get it." We never gave it a second thought. Fat chance that'll happen! Fifteen minutes later he returned with a nice shiny wooden prop.

Unbelievably, the mounting holes matched and the prop was slipped into place as if it had been made for the airplane. The airplane was cranked up and it got full static RPM. That was a promising sign, so the pilot made a test flight with it and to our amazement, it flew better than it did with the original propeller! It was a tale out of a storybook! A wall decoration yanked from its place in a tavern over the bar that saved our day. The TV crew couldn't have written a better script.

After we had settled the propeller problem, I thought about the formation footage above Dunsmuir and the single high-speed distant pass made by Ace who was supposed to fly next to us for some beautiful footage with Mt. Shasta in the background. I asked Bill Bacon, the photographer, who was with this retired "Air Force Colonel", what happened and he offered a concise statement," Didn't you see through that guy? He was a fake from the start. He couldn't fly that Citabria and he didn't want to get within 200 yards of you. As he made his pursuit run out in space he yelled at me, 'Get it now.' I figured what he was going to do and I had the camera set on a long telephoto slow motion shot." Bill got a beautiful shot of us struggling to maintain a tight formation in the thin air with Mt. Shasta as a backdrop.

Pete was planning to fly to Merced again the following year and promised to return the propeller and he kept that promise by strapping the propeller to the side of his little Flybaby and hand delivered it to the Enterprise bunch.

ONWARD AND DOWNWARD

That title would be a double entendre, because we were going south on the map and for some of us, to a lower altitude. Going from our struggles in the mountains to flying over the pool table flatland of the San Joaquin Valley was total boredom. Vast stretches of gray and tan grasses and rice fields as far as we could see.

The Pietenpol dropped down to skim the light gray fields at five feet or less and took a bead on a poor farmer chugging along on his tractor as he pulled a harrow. Coming from behind, he pulled up and over the guy and continued on his way while the farmer really messed up his nice straight line of tilling his field.

A cameraman was with me and he thought that we should form up with and above the Pietenpol to get some footage. Good Move! We were coming to the Sacramento River as it was winding through valley and the Pietenpol had dropped down to fly the river at something like 20 feet. We were tracing the twisties of the river and I had to concentrate on our course as we flew along with the Pietenpol just below. We had to dodge the tall trees lining the banks and I could only glimpse fleeting sights of the Pietenpol as it weaved its way around the tight curves. I did get a long enough look at a colorful scene of the little red and cream airplane up on one wing rounding a curve and darting between the dark green trees, the dark water just below it.

"Did you see that fisherman?" Joel, the cameraman, blurted out.

"No, what did he do?"

"When the airplane came around the bend, he tried to scramble up the bank but he slipped and slid into the river!"

This episode got us some good footage that was used in the TV program. We flew the river until we had to break away to get over to our instrument course, Highway 99 and more boredom.

We arrived at Merced in the late afternoon and noticed that there was a spot-landing circle painted on the runway so all of us tried it. The L-3 landed dead center in the circle but the Pietenpol put the wheels on the line in the center of the circle and the pilot won the spot-landing trophy. I looked at the score sheet that the girls were registering for each airplane and noticed that the winning airplane was listed as the "Pete and Paul."

We traded airplanes and lies for two and a half days and I got a wonderful surprise when my wife appeared unannounced! She had flown down on the Big Tin Bird and joined us for the fly in and the trip home in the L-3. When we left for our return flight, she was a bit abashed when I told her that the luggage and nice clothes had to be shipped home and that her "wardrobe" would consist of several changes of underwear, a toothbrush and hairbrush. Being a good trouper, she obliged and we left Merced in maybe not good shape, but light shape. There were some big rocks that we had to get over.

We were scheduled to stop at a friend of Pete's in the mountains east of Yuba City, Aero Pines. After refueling at Yuba City we, again, were challenged by the weather God and we had to snoop under the clouds through numerous canyons and draws to locate the place. We finally found it and had a very nice overnight there.

We departed in the same weather as the day before, but we were going downhill and out of the mountains so it wasn't so bad. We headed for Red Bluff on I-5 and planned a turn north for Redding. When we reached Red Bluff, the weather was rapidly deteriorating from low clouds to what looked like a cold front. The ceiling was dropping as fast as we were approaching Redding and by the time we got there it was black and down to the treetops. It started raining south of Redding and the visibility was extremely limited.

The rain increased and a strong gusting quartering tailwind arose as we were approaching the town. I saw on the sectional (aviation maps are called Sectional Charts) that there were three transmission towers up ahead, two on the left of the highway and one on the right. I wasn't going direct to Enterprise because I wasn't sure where the towers were in the murk.

Down to several hundred feet, we stayed over the highway and made a right turn at the stoplight and headed for the field. In the dark I spotted the airport ahead and to the left. By this time the raindrops were the size of grapes and the wind was howling. We couldn't hear the engine from the noise of the rain as we scooted diagonally over the field, passing over the office. Our groundspeed must have been over 100 MPH and I figured that we had just one chance to get down.

I made an early flat turn to the left and straightened out far to the right of the runway and let the howling gusting crosswind wind carry us to the threshold. I needed almost full power on the approach, because of the powerful gusts that began to kick us around in all directions. Right wing down and forward stick along with heavy right rudder as we passed over the end of the strip. Try as I did to outguess the gusts, I failed on the last one and we hit with a loud BANG on the right wheel. Poor Judy let out the only yell on the entire trip but she had good reason to, we were in a grip of a powerful black storm.

I kept the stick forward with right rudder and right aileron applied and almost full power to keep the airplane down because it was still leaping into the air as gusts came in. I didn't know what we were to do when we reached the area of the hangar; the airplane was still trying to fly. But then I saw four or five guys running toward us in the rain and, God Bless them, they grabbed the airplane and walked it to a spot where they chained it down.

The same routine was applied to the rest of the airplanes when they landed and all of us drenched to the skin gathered in the office and thanked our saviors. Then they took us to a motel to dry off and get wet again in a hot shower.

Later that night, Judy commented that it was the only time that she had landed sideways and going downhill.

We were there two days waiting for the weather to let up. On the third day we thought that we could make it up the Sacramento River Canyon to Dunsmuir. There were still many low wet clouds but that is the way it is in this country around the first week of June. We got across Lake Shasta, but as we climbed higher the clouds got thicker and about half way up the canyon I was in and out of it, so I flew with the terrain on my left so that I could see something.

The Pietenpol would appear sometimes on my right and I didn't know where Pete was but he was somewhere behind us. A turn to go back was out of the question now so we kept climbing up the canyon because we were being teased by the intermittent visibility.

Nearing the top we hit a brief break in the clouds and maintained a short period of contact with the terrain, but then all of sudden we entered a heavy column of rain. With a total of seven instruments including switches, I was IFR, Instrument Flight Rules, now called IMC, Instrument Meteorological Conditions.

I stabilized the airplane with a slight rate of climb, a heading of due north, an airspeed of 65 MPH, and centered the skid ball. Since there was nothing to see outside, I stared at the instrument panel and waited to detect any changes in what I had set up. An increase in airspeed and a decrease in altitude would indicate a dive. A change in the compass heading would indicate a spiral or a turn.

After what seemed like an hour, we broke out into sunshine slightly off course to the right and the right wing low. Not much fun but I felt better when I could see open country up ahead so we flew to Yreka-Montague and landed for fuel and a much-needed rest.

The clouds were hanging at about 4000 feet and from our viewpoint they obscured the high pass that we had to cross. Good ol' Siskiyou Summit was toying with us again. I had a feeling in my gut that we weren't going to make it without some kind of wrestling match. I was correct. The L-3 didn't want to climb the last 500 feet when we got there and we watched Pete and the Pietenpol cross in a break in the clouds, the deck of which had formed on the north side of the summit.

We had to cross on top and look for a hole so I had to borrow 600 feet of altitude from something. Off to the right there was an old deteriorating spire that had shed tons of dark rock that had formed a shale slide and it looked like it may be worth a look. We crossed near the base of the jagged monument-like chimney with the wind to our right. AHA! A little bump in the butt! There WAS some lift there. I turned out to the right at a 45-degree angle and circled back to cross the rockslide and there was another little lightness in the feel of things. After four or five passes, we had some more altitude and skimmed across the summit just over the undercast.

Up ahead there was some irregularity in the cloud deck and both of us yelled, "THERE IT IS!" A hole just sitting there waiting for us to spiral down through it and that's exactly what we did, just in front of the butte that sits north of the summit. We watched auto traffic to our left as it traveled down the mountain and cruised with it down into the valley and headed for Grant's Pass.

We flew IFR (I Follow Roads) all the way home staying over I-5 in good weather. North of Eugene, Oregon the road is a long straight boring grind and we had a strong headwind. I noticed a little Volkswagen Bug smothered with a huge stack of camping gear on its top. It was gradually pulling ahead of us and my sweet wife noticed it.

"Do you see that Volkswagen down there?"

"Yes! And you don't have to remind me that it's outrunning us!"

We made it home safe after a wonderful adventure. One week later the L-3 was destroyed in a fatal mid-air collision while being flown by an acquaintance. So the little WW2 warrior finally met its fate after a long and checkered career. It had served during the war as a liaison plane and spent 20 years flying as a civilian. It gave many rides to youngsters when we had it, and my 16-year-old son, Kris, learned to fly in it. So, it had a good and useful life.

I was able to fly a bit longer in many other airplanes due to the generosity of my friends at Thun Field but it wasn't the same even though I was able to fly in some unique and rare birds. The airline pilots and those flyers with a few bucks were fortunately invited me to fly with them or to fly their little airplanes. Another antique airplane lover was an airline pilot named Jack Leffler who was a Jonathan Winters clone and kept us in stitches most of the time. He owned a beautiful Monocoupe 90 AW with which he generously shared the right seat with me and many times I got to fly one of the finest restored Monocoupes in the world. Then in 1966 he purchased a 1933 Boeing 247 that was put on the block and flew it up from California. The day after he arrived was TV news day and when that was concluded he asked me if I would go fly it with him. The next hour was one of the most memorable of my life.

I had watched these airplanes in awe when I was a little kid at Hoover Airport in 1933 and to fly one off Renton airport 33 years later was an unbelievable thrill. But what an old tub! It was slow. It was stable AND it wanted to stay that way. I'm sure that its flying characteristics were passed on to the B-17.

Jack was a legend at United Airlines and a man of never ending mirth and practical jokes. His close encounter with dismissal came when he had purchased a rubber gorilla mask and just HAD to something with it. Perhaps you remember the old days when the DC-4 pilots had the passenger manifest passed to them by a long stick before they pulled away from the ramp. If you have guessed that Jack was wearing the gorilla mask when he reached for the manifest, you are right on!

The flurry of commotion by spectators was nothing compared to what was to take place in the airplane after takeoff. Jack had quietly told some of the cockpit crew that there was an animal being shipped and they were not to say anything to the "stews". He knew very well that the flight attendants would know about it.

As they were climbing away from the airport Jack called for some coffee and then stood in the recesses in the flight deck, wearing the mask. The girl faithfully appeared with the tray of coffee and Jack tapped her on the shoulder. When she saw what was behind her, the coffee went skyward into the overhead panel, shorting out many circuits. The finale to this scenario was the girl running down the passenger aisle screaming with Jack running after her shouting, "It's me, it's me."

"I was THIS close to getting fired!" he told me.

As if to taunt the brass again, he allowed his hair-trigger humorous imagination to rise when he learned that the famous pianist, George Shearing, was on his flight.

When they landed in a refueling stop in the Midwest, Jack asked Shearing if he would want him to take his Seeing Eye dog out for a walk and a pee. Shearing thought that would be nice so Jack made certain that he circled the airplane several times while it was on the ramp when he was wearing dark glasses, being led by a guide dog, and tapping with Shearing's cane -- while wearing his United Airlines uniform.

"I was THIS close to getting fired."

Jack wasn't the only joker in our group of flyers. There is a strain of wry humor that gives color to flying community one never knew when he would run into it. One old enclosed cabin antique had a hinged placard posted on the overhead. It said, "Open to see the last word in aviation." Pulling it open revealed a prominent answer, "JUMP!"

One of the homebuilts had an important looking black box mounted on the instrument panel with a single toggle switch labeled "Automatic Shutoff." Shutoff what shutoff? You found out when you flicked the switch up. After a period of loud grinding noises the lid opened and a little green hand came out and shut the switch.

There was always some black humor in the bunch, too, as could be seen on one instrument panel, "If we are going to crash don't go grabbing for the seat or you will die all tensed up!"

And from one SBD dive-bomber pilot who survived the war, there was no humor in tempting your fate and his N3N displayed a placard on the instrument panel, "FOREVER VIGILANT OR FOREVER ASLEEP!"

600 DOLLARS WORTH OF JUNK FLYING IN LOSE FORMATION

Before the L-3 saga, my friend and I hatched a crazy idea on one lazy sunny day and we wondered if the Champ would fly with one aileron. After taking a look at the aileron control system and seeing that it was a closed loop cable arrangement from which the ailerons operated independently we decided to try it. Since it was his airplane, he was the pilot and everything worked fine.

Soon the idea for an air show act evolved and we designed a fake Styrofoam aileron and the mechanism to trigger it off in flight. A typical Boeing-style functional test and flight test proved it to be workable so the next step came from my clownish mind and we worked up an air show scenario full of sight gags and verbal patter with the crowd and air show announcers.

A perfect venue to show our masterpiece happened to be at Thun Field on a beautiful sunny Saturday in 1966 the terrace in front of the café was filled with "Bird Watchers" and many visiting aviators when my partner taxied out in the Champ and took off. When the bright silver doped aileron fluttered to the ground on of the visiting pilots was waving his arms hard enough to get airborne himself and started screaming that we were going to see a crash.

He stood in stunned confusion that no one else was bothered and soon caught on when they started to laugh at the "wounded duck' antics that the Champ started to perform. Then it went through a full aerobatic routine at 900 feet with "one aileron rolls", loops, square loops, spins, snap rolls, and a few unrecognizable contortions. When it was over, the Stinson 108 pilot stomped over to his airplane and left.

Clowns and Clown Plane. Credit: Jim Larsen

Maybe we should get another propeller. Credit: Jim Larsen

ON STAGE

We did several small air shows the summer of 1967 and then we were asked if we could perform at the big upcoming Centennial Canadian air show in Abbotsford. The Canadians knew about us because we had attended their air show the previous year when they were running a test show in preparation for the big Canada Centennial Air Show in 1967. The 1966 show was an absolute blast and one that I will always remember with humor.

My partner and I sort of weaseled our way into the show, because so many of our friends were in it. We didn't have an act yet so we painted the Champ with the very imposing logo as the "Thun Field Ground Crew" and took off with everyone else and headed for Abbotsford.

After clearing customs in Bellingham, Washington, we headed out on a NE course in the rain. As we were plodding our way over the dark country below we were passed by one of the performers in a very specialized Great Lakes biplane. One would not have recognized it except for the spraddled landing gear struts and vertical fin, the rest was transformed with elliptical wing tips and single wing struts instead of the "N" configuration. To be passed by a faster airplane was nothing new when we were cruising at a paltry 70 MPH, but this one went by inverted. At least one of the open cockpit pilots was not getting wet.

Our arrival in the drizzle was a show in itself. As we circled overhead, we watched the earlier Thun Field gang arrivals make their entrance. Mark and Grace landed in their matched "His and Hers" white Ryan's, Dean E. landed his Smith Mini-plane ACROSS the runway, somebody else landed in the grass near the ramp, and we waited for and got the green light and landed like normal people.

After clearing customs, we had to confront the air show people to convince them that even if we weren't on the manifest, we had to be there for the Thun Field crew. In spite of our phony pleading, they allowed us to be included in the air show. So, at least we could be at the show with the gang but where to sleep? Obviously on the floor in somebody's room. But wait! We were given a room in the little hotel in town with everyone else! Not only did we get a room, it was the only one with an inside bathroom AND a shower. The rest of those officially listed had one bathroom in the hall that served all of them.

We didn't dare walk around or lay in our room scantily clad because there was a steady stream of air show people, men and women, coming in and out of our room for a bath.

The show was bigger and more exciting than the earlier shows that we had seen. The RCAF was in it as well as many aerobatic performers. They opened the show with a fly-by of seven CF-101 Voodoos. That doesn't seem too special until we realized that they were coming in out of the Frazer River Valley at 100 feet, almost wide open, and right over the ramp that was full of unsuspecting spectators. They had no warning because the sound is behind the planes, but they heard them loud and clear when they lit their afterburners. It was like getting hit with a heavy pillow as they blasted over. The most unusual thing was the ethereal whistling and rushing of the air as it equalized to fill the hole that the Voodoos left behind them. Yeah! The Canadians knew how to open a show!

Excitement continued when the performer in the Great Lakes Special crashed in front of the crowd while trying to outdo another flyer with whom he was competing. For guess what? A girl, of course. A big ego drove him to try five snap rolls at a very low altitude. He completed four before the airplane stalled and went in. He survived with only a broken nose and we could see him moving in the cockpit in the overturned fuselage and we couldn't keep from laughing when he unfastened his seat belt and fell out on his head. His final act in his embarrassment was to punish the airplane by kicking it several times.

The Monday morning after the show, we were waiting at our fine Attangard Hotel for transportation back to the airport and we were missing the companion of the crash expert who had already departed. She was a striking young model who liked to party.

While everyone was assembled in the lobby, a chambermaid appeared at the balcony for everyone to hear that she couldn't find Mr. "M" but his "wife" was asleep in the bathtub. When asked if she couldn't awaken her and get her down stairs she said, "I don't think so 'cause she hasn't got any clothes on." That turned on one of the mouthier members of the group who loudly expressed, "Well! I'm really disappointed. I thought that Jim M. treated his 'wives' better than to let them sleep naked in a bathtub! It's terrible how poorly Jim M. treats all of his 'wives'!"

During the winter of 1966-67 we not only continued to hone

and prepare the One-aileron act, but that was when we acquired the "basket case" of the L-3. It cost $600, the same price that my partner paid for the clown plane, a 1946 Aeronca Champ. After clearing the leaves and mud away from fuselage, we saw the data plates on the kick board in the cockpit and discovered that it was an ex-WW2 liaison plane that started service in 1942 as an O-58B and later re-designated as an L-3B. So, it wasn't just another old light plane. The house became a bachelor pad in 1964 and by 1966 it housed my four boys, a black Labrador, my flying partner, three airplanes in pieces and me.

When the L-3 became a fairly valuable restoration project, the carport was closed in and became a shop complete with an old gas heater so that we could work through the winter. The fuselage was ensconced in the shop, the wings when placed side by side were the exact width and length of the ceiling in the rec room and they were pressed into place and stayed there without any support. Several pilots dropped by to see for themselves what they didn't believe.

The engine was pulled off the nose and took position on the workbench that was built along the long wall in the now "wreck room". We made a plan to start work on New Year's Day, 1967, to rebuild the L-3 in time to fly it to the Abbotsford Airshow in August. That was eight months away and the airplane needed a complete rebuild.

By the end of New Year's Day the fuselage had been stripped of fabric. Number two son, Dana, eleven years old, had started stripping paint off some of the frame tubing for repaint. And so it went for three months until we were ready to recover the fuselage. All the wood fairing strips and floors were rebuilt and the seats were taken in for upholstering. The 1942 construction techniques were a revelation when we saw the way the fairing strips were attached -- with surgical tape.

At first we thought that it was a backyard fix by someone, but when we got the factory drawings that was exactly what was specified. Another surprise was the elevator trim tab control. It was a window crank and regulator quadrant specified as that from a 1937 Ford automobile.

The summer of 1967 was one of those that come along once in a hundred years in Seattle. It warmed up and stayed dry all spring and summer and we moved a lot of the work to the front lawn and patio and the pace accelerated.

Right in the middle of all this progress, we had to remove the wings from the Champ to apply some much-needed patches. But where to do the work? The only open space left inside the house was the living room and dining room but that didn't last long. The two wing panels took the space from the front window of the living room to the back window in the dining room. One wing rested on the dining table and the other was on sawhorses.

About that time my 19 year-old niece, Leslie, had finished her freshman year at Seattle University and came to the house to see how we were doing. Well, she must have gone into permanent shock because she decided to stay with us that summer and try to help out with the household duties like cleaning and cooking. Don't get me wrong here, I know how to cook good stuff and I usually did, but the strain of my day job and trying to get two airplanes repaired in a short time sort of took its toll. I realized that my cooking was known to all the bachelor pilots who always "just happened to be in the neighborhood at dinnertime."

Every payday I went to Safeway to spend at least $80. I filled two and a half carts sometimes and ladies in the checkout line looked at me like I was shopping for the Russian Army, but it was only for us to survive for two weeks. Chuck blade roast was about $1.30 per pound and we ate a lot of it along with teriyaki chicken, salmon and stew. Plenty of vegetables and gallons of milk kept us going. Before leaving for work, I put a chuck roast covered with potatoes, carrots, and Lipton's dry onion soup mix in the timed oven. When I got home it was already cooking and the aromas kept the kids home for a couple of hours. The faster pace of the airplane work began to bite into the prep time and quality and that's when Leslie saved us.

She cooked and cleaned and gave the younger kids the big sister attention that they sometimes needed. One Saturday after a very strenuous day on our projects, she announced that the meatloaf was ready. We cleaned up and never thought about where we would eat it. Leslie, without missing a beat, had set place mats and silverware on the wings and we adults ate a delicious dinner there while the kids sat underneath on the floor. It went that way for the next several months as we rushed to finish the L-3. At times Leslie complained about the weird odors coming out of the oven but we assured her that it wasn't her cooking; it was normal after baking brake shoes to drive out the solvent after cleaning them. We did quite well under her loving care.

The long hot summer continued to hold through June and we had the L-3 fuselage and tail feathers covered and painted and work shifted to the greenhouse structure and glass. Hundreds of little details cropped up that took millions of valuable hours and by the middle of July the rebuilt engine was ready to hang on the nearly complete fuselage that stood on the rebuilt landing gear.

On a Sunday night near the end of July at 9:00 PM, we lashed the tail of the wingless L-3 to a tree in the front yard and cranked up the engine. Ah! What a sweet sound that was! The next morning the fuselage was tied to the back end of our VW pick up and taken to Bellevue Airport just below where we lived. Then the wings, long since removed from the "wreck room" ceiling and redone, were loaded onto the little truck and taken to down to mount on the fuselage and get the controls hooked up. It was Monday and we had to have the L-3 in Abbotsford, Canada by the next Thursday no later than 5:00 PM.

Still many details dogged us including getting the wing struts stripped and painted and when we were in that process, we uncovered a serious problem. An illegal repair on one strut had been covered up by epoxy. The strut HAD to be repaired before anything else was done because the airplane would otherwise be un-flyable. Frantic calls to our flying buddies to locate another strut were fruitless, but a call for someone to repair it netted results and a certified welder was identified in Tacoma. A homebuilt airplane buff and fellow pilot arrived in his Cub Special and strapped the strut to his airplane and flew it down to get it repaired.

Wednesday night a little bit after sunset, we spotted the Cub in the valley south of the field on short final landing by the lights on the hangar. We untied the strut from his airplane and started final assembly. The L-3 had been set on its main gear with the tail up to level position, the right hand was wing installed and supported by 2 X 4's and we began an all-night session of painting, fitting, aligning and adjusting and by 0800 we had what looked like a whole airplane. BUT, it had to be inspected and signed off by a certified A&E mechanic and test flown. We knew a good friend who was an A&E and he lived nearby.

He arrived mid-afternoon and took FOREVER checking,

looking and checking. Finally he hooked up and safety wired the turn barrel on the aileron cables, but caught one item that had to be done before sign-off. "The airplane will have a compass mounted, etc." My partner, losing an argument that we knew how to get to our destination, grabbed the compass and strapped it in the rear seat with the seat belt.

The first flight occurred at 3:15 PM, the hour that we were supposed to leave for Abbotsford. My partner rushed back to the house, packed a few clothes and thankfully took a quick shower while I sprayed the final O.D. color on a closure plate on the tail. When he returned, I left and did the same and rushed back to the airport to load the TV photographer and our gear into the Champ.

TV photographer? Yeah, KOMO-TV had heard about our crazy act and wanted to do a feature about it so they assigned the biggest photographer on their payroll. Not only did he weigh 200 LBS+, he had a huge suitcase and a huge 16 MM camera. He and his gear weighed more than the Champ and something wasn't going to work, like getting the Champ off the ground. So we loaded all the clothes and film gear into the L-3 and I took the passenger and his camera in the Champ. It was a 90-degree day and I didn't look at the takeoff with much joy.

We taxied all the way to the very end of the field and managed to get airborne from a runway that somebody must have shortened overnight. The Champ wasn't going to get any faster than 55-60 MPH and the climb was maybe 50 feet/min. Any attempt to do more than that was met by a firm refusal. The terrain south of the airport rose and was covered by tall fir trees but there was a valley at the base of the rise that led to Lake Washington.

With the Champ running wide open, we skimmed over the trees at the lowest point and headed for the lake, gaining a little speed as we slowly descended. The stick still felt like a piece of wet spaghetti but we were able to fly a bit better as we turned north. Flying the length of Lake Washington over cooler air helped us to get to 150 feet and we headed to Arlington Airport where we were to pick up the company of another airplane.

I could tell when we were on final approach that I shouldn't retard power because we were rapidly coming down just fine with half throttle. After landing, the loads on the L-3 and Champ were redistributed and while this was going on I installed the closure plate on the L-3 that had been hanging in the back of the Champ to dry. The L-3 was finally complete fifty miles down the road. In the rush to change the loads, I ended up with all the clothing and no sectionals. I didn't realize that until we left Bellingham and here I was leading the pack to Abbotsford. I headed on a northeast heading as darkness turned everything to a purple haze and figured that I could find the airport. I ended up wandering off too far to the east but I caught the beacon out of the corner of my left eye when they turned it on. Like a good pilot, I entered the downwind leg and turned on the base leg when the bright approach lights came on. Humm, how nice of them, maybe I can make a good night landing since I hadn't made one in 20 years. I flew the Champ on with a chirp and taxied off the active just in time to see a C-130 landing behind me. I then figured that the lights were for them, not me. That made sense, too, when I remembered that the Champ didn't have any navigation lights and I had made my entrance unseen.

THE BEST OF THEM ALL

The Centennial Abbotsford Air Show was unlike any that we had experienced. It was programmed to be a cavalcade of aviation history with aircraft from WW1, between wars, WW2, and up to the contemporary. It was a three-day show and the crowd that appeared on Friday morning was staggering. The ramp was full of spectators and static display aircraft. The "infield" was lined with military and civilian aircraft of every vintage from 1913 to 1967.

Daily program was crammed with performances and acts and the timing for the six-hour show was as precise as a military assault, not paced in minutes but half minutes. I flew the L-3 in the WW2 section of the parade of history and as I was crossing the runway threshold to land, I could see the next airplane pulling out for takeoff as I went over him.

The show was filled with an array of beautifully restored equipment from every age: Pete Bowers flew his 1913 Curtiss pusher, the Canadian National Museum flew its WW1 duet of a Nieuport 17 and an Avro 504K, then there was a Fokker Triplane, a Sopwith triplane, a Thomas Morse Scout, a 1917 Sopwith Pup, numerous old planes from between the wars, and then from WW2 there were Spitfires, P-40's a P-38, F8F, F4F, P-51's PT-13's, and our own L-3. Art Scholl and many other aerobatic acts were interspersed between the big iron stuff, as was our clown act.

The spectators were completely fooled by the makeup that we had put on the Champ. We made it appear as if it had been in some sort of mishap. The left landing gear strut was a piece of water pipe shortened as if it had been collapsed, the rudder was missing, the right aileron was missing, the door was gone and the cowling and prop was off. Bushes and junk had been jammed into every corner and it looked like a wreck.

As we pulled it out to flight line, one gentleman rushed forward and offered us 50 dollars for it if we didn't burn it. All during the afternoon show we were trying to get the Champ to run and we were "stealing" parts from other airplanes to put it together. Actually the parts were taken off the Champ earlier and painted different colors to appear that they were from another airplane. The aileron kept falling off and the old wooden propeller fell off when we tried to start the engine.

Good to have helping hands.

The crowd loved it as we went through all sorts of antics to get the airplane put together and running but they didn't notice that we had the rudder back on, the landing gear fixed, the aileron finally stayed put, and a propeller was on it.

At 1413 we had to fly per the schedule and we "finally" got

the engine to run. Charlie pointed the Champ away from the crowd and took off ACROSS the runway. Fifty feet in the air the right aileron fell off AGAIN. The crowd actually screamed as they thought that a disaster was about to take place, but Charlie hung in there and the plane lurched down toward the runway, then gained altitude and struggled to 900 feet where he put on a complete aerobatic routine with everything but sustained inverted flight. He killed the engine in the top of a loop and landed dead stick with a ground loop in front of an applauding crowd. As he fell out of the airplane, the next performer was taking off.

That first show completely fooled the crowd and earned the praise of some of the big names in the show like Bob Hoover and Art Scholl who ducked his head into the cockpit of the Champ when I was taxiing to the fuel pumps and said, "You guys are absolutely nuts!" Well, maybe, but we had more fun than anybody and we gave the crowd a big laugh and proved that an airplane CAN fly with one aileron. B-17's did it many times during the war.

Even the FAA was doubtful when my partner had to demonstrate that he could control the airplane in order to get the waiver. In fact, they didn't want to see him "attempt" anything else but straight and level flight, once around the pattern. When he asked if they didn't want to see some of the maneuvers, they said, "Nope! If you want to kill yourself you can do it on your own." Little did they know that we had been messing around for two weeks with only one aileron on the airplane and my partner had done everything that he could think of without mishap.

During the off-season, I invented more sight gags and worked up a vocal scenario that we could perform in cahoots with the announcers at the shows. It worked beautifully. Typical of what we did happened at the Abbotsford show the next year when we had short conversations over the PA system with the announcer, Toby Trowbridge, in between acts.

After showing up with different colored parts to complete the Champ that was missing a rudder, the door, half an elevator and an aileron, Toby asked us where we were getting all this stuff and, of course, the answer was "from some of the planes in the parking area." All during the show we were putting the Champ back together with its own parts that we painted with water paint but the crowd wasn't sure and Toby warned every pilot to check their airplanes carefully before takeoff.

We had engine problems, too! A twittering when we attempting to start it! Toby said that we should check the engine and when we pulled the upper cowl a flock of pigeons flew out. The next day the same routine caused by something "fishy" produced a three-foot salmon. Another day we had to remove a bad engine part after telling Toby that "The generator wouldn't gen, the carburetor wouldn't carb, the starter wouldn't start and the pistons wouldn't pi ... work either!" Then we threw out a fake over-sized piston and rod. The crowd loved it.

We had completely fooled and amused the crowd. Art Scholl told us that we were nuts and we even had Bob Hoover laughing. But the best comment came in a personal note from the Canadian Prime Minister, Pierre Trudeau, telling us how much he enjoyed our "silly act."

Chief of Flight Taste

BLUE BLOODS

Our shows in Abbotsford exposed us to the Blue Angels close up and personal since we were in the same show and that was the extent of it, the same show. I don't recall any of them, or even one of them at the morning pilot's briefings and they sort of appeared at their airplanes from somewhere when they had to do their show. We never saw them at the dinner dances on Saturday night. Those Saturday night dinners were a joy and we met everyone in the show: Art Scholl, Mira Slovak, Joe Hughes, wingwalker John Kazian, Bob Hoover, actress Susan Oliver, all the wonderful Canadian hosts, and all the others who performed with us. We all had name tags to identify us, mine said "CLOWN", my spouse's said "WIFE OF CLOWN", and so it went.

Previously that Saturday when my partner and I were pulling the Clown Plane out for our show, we positioned it near the line of the Blue Angel's F4's to take a picture. Our steed was dressed in all the worst looking things we could think of. It sagged to one side with a "broken landing gear" and there were shreds of torn fabric hanging from it along with bushes and wires dragging out of the hole left by the missing door. A huge black bumbershoot was taped to the vertical fin as a "drag chute".

Before we could get set up a Blue's mechanic ran out with arms waving and yelling, "Get away, get away!" We asked what the problem was and he told us that we were improper and we weren't sophisticated and we shouldn't get any closer.

My partner stood there in his filthy grease stained white coveralls, a black swallow-tailed coat, and wearing a top hat with the lid blown open and asked the mechanic, "Now where the hell did you get the idea that we weren't sophisticated!"

So we got properly cut down to our proper level and left the Blues alone to do their wonderful thing. We were scheduled to perform in other shows in the states and one of them at Paine Field had the Blues also scheduled so we couldn't escape them. As the show went on, one of the performers caused a 15-minute delay. That would extend the schedule of later acts and the show would go beyond the listed times. The boys from the Navy immediately announced that if they did not fly precisely at 1700 hours they would not fly at all. So after we had the Clown plane set, running and ready to take off do our act, we got a red light and had to stand down so the Blues could have their way.

The following summer we performed at Paine Field when the U.S. Air Force Thunderbirds were scheduled. We had a wonderful experience with them. They had never seen the Clown Act and before we flew, we could see that they were feverishly talking about our airplane. Finally one of them sauntered over to look at the wreck and asked, "You guys aren't really going to fly that thing are you?"

Of course my partner answered, "Gosh, no. That would be crazy!"

As the show continued we were "trying "to get the Clown Plane started without success and another of the Thunderbird pilots came over and asked, "You guys are going to fly that, right?"

I answered, "Certainly! That's what we're here for!"

So, we had planted a seed of doubt with them and we could see that there was something going on with them when they were talking and pointing at our airplane.

After we had flown our part of the show, their leader, Stan Musser, came over to us and said, "Dammit, you guys cost me 100 bucks, I could'a sworn you weren't going to fly that pile of junk!" He then hack-sawed a piece of the junk off the plane for a souvenir. Sadly, a short time later we learned that one of them who befriended us was killed in the crash of his plane, Capt. Howard. They were a different breed and they always welcomed us.

The next summer at Abbotsford, the Blue Angels front man, a Commander, ascended the stairs to the control tower to tell the tower chief that he had to make a change in the schedule that more suited the Blues in their performance. Bill Warn, the tower chief assured the Navy Commander that he was not in charge of the tower or the schedule and physically escorted him back to ground level.

We had one more experience with the Navy.

WONDERS NEVER CEASE

After several more shows that summer, we finished the season at the Whidbey Island Naval Air Station's 25th Anniversary show. We were supposed to do the Clown Act, but we were in conflict with a Naval Officer who performed a "Drunken Professor" act in a Cub and he demanded that we should be cancelled. So, we brought the L-3 to represent the "Grasshoppers" of WW2 and flew it in the aircraft parade. In the presence of high powered and flashy naval aircraft, the L-3 stood out with its olive drab finish and its diminutive size and we were visited by the base commander, Admiral Ramage, his wife, and their daughter and son. The kids wrangled rides in the L-3 with their parents blessing and enjoyed riding in the "greenhouse" of the little observation plane. At the end of operations that day, Mrs. Ramage invited us to attend the reception at their home that evening. All air show performers were invited for cocktails and food.

Mrs. Ramage was much younger than the admiral, but she was a very competent and comfortable lady in her position. I couldn't hazard a guess at her age but I did notice that she was a trim and voluptuous brunette who obviously was in charge. My partner and I hadn't had anything to eat since our early breakfast that morning and when we saw the fare in the dining room, we quickly downed our drinks and loaded finger food into our glasses and clumsily tried to eat it with our fingers and olive sticks. In the middle of smoked salmon and beef tenderloin being extracted from our cocktail glasses, Mrs. Ramage appeared out of the crowd and asked us if we had eaten. Our answer prompted her to take us into her huge kitchen and instructed the cooks to, "Please give these men full plates of anything they want."

After a wonderful dinner we returned to the reception to mingle with the guests and Navy pilots, many of who had just returned from action in Viet Nam. I noticed that the house was filled with furniture and artifacts from all over the world and near the front window was a huge ornately carved trunk from the far- east. As I was admiring it, Mrs. Ramage approached and asked if we had been well served and we of course told her that we had been. This was the instant when I was stricken with foot-in-mouth disease,

"Mrs. Ramage, I have been admiring your beautiful chest."

My partner looked at me as if I had lost my mind but she riveted me in an eye-to-eye gaze with her beautiful brown eyes and smiled,

"Well! I've heard a lot of "lines" but not one quite that direct."

"Oh", I stammered. "I didn't mean YOURS, uh... it's very nice, uh... I was referring to the one by the window."

My partner quietly uttered, "Parks! Shut up!"

"Yes, I know. THAT chest came from the Philippines. I got mine when I was 13."

She patted my arm as she walked to join the rest of the party. She was quite a gal.

Chapter 19.

A look at some interesting flying and air shows.

AND THEN, THE PRINCESS

On my return home, I called my son from the airport to pick me up and he told me that he couldn't. I asked why and his answer was, "Well, do you remember that VW bus that you used to like?" If you don't think that was a wake-up call, you haven't had kids. This answer carried tons of visions and scenarios so I asked precisely what that meant. He was driving home from a friend's house through an area that was wooded and tried to avoid a deer and rolled the bus five times, two on the road and three while going down an embankment. Well, that was special! He was unbelievably okay but that left us with an old beat up Volkswagen pickup. I had an appointment to keep that night, a blind date with a beautiful girl, I had been told. So, off I went to my blind date, late and driving something that not even a homeless junk dealer would be seen in. It was three or four shades of green with primer in between them. The front and rear bumpers were missing and the heater and turn signals didn't work. We used this fine vehicle to haul airplanes and airplane parts, not socializing. Its saving grace was simple -- the wheels went around and the engine made noise. So, off I went, clattering into the night for my blind date.

She was a thirty year old widow, she had three children, she wasn't happy with being set up for a blind date and she was beautiful. I was interested. She was not. I called her the next day for a dinner date; she accepted. I had been given tickets for dinner for two at the Space Needle because I had served as a model for a sales promotional film for the forthcoming 747 airplane. I had it made! A free dinner for two in the swank Space Needle Restaurant with a gorgeous young lady. The only thing that I lacked was the mental awareness of a normal man about town who would put on his best bib and tucker when he was about to call on a lovely lady. Oh, I had nice clean clothes on but I never thought about the pick-up truck. It was October and a bit chilly and I was arriving in a cross-eyed chariot with no heater. Luckily, I had a blanket to keep the chill away from my date who gracefully wrapped her legs and upper body without comment.

Judy was quiet and a bit nervous as we drove down town but as our dinner progressed she and I found that we liked the same things and the conversation got easier as the evening wore on. The beat-up junker truck never entered the conversation and I really didn't think about it until my kids read me the riot act about driving a first date in that "groaty piece of crap." Well, all that I owned was "groaty" but the pickup was the only thing drivable. I had to plan an attack on our vehicular shortfall and my plan was kick-started when one of the bachelor pilots in the clan wanted to buy the bus engine and all the undamaged running gear. That was no problem since we replaced one bent wheel, refilled the gas tank, and got it running again. The next step in the plan was to drive it 10 miles south to Renton and leave it at the new owner's shop. So, my partner and I cranked it up and started the bus's last journey. Halfway there we were startled by flashing red lights behind us and we were pulled over by a Washington State Patrol officer.

"Driver's license and registration."

After presenting the documents we watched the officer stare at us and at the bus for a few seconds. He checked everything as okay and continued to assess us with a questioning look.

"Okay, where was the accident?"

"Back on Richard's Road -- last week."

"Last week!"

"Yes sir, my son rolled it down an embankment."

"What are you doing driving it like this!" He was still perplexed by what he was seeing.

"A friend bought it for the engine and running gear and we thought we would drive it down to his shop for him. Everything works: headlights, tail lights, turn signals and even the horn."

"The two of you step out please and follow me back here."

We walked with him to a spot 30 feet behind the bus and we stood looking at our vehicle.

"Do you see what I see? Do you have any idea of what this thing looks like driving down the road with two guys wearing leather helmets and goggles! Look at that thing!"

The two of us stood there in our dirty flight suits and helmets and goggles looking at it and had to agree with him. The helmet and goggles were required because the windshield was missing and there are more bugs out there than you realize. All the glass was broken out and shreds of the headliner were flapping out of the openings that the windows once occupied. The headliner looked like a mad slasher had cut it to shreds. The thing that caught the officer's eye was the lopsided body that had been knocked into a ten-degree parallelogram leaning to the right and there wasn't a body panel that hadn't been caved in by the rocks and stumps. Yeah, it did look pretty bad to be driving on the freeway.

"How much farther do you guys have to go?"

"Officer, we have about three more miles to the shop up there on the hill."

"All right! You can go three more miles but no further, do you understand? If I see this thing on the road again I'll cite you for driving... huh... driving a MENACE and uh... uh... a distraction."

He was correct on that one because there were several cars stopped on the other side of the highway trying to figure out what the hell was going on.

"Yessir, we didn't intend to do anything else, anyway."

As we drove away, I thought, what could he do? I was driving under the speed limit, everything operated properly -- except the windshield wipers because there was no windshield and no wipers. It looks like it was just a little problem with cosmetics.

The bus was soon replaced with a used VW bug in which the heater worked so my meetings with Judy were warm in more ways than one. Our next date had to be spent at her little house because she couldn't arrange for a baby sitter. We had dinner and wine -- and little girls. While Judy was fixing dinner and I was having a little pre-dinner Martini, I looked into the back room that was separated by French doors that were ajar and saw two of the cutest little faces peering at me. I think they were supposed to stay in their room but I smiled at them and wiggled my finger to come out and before I knew it I was looking at school drawings and writings and had them cuddled up to me to show me all their work.

Well, that did it! How could one resist this clan? A beautiful gentle mother, three sweet pretty little children, all of whom needed some support. Judy was doing her best as a single mother recently widowed and had things pretty well under control, but it was obvious that it would be better if they all had some help. But hold on, this lady wasn't casting the waters for a big daddy fish.

She was very conservative and had a secure little clan under her wing so as our relationship progressed we just let it play out. After all, who in their right mind would consider marrying a divorced 40 year-old air show pilot with four boys and a house full of airplanes?

Three months later we got married. But not before we had cleaned out the Aegean Stables-of-a house so we could accommodate all the kids in some sort of "normal" household. The "wreck-room" was cleared of the engine rebuild workbench, tools and an assortment of landing gear parts and thoroughly cleaned. A king sized mattress and a dresser completed the job for the little kids and my kids had their own spaces so it all worked out. The big redwood picnic table in the dining room seated everyone for meals that sometimes were like an army chow hall.

Thanks to hours of scrubbing, painting, cleaning, decorating and polishing, Judy changed the house/hangar to a home. Many times before we were married, I would come home from work to find Judy already there scraping or using a jack hammer on something -- well, almost. And somehow her little girls and two year old boy were accepted and cared for by my boys to everyone's amazement.

PART FIVE
Chapter 20.

The last air show. Lay off at Boeing and turning into an artist.

My first attempt to paint aviation subjects.

ON WITH THE SHOWS

In the following years we were asked to perform in many more air shows. One that will always have a special place in my mind was the 1969 Spokane Air Show. There were lots of hot performers including Art Scholl and his new back-to-back act with a new pilot. There was a new guy that did a routine with a T-6 including a Lomcevak. There were flybys by the Air Force and a special act, "The Great Race" where my partner flew Pete Bower's 1913 Curtiss pusher in a takeoff duel with Larry Blumer's 1913 Cadillac. We didn't have a good feeling about the show set up and where it was set up. Things just didn't seem to be organized well and the field was an operational airport. So the show was running on an unused runway on the south end. Not good to have airliners coming and going when you're trying to do an air show.

The first day of the show started with a low attendance that foretold us that there wasn't much interest for air shows in the Inland Empire. Then during Scholl's back-to-back aerobatic routine, his partner lost contact with where he was and wandered low over the crowd and was headed south when Scholl broke away to end the act. After a head-bashing session they decided to cancel the act for Sunday.

Then it was time for the Great Race and the Curtiss and Cadillac put on a cute display but my partner, following the FAA directions, had to take the pusher through a complete landing pattern instead of putting it down at the end of the runway. Half way around, the engine died and he disappeared into the complex of housing on the field.

When there is no power, the pusher has a glide angle of a rose bush, and the pilot became a passenger riding it down through two sets of power lines and crashed into a child's swing set after bouncing off the roof of the kid's house. It was difficult to discern the frame of the pusher from the frame of the swing set but he got away from his unscheduled landing with only a bloody nose.

The show continued to unravel when the guy doing the T-6 act ground looped his airplane in front of the crowd and knocked the landing gear off. Time for a break! The show ended that afternoon with an exodus to the fancy hotel where we were billeted. Showered and sweetened up, we convened at the indoor pool where there was food and cocktails for an evening bash. All the girls fixed themselves up to make-believe they were beautiful and the party started. Making a lovely entrance after spending 60 bucks on a fancy hairdo, Elaine, the wife of Fred, the Moncoupe pilot, was met by Blumer, who by then had a snoot full. He put his arm around her waist and walked her into the atrium, walked her into the dining area and serenely walked into the swimming pool. Then the party really started.

Not much of a show on Sunday, so Art Scholl came through with a new twist on his solo aerobatic routine. He had fitted his Chipmunk with flare launchers that fired photo flash grenades all during his maneuvers. I should have mentioned that the summer had been hot and dry in Spokane and the grass was tall and dry. When we left the show and headed west for the mountains, there were six or seven columns of thick smoke rising from the fires on the airport.

There was no Spokane Air Show in 1970.

1969 AND THE BEST LAID PLANS

The Spokane Air Show seemed to be a precursor to other events that were coming apart. Boeing had entered proposals in several competitions, the new fighter-bomber called the TFX, the U.S. Super Sonic Transport, and the C-5 giant cargo plane for the air force. The company was also successfully involved in space projects and helicopters. So in 20 years I had seen it grow from a fairly large airplane company to a giant aerospace force. It seemed that there was no stopping it, but then we lost the TFX competition to General Dynamics. We failed to configure a viable SST before the government canceled the program. Then we lost the C-5 proposal to Lockheed. What appeared to be a cloud of doom at that time was eventually to lift the company to unimaginable heights, but it would go through a difficult transition.

The C-5 proposal generated a wealth of data in the design and production of a large airplane and its time had come. The flying public had embraced the new jet era with much enthusiasm and the airplanes were making so much money for the airlines that Boeing could see that a new class of airliner was needed.

The company took the C-5 engineering data and applied it to a new concept: the biggest commercial airplane that anyone had ever attempted, the 747. In 1966 I witnessed the first computer-generated parts drawings emerge while we were still laying out the loft and detail parts by hand. For the life of me, I couldn't understand how this could be done. The new age had arrived.

In the middle of designing training programs for the 747, I was assigned to the SST proposal team to develop training programs that were stipulated requirements in the contract. I moved up from learning the engineering concepts of the subsonic machines to learning the supersonic disciplines. On top of that I was saddled with a monster training assignment to develop training for something invented by McNamara's "Whiz kids" called PERT (Program Evaluation and Review Technique) and PERTCOST. When the brains who designed the process presented it to McNamara they, in their infinite wisdom, had entitled it the "Financial Analysis and Review Technique". I'll let you figure out why McNamara told them to find another name for the program. It is too complicated to go over it in this essay, but it was a brutal assignment and my good health and sanity was saved when the government killed the SST.

One of the most interesting incidents occurred while I was digging for engineering inputs on the SST design concerning flutter. I was directed to talk to a renowned flutter expert, "Pete" Plunkett. When I reached the expert's office I was surprised to meet a lady sitting at her desk. "Pete" was Elizabeth and she invited me to sit down for what was to become an amazing hour telling me about flutter.

"Pete" was the one who solved the Lockheed Electra's mysterious in-flight failures. Perhaps you remember that the airplane's wings disintegrated after a loud bang according to witnesses on the ground. In one incident, the fuselage plummeted to the ground and buried itself and its passengers in a deep hole that was never exhumed. She had a theory about the cause and designed a flutter model of the Electra and proved her theory in wind tunnel tests.

Her investigation proved that the structure in the engine nacelles was too flexible and when the airplane encountered turbulence. The propellers fed gyroscopic precession loads back into the nacelle and the wing, both of which were too flexible. They fed the torsion back into the nacelle that then fed it back into the wing until the height and frequency of the oscillations, fed by the propellers, failed the wing. One can see her corrections in the upward angle of thrust on the modified Electra's nacelles, witnessed by a break in the upper surface curvature in the contours. One cannot see the increased thickness of the nacelle skins and wing skins that successfully stiffened everything.

Many nights I hear the Navy's Electra-based Orions drumming overhead and I think of "Pete Plunkett."

I went to Everett to work on the 747 where, after hundreds of hours of dedicated overtime work (much of it on my own time) I was laid off with thousands of others. It was ironic. We were called the "Incredibles" because we got the airplane out on time after some horrendous hurdles. The loads on those who were attempting to produce the world's largest commercial airplane were staggering. It was a man- killing program where missed schedules and part shortages were not accepted and the managers applied pressures that were literally deadly. "Come to God Meetings" were called at any time of the day or night and held in "War Rooms" where responsible supervisors and managers were put on the carpet to explain why they were not able to meet their schedules or part acquisitions. After an explanation and plan to correct the deficiency, they were scheduled to be the featured guest at the next meeting to attempt to save their ass. I remember on one occasion where one foreman, after 14 hours of hard work, was called back from home late at night to justify his performance.

Self-protection became a prime assignment for most of the assembly line people, but one Saturday late in the program when the number one airplane, RA001, was in functional test a program near-disaster took place. Someone somehow disregarded orders from above that the airplane was not to be jacked up until the new stronger jacks arrived. "Above" was the manufacturing manager, a bulldog of a man, who had no compassionate inclinations for anything or anybody. He was correct in his decision to wait for the heavier jacks, but somehow his instructions were ignored. The landing gear retraction tests proceeded with the lighter jacks. When the landing gear was fully retracted, a forklift trundled down the transportation aisle in front of the 747 and the wing jacks, extended to their limit, began to vibrate. Mechanics scrambled to get clear of the airplane that then came crunching down when the heads of the jack shafts sheared. The wing jack shafts punched through the wing skins in four places but the airplane was kept from reaching the floor when the inboard jacks encountered an extra wide stringer 18A in the lower wing surface and stopped the fall.

When the manufacturing manager returned on Monday from his company trip there was no self-defense in the world that protected one from his wrath.

On the wall of one of the War Rooms there was a boldly printed slogan.

"You better be bright!
You better be right!
Or you better be gone!"

AND THEN WE WERE GONE

If I remember correctly, the Boeing population in 1970 was 134,000 and after the layoff it was well under 100,000. That's when the billboard appeared along southbound Highway 99 that said, "Will the last person leaving Seattle please turn off the lights?" I couldn't get work due to the collapse of Boeing. Loss of the SST and a failing economy killed any orders for the 747. The local economy had collapsed in Seattle and nobody would hire an ex-Boeing mechanic/training supervisor/draftsman/illustrator/forty year old. I had a new wife and seven children, and a new huge house that eventually was sold at a loss. We were able to rent an old house south of Seattle and I tried to see if I could paint something artistic that would sell.

I tried selling a couple of airplane paintings by hanging them in the Hyatt House motel near Seattle-Tacoma airport. They sold immediately -- for 300 dollars. That was a fortune for us then so I tried several more. At the time, I wasn't what one could call an accomplished artist. I did have some ability, but to paint good pictures of a difficult subject, airplanes, was a long shot at best. I had to teach myself how to use a difficult medium, gouache, as well as how to draw the subjects. I painted my favorite subjects, old airmail planes.

Chapter 21.

Adventures as an artist and flying on San Juan Island.
Back to Seattle.

My second aviation painting. | *Robert Parks*

"DB"

Thanksgiving Eve, 1971, I was working on my first attempt to paint with oil colors and listening to my radio which was set on the airways band and thought that I had heard someone say that their airplane was being hijacked. I let it pass and kept painting because I was sure that I didn't hear it correctly. One minute later I put down the brush and listened intently because there WAS a hijacking in progress at Seattle-Tacoma airport. I couldn't believe what I was hearing! The Northwest Airlines pilot described the situation to the tower told them their sole remaining passenger had a bomb and demanded $200,000 and four parachutes. I have no idea how long the ground preparations took, but the NWA 727 was closed up and cleared for departure.

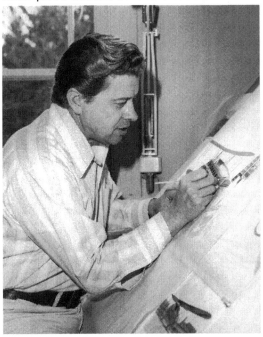

Robert Parks

We lived southeast of the airport and air traffic was departing on runway 16 to the south. I heard them get their clearance and then heard the 727 as it flew over the house while they were still talking to the airport. As they climbed away, they were patched in to the head office in Minneapolis where they talked to NWA officials. I can't recall all of the conversation, but I do remember that the pilot told them that his passenger had instructed him to maintain an altitude of 5000 feet and that he had to convince him that if they did that on the present heading they would run into some awfully big rocks: the Cascade Mountains. The pilot mentioned that the "stews" were doing a great job and the official in Minneapolis told him that they were all doing a good job.

I listened to the radio long after the sound of the airplane faded, but soon they were out of range. The next morning's newspaper was full of the story about the D.B. Cooper "skyjacking". Some months later, one of my flying buddies told me that the parachutes that were put aboard the 727 came from the sport flying and skydiving outfit near Seattle and that they disabled the parachutes before they were delivered. I was never able to corroborate the story but it makes it a lot more interesting to believe that they did.

Back to the drawing board! I completed four paintings and they caught the eye of my friend and airline pilot, Jack Leffler. He purchased one and showed another to his friend, Ernest Gann, the author, who purchased it. This led to a long running series of historic aviation paintings that illustrated stories by Gann that were published in a prominent aviation magazine, "FLYING."

Since we had nothing to anchor us to the Seattle area, we moved to San Juan Island where Gann lived and we worked on the series there. The series eventually was published in a book titled, "Ernest K. Gann's Flying Circus" and it kept me busy painting for three years. During that time I was able to make friends with the pilots flying for San Juan Airlines and I flew with them many times when they were flying freight and mail. The word, "Airlines" connotes a vision of large multi-engine equipment, but this airline was anything but. Most of the equipment was single engine Cessna's and the type of flying on some of the routes did not accommodate a large twin.

One of the "stations" was a strip of beach on Waldron Island. Another was on the spine of a ridge on Spieden Island. After taking the FAA inspector to land on these strips, a bit rattled, he decided to terminate the rest of the inspection tour. Another unique strip was on Shaw Island and I was able to enjoy landing there several times.

The strip was cut through the woods on a hill. At the lower end of the strip there was a telephone line stretched across it that required the pilot to duck under it at the point of touchdown. After passing under the wire, the hill rose sharply; to make it to the top of the incline, a healthy application of throttle was required. Then a quick pull back and right brake would get you on the parking pad at the top. There was no building, counter clerk, or ticket counter: just a passenger with a small bag waiting in the trees.

Possibly one of the most interesting airplanes they operated out of Friday Harbor was a Stinson Bushman: a metalized SR10 powered by a P&W R985, 450 HP. It was a great freighter and hauled anything that they could stuff into it -- from stem to stern. It was used to haul mail and freight into the islands from the mainland, Anacortes Airport. One beautiful summer morning at 0700 I was sitting in the right seat (an apple box with no seatbelt) while the pilot, Terry, was flying us to make the morning pickup. Looking out of the pilot's side,

I could see the "redeye" ferry making its way through Thatcher Pass and I just happened to ask Terry if they ever looped the Bushman.

"Oh sure, Lemme' show you."

The apple box and I remained planted to the floor all the way around as I watched the ferryboat twirl around during the loop.

Flying in the San Juans is not always fun. The weather can be extreme in the winter when the winds can reach 60 and 70 miles per hour and in the spring and summer the fog can be a serious problem. The pilots who sometimes made as many as 30 to 40 landings a week became extremely good at their trade. They were in constant touch in bad weather and I listened to them one morning when two sections were headed for Anacortes. The guy in the first section was following the shoreline at low altitude and came on the radio with a quick warning,

"Jesus Christ! Watch out for the barge with a crane on it near the Lopez Island ferry dock! I had to lift a wing to clear it!"

"Yeah, I see what you mean," as the second section successfully passed it.

While helping a friend to fly freight into Blakely Island in a Cessna 206, I called in to announce a 45 entry to the downwind leg and got the response that there were deer on the "blind end" of the runway. This is something that one never hears at a normal airport so I noted it and hoped that they were gone by the time we got over the crest of the high hump in the runway.

Back to painting -- the toughest job on the island. The magazine series and the book had been published so one would think that this would have spawned a rush of commissions. It didn't. Aviation art was not considered real art as it is now, so we again were in rather tight circumstances. One rewarding event did come out of the book being published. I was asked by the Smithsonian Museum if I would be willing to prepare a painting of the Graf Zeppelin to hang in the halls of the new Balloon and Airship Wing to be a part of the Bi-Centennial opening. Of course I did it and it is there somewhere in their collection.

Then my beautiful young wife had a stroke and it was necessary for us to return to the mainland and I eventually got a job with Boeing again. Somehow she recovered to ninety nine percent of her previous health and we charged ahead.

In the Smithsonian: Balloon and Airship Wing | Robert Parks

Chapter 22.

Back to the Kite Factory.
Working on the 777.
Salute to the B-29 and then Retirement,
but returned twice for a total service of 48 years.

BACK IN THE SADDLE

After a short stint in 1977 as a draftsman in 767 body structures, I was asked if I would like to go to work in 767 Product Development (PD), also known as Preliminary Design. After considering the offer for a lengthy microsecond, I agreed to a move that was to be the best position I would ever know. My creative and inquisitive nature was not suited to a project type environment where everything was ruled by lists and bound by accounting for repetitive minutia. In PD, one was constantly stimulated by ideas to improve the present configuration or to invent something better. Almost every day there was something new to work on and there was no chance to be bored by repetitive processes and best of all, my boss would present me with a proposed change or entirely new idea and say, "See what you can do with this." There was hardly any area of the airplanes on which I didn't work: hydraulics, structures, electrical installations, all systems and lofting. I looked forward to going to work every day not only for the work, but also to be with some of the finest people in The Boeing Company.

Twenty-five years of working through the Company from a flight line mechanic through almost all the manufacturing disciplines and some engineering associations seemed to be a natural progression to being a technical designer and I enjoyed every day at my job. One day several of us were discussing the problems of the cantilevered landing gear of the KC-135. Our discussion went into the metallurgy and the occurrence of undesirable martensitic conditions in the support rib. After a lengthy discourse on the mistakes and what Boeing learned from the design, a young engineer who had been listening to the discussion said, "Well, I went to school for four years to study engineering but I got an education here in the last hour."

THE FINEST OF THEM ALL

One day in 1988 I noticed a man whom I had never seen before come into the boss's office. He was there for quite a while behind a closed door. That afternoon I was told that I was going to Renton with six others to work on a new program.

We had been working on a 767X project to design a new larger longer-range transport and we surmised that the program had been solidified into a firm program. We were correct. Our studies had been moved into an active design project for our next model.

For the next three years we not only worked on the next generation long range large airliner, but went to schools to be trained in the use of the CATIA computer program with which we were to design the airplane.

The transition from meticulous work on the drafting tables and aluminum sheets was difficult, but workable. We designed, for the first time, a very big airplane on the computer. There were no paper drawings in the process and we designed what we felt then and know now, the finest jet airliner ever produced: the 777.

THE WGA

This wasn't just another airplane program and we knew from the beginning it was something special. It was somewhat like the 707 program but without the groundbreaking pioneering aspect of it. But then, it did have some of that because we were fighting a new and aggressive competitor and the sense of urgency. Survival permeated the atmosphere at work. We were attempting to fill a niche between the smaller wide body transports and the 747 class that included the Airbus A330 and 340. We had to design something that would beat Airbus and all the stops were pulled out. In addition to that, the company decided to use the CATIA system and we spent as much time in training as we did on the design operations. Soon it all came together and the airplane took shape. The elimination of the time-consuming hand layout and incremental mathematical calculations in the lofting phase saved an enormous amount of time. Then more time was saved by the elimination of the full-sized master models to define complex shapes and contours. That, in turn, eliminated the need for the casts and trim jigs that were taken off the master model. It was all extracted from a single source of digital data in the computer and the accuracy was wonderful.

Design elements were freely transferred between groups in real time instead of one group waiting for another to finish its work. Customers were integrated into the design process as were contractors and vendors so that everyone had an input to mold the design to their needs. Many meetings took place with everyone involved -- even airline pilots. As the airplane became an actual piece of hardware in the final stages, a new and controversial operational feature came to the surface, ETOPS. That stood for Extended Twin Operations. The 777 from the beginning was a twin engine airplane and the prospect of losing an engine over the ocean loomed ugly as operational planning reached its peak. In one of the meetings with our airline customers to discuss ETOPS, a pilot spoke up and said, "Hell, I know what that means: ENGINES TURN OR PEOPLE SWIM."

In the beginning of the design I had been charged with the task of investigating the possibility of using three 767 air conditioning packs in the airplane to save the expense of designing new packs. I successfully crammed three packs and the associated intake scoops, plumbing, ducts and heat exchangers into the A/C bay under the wing -- but it was ugly. It looked like a snake pit. As I was getting on the elevator from the plot room with my plot of the system, a gentleman whom I recognized as one of the executives joined me and wanted to know what I was working on. I told him what I was trying to do and I had just gotten the three dimensional plot of the entire system.

"I would like to see that, may I?" At his urging, we laid it out on the lobby floor and both of us on our hands and knees looked at it and he said, "I don't think that is a very good way to do that. It's too complex and the reliability rate wouldn't be good with three packs. I really think that we ought to go with two new packs. Don't you?" I agreed.

He introduced himself, "I'm Alan Mulally. Nice to chat with you."

Several days later I was instructed to lay out a two-pack system.

This happened in the first few weeks of the program and in the ensuing months we were to have many meetings with every discipline involved: project engineering, production planning, tooling, manufacturing, materiel, airlines and contractors. Everyone was involved and making their inputs. Several times at 0730 in the morning or at 1800 in the evening, Alan Mulally could show up to see how things were going. One never knew when he was going to pop up and his pep talks were always well received. This program was not at all like the exciting pioneering 707 that I remembered. It wasn't the backbreaking desperate effort of the 747. The 777 was a well organized, carefully planned, staffed with the best personnel, and a fully funded in-house program to make a decisive thrust against the competition. One glaring new change was the break from the detached ascetic corporate image to one of almost juvenile humoristic behavior by the new executives. In all-hands pep meetings in a large rented theater, each of the section representatives gave his own self-reflecting pep talk. As an example, the finance VP of Scandinavian descent came rushing onto the stage dressed in Viking garb complete with the horned helmet. He gave us a fun-filled pep talk that left an impression that this could be a hard-working and fun-filled program. It was.

On top of all that, they decided to go with a new computer-based design system that cut development time by three years and it all worked to produce, as the airline pilots call it, the WGA, the World's Greatest Airplane.

Still vivid are the memories of struggling with the three-dimensional computer system while we learned it and the elation when we could see what miracles it could perform. Eventually we put the entire airplane together on it and produced the first digital inboard profile. The kinetic feature of it blew us away when we could assemble the entire landing gear and watch it retract into the wheel well structure to check for interferences. We ran the flaps through their cycle and when a colleague and I were lofting the upper body aft of the cab we ran airflow studies on it to identify possible area of sonic shock and we did find some. It was magic like the "glass" instrument panel and other things about the airplane. The "glass" instrument panel did away with the old analog dials and displayed data called up from multiple sources on a flat screen. Soon the airline pilots had a word for the new panel and they simply called it "Magic." The old analog dial clustered panels were called "Steam Gage". And more magic came in the form of a little computer "fly" that we could move around inside the structure and look at possible interferences. Amazingly, it was called "Fly Through"

My old Production Illustration Group was still in operation and they used the fly-through to good advantage in routing the wiring and tubing by the CATIA computer. It was destined that the Production Illustration Group's (PIG) adaptation to Fly Through would be officially identified as PIGS FLY.

CELEBRATIONS FOR THINGS WELL DONE
1985 and 1992

While all this magic was happening in 1992, the 50th anniversary of the B-29 was upon the company and I was asked to do a full color cutaway of the airplane that was to be a hand out at the celebration. A position on the celebration committee was also an assignment and while working the flight line, I was fortunate enough to get a flight in the famous and the only flyable B-29: FiFi. Flying for one hour in the bomb aimer's position was an exciting experience, especially when the pilot, the late Tom Cloyd, was landing the bomber. This flight was a great addition to my being able to fly in a B-17, B-25 and a P-51 during the B-17 anniversary celebration seven years earlier.

Those 50th anniversary celebrations were the most interesting operations in which I had ever participated. The B-17 party in 1985 was huge because at that time there were many veterans still alive that flew in the B-17 and their bomb group associations were full and active. I was honored to meet several Medal-of-Honor winners and I could readily see that they were special human beings. Their demeanor, their stature and their presence spoke of their status. But even with these exemplary people and Curtiss Le May in attendance there were a couple of clowns who flew into the show in a B-25 from Wyoming. After landing, they taxied along the ramp in front of the crowd "firing" the fake .50 caliber machine guns powered by acetylene gas that they sparked off. While we were getting them backed into their parking slot, a group of very high-level Boeing executives gathered in front of the airplane and asked about the acetylene gun packs on the side of the airplane and wanted to see them fire again. The pilot, a young ex-air force veteran, was very accommodating and told them to stand directly in front of the nose so that they could get the "full affect". There they gathered as they were told in their Brooks Brothers suits and got "the full affect" as the nose gunner hosed them down with a fake .50 cal. giant water pistol.

The soggy executives laughed as hard as the rest of us.

The B-25 crew never stopped with their pranks. When I flew with them on Saturday when all the WW2 airplanes performed an aerial parade, I got wind of something that they wanted to do during the flyby the next day. They failed to get permission from the FAA but I went with them anyway. A low-level pass over the runway in front of the crowd was wonderful and we pulled up to the right and over Beacon Hill and headed south to Renton airport where they got permission from the tower to make a low pass for them. The north end of the runway terminates at Lake Washington and at that time of year, July 15th, it is full of salmon. The Cedar River empties just to the right of the runway and the fishermen congregate in the south end of the lake near there. Flying low over the lake they opened the bomb bay to "bomb" the fishermen -- with 50 beach balls. The sight from the tail gunner's position was hilarious with the fishermen either waving and cheering or standing in their boats in shock.

The next day as I was returning to the flight line, one of the P-51 pilots asked me if I would like to ride with him in the parade of aircraft that would pass in front of the crowd. Of course, I jumped at the chance to fly in the greatest WW2 fighter plane. So, I got to fly in two of North American Aviation's great warplanes, a B-25, and "Worry Bird", a P-51.

As counterpoint, the day before the celebration we were very busy welcoming the airplanes coming in to be on display or to fly. At approximately 1700, the scheduled KC-135 came in and was parked in its slot. Before any salutations could be offered, the aircraft commander, a cute little blonde, stationed herself in front of the number two engine and stood there while the crew attacked some sort of problem. She stayed there until the crew had solved the issue. Her display of discipline and dedicated command responsibility was striking to me. She couldn't have weighed more than 120 pounds but she was unequivocally the boss. It was difficult for me to digest the changes since I was in the service when women were relegated to typing duties in a colonel's office.

An hour after we got her KC-135 parked and darkness was creeping up on us, lights appeared in the golden colored sky south in the Green River Valley. We immediately recognized them as a B-52 on a long stable approach. Here it came, characteristically rolling from side to side while trailing eight streaks of black smoke. It flew onto the runway in a cloud of blue smoke and eventually waddled up to our area where we parked it next to the KC-135. The crew deplaned and the pilot finally appeared, making a beeline to the KC-135 pilot who stood nearby. Again, we were taken aback when they embraced and conversed in an intimate nose-to-nose confrontation.

Well, the air force was certainly different than when I was in! After watching this display of decidedly un-military behavior, we were told that they were husband and wife. She had refueled his B-52 on their way from Barksdale Field, then landed and waited until he had completed his training mission. Darkness settled as we were securing the airplanes for the night and I could not stop thinking about the beneficial changes that had occurred in the air force since I was in it 40 years before. The B-52 pilot was 27 years old and I commented to my son, Kris, how young he was and my son looked at me and said, "Dad. How old were you when you were in the air force?" I thought back to 1943 when I enlisted at age 17.

We were blessed with warm clear weather for this extravaganza and the celebration went on without a hitch. The fly-by's of aircraft were flawless with B-17's, P-47's, P-51's, C-46, a P-12, a PT-19, PT-13's, a B-25, and even some lowly " Grasshopper" liaison planes participated. I was in charge of flight line operations and I was fortunate to meet all of the pilots who brought airplanes to the event. The most gratifying was to meet many of the surviving crewmembers. Some, hair laced with white, were still able to do the chin-up maneuver to get into the B-17 forward entry door and others were able to get into the ball turret that they had ensconced themselves in to ride for hours scrunched up like a prenatal fetus. Some of them were wonderfully happy to re-live their days of danger and strife. Others were silent but happy to be involved in the celebration.

Before a photo session to record a group of the five surviving Medal-of-Honor recipients, I was able to chat with them and from the very first words you knew that they were special men. There was an aura of strength coupled with peace and confidence about them. I know that this is a clumsy effort to describe them, but they were definitely different from the rest of us and to a man, they were self-effacing and unimpressed with what they did. Then there were some of the veteran pilots who were still able to wear their uniforms from the 1940's, one of which was a famous used car dealer, Cal Worthington, who was still as thin and athletic as he was when he flew B-17's 40 years before.

The ramp was lined with as many WW2 airplanes as we could get. The veterans, their wives and family members swelled the attendance to well over 150,000 and the reunions of old squadron mates caused many spontaneous but brief parties out on the ramp. Early on the second morning of the celebration we were presented with an unexpected and uninvited surprise when several groups of restored WW2 military vehicles arrived. There was space for them so they were invited to set up their display of Jeeps, command cars, 6 X 6 trucks and line tugs. They were a big hit with the veterans as were the airplanes. One old aerial gunner pointed with glee at the command car and exclaimed, "Look at that! I was hauled off to the stockade (jail) once in one of those." All three days were filled with euphoria and joy as the vets relived their days of companionship. But one of them was gripped by a less giddy emotion.

As part of the anniversary celebration, The Boeing Company commissioned company artists to prepare 20 illustrations of outstanding events in the history of the B-17 and I was asked to do one as well. I chose to paint a picture of a B-17G that survived 138 combat missions, "Ole Miss Destry", one of only three that was able to rack up over 100 missions and return safely. Lithographs of these illustrations were given to all the members of the bomb squadrons in attendance. I wasn't thinking about the art when I was on the ramp tending to the movement of aircraft when a message sounded on the PA system for me to report to the command trailer. My first thought was that I had failed to accomplish some of my duties and I rushed back to the command post to receive my admonishment for -- I had no idea.

To my surprise, the trailer was almost empty when I entered, except for two men. One of them was seated with his head down, staring at some papers on the table and obviously in a stressful condition. A younger man stood by his side rubbing his back and as I approached he introduced himself and said that he was with his dad for the reunion. They wanted me to sign the lithograph of my painting for his dad, Joe. I couldn't understand the urgency of my presence until Joe looked up at me with tears streaming down his cheeks, a painful and sad look in his eyes.

"You did a picture of my airplane and it really got to me to see her again just like she was."

He continued to tell me about his flying with her for her last 30 missions as her navigator while both of them took wounds and more patches.

"I'll never forget the day that I arrived at Chelveston and went out to see the airplane that I had been assigned to. After checking her over, I had my doubts about flying in her. It was pretty beat up and there were still some signs of damage that hadn't been fixed "too good." She smelled bad and I could see some dried blood and vomit that were still in some of the hard to clean spots."

He told me how he decided to grit his teeth and honor his assignment. After a couple of missions, he became a part of "Ole Miss Destry" and stayed with her until the end of the war. After autographing his print I left him and his son alone in the trailer I imagine to try to "put things back together". His son told me that when he saw my painting he simply "lost it" but had the wherewithal to ask for the artists autograph. A small thing for what he and so many others there had done for their country.

This Joe wasn't the only "Joe" who was familiar with this airplane. The other Joe was right here at Boeing, Joe Harlick, a company photographer. He served with the 8th Air Force at Chelveston with the 305th Bomb Group as a photographer and many of his photos of 8th Air Force B-17's, including "Ole Miss Destry," have been seen world-wide so he knew about the airplane too.

I chatted with him when the paintings were displayed at a special dinner event showing at the Boeing Red Barn and he told me that he had a chance to fly back to the states in "Destry" but he declined.

"That airplane didn't have one tight rivet or bolt in it and it flew like it was made of Jello."

"Ole Miss Destry" made it back to the states okay where one would have expected her to be saved and honored for the brave warrior that she was.

She was scrapped soon after her return.

FINALE'

On the last evening of the celebration, we held a dinner/dance in a rented hangar on the east side of the field with Tex Beneke and a reconstituted Glen Miller Band and remnants of the Andrews Sisters singing group. When all the attendees were having their dinner and listening to the band play "Sentimental Journey," the hangar doors opened and there facing the crowd silhouetted in the glow of the setting sun were four B-17's, one of them "Sentimental Journey", saluting those who had given so much 45 years before. There wasn't a dry eye in the house and sadly, it would never happen again. The ranks are now thinning at the rate of 1000 a day and we will soon be memories, immortalized by the ink and paper of records and writings.

THE FORTY-SECOND YEAR

Nineteen fifty was a long time ago to some but in 1992 it seemed like just a few years to me. Yet, there was a long trail marked with memorable incidents that would not have happened if I had been seriously chasing a lofty career position. I was never built to do that anyway so what happened just simply happened. I was never focused on a single career target and that allowed me to travel through a series of varied experiences. Some of them were not so good, but I feel that the good things canceled the bad so I'm comfortable with what I see when I look back. However, in 1992 I still had the curiosity to see what was down the road or over the hill so I retired. I shouldn't have. I was at the top of my game. I had managed to join the younger set by abandoning the pencil and learning to design things on a computer screen where I joined 42 years of experience with new technologies. I could have and should have stayed for another 10 years. Now what was it they said about 20-20 hindsight?

Retirement was not nirvana. After four years I went back to the Kite Factory to work on future versions of the 777 and 747 and I spent another four years at it working with the CATIA computer system to modify the things on the 747 that eventually transformed into the 747-8. I was finally released in 2001 and turned out to pasture after 51 years of my association with Boeing that up till now has never really been broken.

And it never will be. Shortly after I retired for the second time, I was suckered to come in for a "15 year pin celebration for someone." When I was settled in the conference room with a large crowd, I was surprised by having my wife escorted into the room and shocked by being presented with the honor of my name being installed on a plaque on the WALL OF HONOR at the National Air and Space Museum's Udvar-Hazy Center in Chantilly, Virginia! The Wall of Honor recognizes those who have contributed outstanding service in the field of aviation and their names are engraved on plaques lining the entrance to the museum. It's humbling to realize that I share a small space with names like Jimmy Doolittle and other truly great aviators. My old group had conspired to do the deed and I will forever be humbled by it.

Some day I must go to see it.

I still talk with my old group and occasionally visit them and the adrenalin picks up a bit when I see what they are doing and I would still like to be with them working on the follow-on designs to the 787, the 777X, or the new 737. But that is all in the past now and when I visit them I have to have an escort. I realize now that I worked with them during the best of times.

As I write this at age 88, I have been involved in aviation for 82 years and I have seen it go from wood and fabric to titanium and reinforced plastic and other materials that are emerging. Speeds have gone from 85 MPH to 2500 MPH and more, but are now measured as Mach. I have flown something like 45 different airplanes ranging from 40 HP T-Craft and a Model B Ford powered Pietenpol Aircamper to a DC-3 and a 1933 Boeing 247. Best of all was a wonderful 2½-hour flight flying a sailplane. And just because I don't have my hands on the stick and no longer have a lot of air under me, it is still a great flight because I live it every day and like they say, "The older I get, the better I was!"

Progress continues to accelerate. I'm not. But I still like to watch, listen, and try to take another lick at that big lollypop of life. Many times I think about our first radio in 1929, a crystal set, and then marvel at what progress has taken place in my lifetime with all the computers and the fast high flying jets. It is a wonderful scene to gaze upon and now, I'm trying to find a seat on a two-man Bobsled. The name is perfect and I haven't tried one of those yet.

XXX

777 Configurations Group | Robert Parks

THANKS TO ALL

JUDY. The steady encouragement from my wife, Judy, kept me whacking away at this idea for many years and she assured me that the writing was good enough to publish as a book. I hope that she is correct but I think that deep down it was her way to keep from hearing them again. She has heard them for 48 years and now that they are committed to a book she won't have to suffer through them again. But wait, I have quite a few stories left and I hate to see them go to waste. Ah yes, I can see her now, rolling her eyes and staring at the ceiling like she did before. Yep, I can see another book in the offing.

NANCY DEMEERLEER organized, formatted, and retyped my rough recollections into a smoother narrative. Her expertise, generous demeanor, and pleasant disposition were instrumental in lightening the workload in preparing an acceptable manuscript. She transformed a framework into a working vehicle that provided a solid base on which the editors and others could work.

BEN AND MARIE ALMOJUELA edited my writing like a couple of teachers from my past, surgical and unrelenting, but on target. I had no idea that my punctuation and sentence construction was so bad until they straightened some things out with their red pencils. Ben commented that my use of the semi-colon was "atrocious." Well, Ben, I managed to get a semi-colonoscopy and I'm doing much better now.

DAWN RICHARD, a successful author and a good buddy, has given me invaluable advice and encouragement through the years. In spite of a busy life with her family and work, she was always generous and patient when I asked her questions that only a neophyte would ask about building a book. This is my first attempt to write a book and I never realized how much work is involved. She made this difficult task much easier.

LILLYAN HENDERSHOT of The Branding Iron is another one of those multi talented young people who performed the final work to configure, assemble, print, and to produce a physical book. Lilly is a most pleasant young lady with whom to work and, indeed, it is a stroke of good fortune to have so much skill, talent, and experience so close by.

MY FAMILY AND FRIENDS. It was wonderful to have so much encouragement from everyone but I wonder if they were urging the old goat on just to keep him occupied. I don't think so, really. I had so many good words and good vibes from everyone that it kept me going. This task would have been very difficult without their support. Thanks to all of you.

Made in the USA
Middletown, DE
13 January 2016